EFFECTS OF INDUSTRIAL CONCENTRATION:

A CROSS-SECTION ANALYSIS FOR THE COMMON MARKET

CONTRIBUTIONS
TO
ECONOMIC ANALYSIS

74

Honorary Editor

J. TINBERGEN

Editors

J. JOHNSTON

D. W. JORGENSON

J. WAELBROECK

NORTH-HOLLAND PUBLISHING COMPANY

AMSTERDAM · LONDON

EFFECTS OF INDUSTRIAL CONCENTRATION:

A CROSS-SECTION ANALYSIS FOR THE COMMON MARKET

LOUIS PHLIPS

Professor of Economics,
Catholic University of Louvain,
Belgium

with the collaboration of

MICHEL BIART

JAYME GARCIA DOS SANTOS

ALBERT GILOT

JEAN-PAUL LOISEAU

1971

NORTH-HOLLAND PUBLISHING COMPANY
AMSTERDAM · LONDON

© 1971 NORTH-HOLLAND PUBLISHING COMPANY

Library of Congress Catalog Card Number: 75-146197

ISBN: 0 7204 3174 3

Publishers:
NORTH-HOLLAND PUBLISHING COMPANY – AMSTERDAM
NORTH-HOLLAND PUBLISHING COMPANY, LTD. – LONDON

PRINTED IN THE NETHERLANDS

PREFACE

This is a revised and enlarged version of a report written for and at the request of the Commission of the European Communities and submitted in the spring of 1969. [1]

There are numerous persons whose names deserve a place because of the contribution which they rendered to the research underlying this book.

First of all, I want to express my thanks to Mr. Schetgen and his associates, Mr. van Belle and Mr. Giacomello, of the statistical office of the communities, who moved heaven and earth to provide the results of the 1963 industrial census within the shortest time limits.

Additional statistical information was also supplied by Messrs. G. Als, Director of the Service Central de la Statistique et des Etudes Statistiques du Grand-Duché du Luxembourg, Charrayre, of the E.C.S.C., A. Dufrasne, General Director of the Institut National de Statisque de Belgique, J. Dumontier and Hamayde, of I.N.S.E.E., G. de Gennaro, Director of the Associazione fra le Società Italiane per Azioni, J.C. Dastot and P. Kende, of the Fédération Internationale pour la Recherche dans le Domaine de la Publicité, W. Knuyt of the Belgian Conseil National de la Politique Scientifique, G. de Meo, President of the Istituto Centrale di Statistica, P. Schmidt, of the Statistisches Bundesamt, van Liefferinge, Director at the Caisse Nationale d'Epargne et de Retraite de Belgique, J.C.W. Verstege, Director General at the Centraal Bureau voor de Statistiek and A. Vincent, Inspecteur Général Honoraire.

---

[1] The Commission is not, of course, responsible for the analysis and opinions contained in this report.

My colleagues, J.M. Blair, H. Glejser, I. Horowitz, A. Jacquemin, R. Leory, J. Miller, E. van Broekhoven, J. Waelbroeck, and L. Weiss commented on parts of previous drafts.

Special thanks are due to Mrs. M. Vuylsteke-Wauters, of the computer center of the University of Louvain: she wrote all the programs used. Computations on desk calculator were carried out by Miss Lambrechts and Mr. J. Peeters.

I am also indebted to the editors of *European Economic Review, The Journal of Industrial Economics* and *Recherches Economiques de Louvain* for permission to reproduce material published in their journals.

Last not least, I wish to give my warm thanks to my research associates. Although this is a joint venture, it is possible to indicate the main contributions of each of those names appear on the title page. Jean-Paul Loiseau computed the series used in chapter 3 and contributed to the early developments of our research. Albert Gilot realised chapter 4 which he presented as a masters thesis at the University of Louvain. Jayme Garcia dos Santos acted as a research assistant for chapters 2 and 3, and devised the statistical tests used in chapter 6. Michel Biart gave his best efforts to chapter 3, for which he also wrote the survey of the literature on concentration and the rate of return. Furthermore, he accepted the unrewarding task of guiding and supervising the computations leading to the tables of the statistical appendix, and the even more unrewarding task of computing (by hand!) the concentration ratios used in part I.

I think I should take my responsibility as the entrepreneur of this undertaking and the author of the final draft, and add that all remaining errors are mine.

Louvain, April 1970   Louis Phlips

To the memory of P.W.S. Andrews

TABLE OF CONTENTS

LIST OF TABLES

LIST OF FIGURES

LIST OF SYMBOLS

B.I.C.	= Bénéfices industriels et commerciaux (France)
C	= four-firm concentration ratio for an industry
D	= dummy variables
D.F.	= degrees of freedom
E	= total employment of an industry
E_w	= total production worker employment of an industry
$\bar{F}$	= average size of companies in an industry
F	= computed F-ratio
G	= annual rate of growth of assets in an industry
GD	= index of geographical dispersion of an industry
GE	= growth of total employment in an industry
I.N.S.	= Institut National de Statistique (Belgium)
M	= % of men in total employment of an industry *
MCR	= marginal concentration ratio
MC_t	= total cost of purchased fuel and materials less the net increase in inventories for an industry in year t
M.S.	= mean square
N	= number of observations
n	= number of companies or establishments in an industry
N.A.E.	= Nomenclature des activités économiques
N.I.C.E.	= Nomenclature Industrielle des Communautés Euro-péennes
P_t	= industry price level in year t (price index)
PR	= productivity in an industry
Q_t	= industry output in year t, measured by deflating S_t
RI_4	= research intensity in the four largest companies in an industry
RI_I	= research intensity in an industry

* Percentage of male employment

RP	= research personnel in a company
RR	= rate of return
$\bar{S}$	= average size of establishments in an industry
S_t	= value of industry shipments in year t
SD	= % of persons employed in large divisions in an industry
SS	= sum of squares
SW_t	= total salaries and wages for an industry in year t
TP	= total personnel in a company
TU	= power of trade unions in an industry
U	= % of unemployment in an industry
W	= hourly wage rate in an industry
W_t	= total production worker payroll for an industry in year t

CHAPTER 1

INTRODUCTION

This is a global and empirical analysis of some economic effects of industrial concentration. It is a global analysis, in the sense that it tends to embrace the entire manufacturing industry of some E.E.C. countries. It is an empirical analysis, as the emphasis is on the econometric verification of alleged relationships existing between industrial concentration and some indicators of economic performance.

The main indicators used are prices, profits, wages and research personnel. The statistical material comprises data for three-digit industries classified according to the Common Market industrial classification, i.e. the N.I.C.E. (Nomenclature Industrielle des Communautés Européennes) [1] or according to national classifications. The analysis is thus strictly cross-section. In principle, all observations describing the industrial structure are for the year 1962, which is the year to which the 1963 Industrial Census of the Common Market refers. Some indicators refer to the period 1958–65.

No official measures of concentration by industry being available, we had to compute these basic data by ourselves. This being in some sense a pioneering study, we decided to stick to a most traditional measure: the concentration ratio. This ratio has its merits and its weaknesses. It is sufficiently good to serve its purpose here, the field being open for the use of more sophisticated measures such as Herfindahl indexes, entropy, and what not. For lack of sufficiently detailed data on shipments, our concentration

---

[1] For details, see the statistical appendix.

ratios and other measures of industrial structure had to be computed in terms of numbers of persons employed. Needless to say that no systematic information is available on financial concentration, personal relations among companies (interlocking directorates), vertical integration, etc. These types of concentration might be more important, in some way, than the object of our study, horizontal concentration within an industry. In the present state of our information, these problems seem to be beyond the scope of a global and econometric approach.

When we embarked in this undertaking, we (somewhat naïvely) planned to use systematically the census data, classified according to the N.I.C.E. and reproduced below in the statistical appendix, to take advantage of their comparability. We soon discovered, however, that we had been too optimistic. Time series on prices, annual surveys of production, data on profits can only be found, for a sufficient number of years, in publications of member countries, which implies that these series are presented according to national industrial classifications. These classifications are definitely not comparable. Wages are the only indicators available in the N.I.C.E. classification.

Under these conditions, we had to divide our report in two parts. The second part, which tries to give an international comparison of industrial structure within the Common Market, could be based entirely on the N.I.C.E. classification, no indicators of economic performance being involved. The first part, on the contrary, devoted to the analysis of the economic effects of concentration − our main objective − had to utilize "national" statistical sources.

The field of national industrial classifications looks very much like a jungle: each country has not just its particular classification but rather several own classifications, depending upon the type of information required. There was no hope of converting all these into N.I.C.E. The only solution was therefore to recompute our measures of concentration according to the national classification, taking advantage of the fact that the 1963 Industrial Census is also available in "national" versions (as explained in the statistical appendix). The resulting waste of time and efforts seemed disproportionate and rather discouraging.

Given these constraints, we adopted the following research strategy. In each chapter of part I, we first concentrated our efforts on Belgium, for which statistical data were the easiest to get — for obvious reasons. It was only when reasonably good results (in terms of specification and statistical significance) were obtained that we turned to other countries, hoping to find data suitable for testing the model that was retained for Belgium. As a result, undue emphasis might have been given to Belgian particularities: researchers from other countries might have preferred another approach. We felt this was the only way to proceed, to prevent our efforts from continuing indefinitely.

As we were, after all, interested in the Common Market as a whole, we did our best to put results for particular countries in a larger framework and to make as many comparisons as possible. Covariance analysis appeared as the obvious panacea. In addition to its intrinsic interest, covariance analysis permits to compensate (at least in part) the non-comparability of some national data and the resulting losses of information.

Implicit in all this is the idea that the Common Market was not, in 1963 (and even now?), truly common but rather a juxtaposition of more or less closed national markets. We thought it would have been premature to treat the E.E.C. as a whole, e.g. by computing concentration ratios for the Common Market as a whole. The reader may not be ready to accept this, and even reverse the argument, objecting to the use of "national" concentration ratios for countries as "open" as Belgium or the Netherlands. This is partly a matter of belief and partly an empirical question. The problem will be taken up in due time (in particular in chapters 2 and 3 and in the final conclusions).

Chapter 2 is devoted to the so-called "administrative inflation" hypothesis, while chapter 3 tries to verify once more an old standby of the industrial organization literature: the profit-concentration relationship. Chapter 4 takes up the wage-concentration problem. Part I ends with an attempt to combine data on individual firms and industry data in an analysis of research efforts in relation to the size of firms and the degree of concentration of industries.

PART I

EFFECTS OF INDUSTRIAL CONCENTRATION

CHAPTER 2

INFLATION [2]

2.1. Survey of the literature

This chapter presents some empirical evidence, for Belgium, the Netherlands and France, on the so-called "administrative inflation" hypothesis. The hypothesis might be defined as saying that price increases are higher in more concentrated industries, given positive changes in demand and costs. Empirically speaking, it implies that, for a cross section of industries, wholesale-price changes are a positive function of concentration ratios, for given increases in demand and unit costs. Although any relevant evidence would be an interesting contribution to the present discussion about the Common Market's antitrust policy, the hypothesis has never been confronted – to our knowledge – with data from E.E.C. countries.

It was G.Means who formulated the idea that prices are characterised by upward flexibility in concentrated industries, in a presentation before the Kefauver Committee. [2] Since then, the idea seems to have gained some acceptance. But the case is rather weak,

It would indeed be difficult to defend the hypothesis on theoretical grounds. As G.J.Stigler puts it, "The traditional economic theory argues that oligopoly and monopoly prices have no special relevance to inflation. A monopolist (to take the simpler case)

[1] This chapter was published in *J. of Industrial Economics* 18, 1 (1969), under the title Business pricing polices and inflation – some evidence from E.E.C. countries.

[2] *Hearings before the Subcommittee on Antitrust and Monopoly of the Committee on the Judiciary*, United States Senate, 1957, pp. 124–25; 1959a, pp. 4746–58; 1959b, pp. 4897–910.

sets a profit-maximizing price for given demand-and-cost conditions. If inflation leads to a rise in either demand or costs, a new and usually higher price will be set. The price will usually be above the competitive level at any given time, but its pattern over time will not be other than passively responsive to monetary conditions." [3]

On the empirical level, there is room for discussion. For obvious reasons, the profession could not accept as valuable evidence the now famous charts presented by G.Means before the Kefauver Committee. The first serious statistical analysis is due to De Podwin and Selden. [4] These authors concluded that their simple correlation analysis of 1953—59 price changes and concentration ratios of some U.S. industries were adequate evidence to "put the administrative inflation hypothesis to rest".

In a more recent article[5], L.W.Weiss emphasized the necessity of introducing demand and cost changes in the analysis, to separate their influence. Utilizing the same sample, he found a small positive effect of concentration on price changes for the period 1953—59; for 1959—63, the relationship became negative and not significantly different from zero, however.

The evidence presented in this chapter is limited to the 1958—65 period, because of the difficulty to collect comparable data for earlier years. As we were more familiar with Belgian data, Belgium was selected as a test case to determine the most appropriate empirical specification of the hypothesis. A few changes in Weiss's approach proved to be beneficial and are discussed in section 2.2 together with the data and results obtained for Belgium. In section 2.3, results for the Netherlands are compared with the Belgian evidence on the basis of an analysis of covariance. Section 2.4 introduces France while the last section draws some conclusions as to the validity of the hypothesis in a European framework.

---

[3] Administered prices and oligopolistic inflation, *J. of Business* 35 (1962) 8.

[4] Business pricing policies and inflation, *J. of Political Economy* (April 1963).

[5] Business pricing policies and inflation reconsidered, *J. of Political Economy*, (April 1966).

2.2. Belgium

Data collection represented a problem – as is invariably the case in Europe. It was possible to construct comparable series for a maximum number of 17 manufacturing industries only, for the period 1958–64. In one case, data were lacking on production worker payroll, in another on materials cost. As a result, some regressions are based on only 16 or 15 observations.

2.2.1. Using Weiss's approach

To facilitate comparisons of methods of analysis, the same concepts were used as in the J.P.E. articles mentioned above. It might be useful to recall briefly the significance of the following symbols:

S_t = value of industry shipments in year t;

P_t = industry price level in year t (always part of a price index expressed as P_t/P_0);

Q_t = industry output in year t, measured by deflating S_t;

C = four-firm concentration ratio for the given industry;

W_t = total production worker payroll for the industry in year t;

SW_t = total salaries and wages for the industry in year t.

We will also introduce

MC_t = total cost of purchased fuel and materials less the net in-increase in inventories in year t.

A simple regression of the 17 price indexes on the 17 concentration ratios gave the following (standard errors are between brackets)

$$P64/P58 = 125.51 - 0.310C$$
$$(6.81) \quad (0.132)$$

with $R^2 = 0.26$. Of course, this does not allow the conclusion that concentrated industries increased prices less than unconcentrated. We have to correct for influences of demand and costs. When the output variable, defined as

$$\frac{Q64}{Q58} = \frac{S64}{S58} \bigg/ \frac{P64}{P58}$$

is introduced, output has a negative effect (as in Weiss's paper)

$$P64/P58 = 169.96 - 0.386C - 0.303 \; Q64/Q58$$
$$\quad\quad\quad\quad (21.73) \quad (0.124) \quad (0.142)$$

$$\bar{R}^2 = 0.37 \quad\quad (\text{D.F.} = 2, 14) \quad\quad (F\text{-ratio} = 5.7)$$

where D.F. designates the degrees of freedom. Industries with greater increases in production increased prices less, which indicates that changing costs (per unit of production) are likely to have played an important role. It is necessary then to introduce changes in such key cost factors [6] as labor and materials costs per unit of production (defined as

$$\frac{W64}{W58} \bigg/ \frac{Q65}{Q58} \quad \text{or} \quad \frac{SW64}{SW58} \bigg/ \frac{Q64}{Q58} \quad \text{and} \quad \frac{MC64}{MC58} \bigg/ \frac{Q64}{Q58}).$$

Table 2.1 gives the results from a set of regressions with different combinations of the cost variables. A striking result is that the coefficients of the labor-cost variables (W or SW) are not significantly different from zero [7], whereas the coefficients of the materials cost variable (MC) are always significant (although with variable sign). This is, to say the least, surprising. As for concentration, it appears with coefficients which are either negative or not significantly different from zero, as in equation (I.3) which stands out as the "best" in terms of explained variance.

One explanation of these strange results is that our sample is too small and/or our data too bad. But another (possibly concomitant) explanation is that the specification of the model has to be improved.

---

[6] Changes in the cost of capital, per industry, are neglected because of the difficulty of measuring them.

[7] We adopt the convention that a regression coefficient is not significantly different from zero when less than twice its standard error.

Table 2.1
Administrative inflation in Belgium. Regression coefficients
(Unweighted cost variables)

	Constant	C	$\frac{Q64}{Q58}$	$\frac{W64}{W58} / \frac{Q64}{Q58}$	$\frac{SW64}{SW58} / \frac{Q64}{Q58}$	$\frac{MC64}{MC58} / \frac{Q64}{Q58}$	$\bar{R}^2$	D.F.	F-ratio
I.1	229.5 (30.7)	-0.500 (0.094)	-0.608 (0.143)	-0.145 (0.099)			0.73	3, 12	13.92**
I.2	89.8 (92.1)	-0.307 (0.153)	-0.157 (0.217)		0.500 (0.559)		0.36	3, 13	4.01*
I.3	87.2 (72.3)	-0.247 (0.137)	-0.209 (0.215)	0.197 (0.339)		0.371 (0.185)	0.79	4, 10	13.89**
I.4	164.1 (91.7)	-0.492 (0.159)	-0.513 (0.261)		0.640 (0.502)	-0.342 (0.123)	0.56	4, 11	5.72*

* Significant at the 95% level.
** Significant at the 99% level.

2.2.2. *Alternative specifications*

The foregoing approach gives equal weight to increases in unit labor or materials cost, irrespective of the importance of these elements in total average cost. It is clear, however, that capital-intensive industries should worry less about a given percentage change in unit labor cost than labor-intensive industries, and that producers of margarine should pay more attention to a given percentage change in unit materials cost than producers of bricks. A natural procedure is then to multiply the cost variables by percentages of wage and materials expenses in the value of shipments. [8] The results are presented in table 2.2.

Improvements are substantial. Equation (II.2) clearly stands out with a remarkable $\bar{R}^2$ of 0.89. It corresponds to the fully specified model with production worker payroll (deflated by production) as the labor cost variable. Firms appear to adjust prices positively to wage increases, especially when production is labour-intensive. But the administrative inflation hypothesis does not derive any support from the results.

There remains an uneasy feeling, however.

First, the regression coefficients of most variables are unstable. Second, standard errors are generally very high, especially for the output variable and the concentration ratio. Third, the regression coefficients of the output variable are difficult to interpret. In Weiss's interpretation, $Q64/Q58$ should measure the impact of demand, once the cost variables enter the regression. But why should an increase in demand lead to smaller price increases or be without impact? [9] Finally, the variables are defined in such a way that $Q64/Q58$ enters in the denominator of the cost variables. As $Q64/Q58$ is itself highly correlated with the concentration ratio, a huge amount of multicollinearity may be suspected.

---

[8] The percentages were calculated for the year 1964.

[9] Weiss offers the explanation that a non-significant coefficient for $Q64/Q58$ might indicate that firms have been working in the range of constant marginal costs. In the standard textbook case, a movement to the right of the demand curve does not affect price if costs are decreasing, however.

Table 2.2
Administrative inflation in Belgium. Regression coefficients
(Weighted cost variables)

	Constant	C	$\frac{Q64}{Q58}$	$\frac{W64 \cdot W64}{W58 \cdot S64} \cdot \frac{Q64}{Q58}$	$\frac{SW64 \cdot SW64}{SW58 \cdot S64} \cdot \frac{Q64}{Q58}$	$\frac{MC64 \cdot MC64}{MC58 \cdot S64} \cdot \frac{Q64}{Q58}$	$\bar{R}^2$	D.F.	F-ratio
II.1	157.3 (18.6)	-0.268 (0.095)	-0.321 (0.101)	0.518 (0.215)			0.77	3, 12	18.51**
II.2	104.2 (32.2)	-0.175 (0.090)	-0.171 (0.137)	1.118 (0.286)		0.303 (0.127)	0.89	4, 10	29.36**
II.3	183.4 (65.1)	-0.298 (0.182)	-0.403 (0.278)		0.336 (0.518)	-0.193 (0.236)	0.50	4, 11	4.75*

The analysis of multicollinearity has been facilitated by the recent contribution of D.E.Farrar and R.R.Glauber. [10] Their paper introduces three tests of multicollinearity:

(a) an approximate transformation of the determinant of the matrix of correlation coefficients, to judge the presence and severity of multicollinearity between the independent variables;

(b) F-tests to indicate the dependence of a particular variable on other variables;

(c) t-tests to determine which variables are collinear with each other.

Applying these three tests to equation (I.3) (table 2.1), we find $\chi^2(6) = 30.8$ where the critical value at the 95% level is only 12.6. The F-tests indicate that all four independent variables are affected by multicollinearity: the $F(3, 11)$ values are 12.0 for the concentration ratio, 16.3 for output, 8.8 for wages and 8.3 for materials costs. Furthermore, each variable is linked to each of the remaining variables, with the exception of wages and materials costs for which the t-ratio is 0.32.

Our weighting procedure makes things worse, as exemplified by equation (II.2) which is gratified with a $\chi^2(6) = 26.6$, F-values of 9.4, 12.2, 18.8, and 12.6 and t-ratios indicating that all variables are dependent upon *all* the others.

These results are not surprising and confirm the objections raised earlier. Furthermore, as the percentage of wages in the value of shipments is negatively correlated with the percentage of material costs, the weighting procedure had to destroy the independence between the two cost variables.

Multicollinearity, however, is a fact of life. In principle, nothing can be done about it. [11] In practice, one has to try to rearrange the problem at hand. In this context, it seemed reasonable to leave the production variable ($Q64/Q58$) out, given its dubious economic

---

[10] Multicollinearity in regression analysis: the problem revisited, *The Rev. of Economics and Statistics* (February 1967).

[11] See H.Theil, *Economic Forecasts and Policy* (North-Holland Publ. Co., Amsterdam, 1965) p. 216.

significance and its high correlation with the concentration ratio. We also wondered whether an *ad hoc* specification, in which one cost variable only would be weighted, would not give a better fit.

Re-arrangements along these lines were rewarding (see table 2.3). When $Q64/Q58$ is deleted, the coefficients of the cost variables have the correct (positive) signs (compare regressions (III.1) and (III.2) with (I.3) and (I.4)). This might indicate that a correct specification of the model does not include the production variable. After all, the influence of demand might already be reflected in the variation of the cost variables. On the other hand, weighting wage cost only leads to a gain in explained variance ($\bar{R}^2$ is higher in (III.3) than in (II.2), although one independent variable was deleted). Notice that the χ^2's are not only reduced – as is inevitable – but also turn out to be above the 95% significance level of 7.815 in table 2.3A and below in table 2.3B.

Table 2.3 leads to the following conclusions:

(a) Belgian firms tended to increase prices when unit wage and/ or materials cost went up;

(b) price changes in response to changes in unit wage cost were a positive function of labor intensity (equation (III.3) and (III.5));

(c) price reacted directly to changes in unit materials costs, in the sense that these changes were given equal weight;

(d) the calculations do not allow to draw any conclusion as to the role demand could have played;

(e) there is no support whatsoever for the administrative inflation hypothesis, all the regression coefficients for C being negative in all cases. Of course, this negative sign does not imply that concentrated industries had a stabilizing influence on prices, [12] since the coefficients of C are not significantly different from zero in the "best" regressions (III.3 and III.5).

---

[12] In the regressions with unweighted cost variables, the negative effect of concentration on prices is probably due to the negative relation between concentration and labor intensity.

Table 2.3

Administrative inflation in Belgium. Final results.

A. Unweighted cost variables

	C	$\dfrac{W64}{W58}\Big/\dfrac{Q64}{Q58}$	$\dfrac{MC64}{MC58}\Big/\dfrac{Q64}{Q58}$	$\dfrac{SW64}{SW58}\Big/\dfrac{Q64}{Q58}$	$\bar{R}^2$	D.F.	F-ratio	$\chi^2(3)$
III.1	-0.134 (0.072)	0.400 (0.265)	0.472 (0.253)		0.78	3, 11	18.3**	11.05
III.2	-0.147 (0.077)		0.510 (0.181)	0.304 (0.351)	0.76	3, 11	15.8**	13.20

Table 2.3 (cont.)

B. One cost variable weighted

	c	$\dfrac{W64}{W58} \cdot \dfrac{W64}{S64} \Big/ \dfrac{Q64}{Q58}$	$\dfrac{MC64}{MC58} \Big/ \dfrac{Q64}{Q58}$	$\dfrac{W64}{W58} \Big/ \dfrac{Q64}{Q58}$	$\dfrac{MC64}{MC58} \cdot \dfrac{MC64}{S64} \Big/ \dfrac{Q64}{Q58}$
III.3	-0.030 (0.043)	0.633 (0.107)	0.516 (0.063)		
III.4	-0.159 (0.102)			1.028 (0.275)	0.086 (0.125)
III.5	-0.050 (0.054)		0.530 (0.081)		
III.6	-0.178 (0.099)				0.127 (0.129)

	c	$\dfrac{SW64}{SW58} \cdot \dfrac{SW64}{S64} \Big/ \dfrac{Q64}{Q58}$	$\dfrac{SW64}{SW58} \Big/ \dfrac{Q64}{Q58}$	$\bar{R}^2$	D.F.	F-ratio	$\chi^2(3)$
III.3	46.66 (7.32)			0.94	3, 11	72.1**	7.28
III.4	6.63 (31.33)			0.62	3, 11	8.6**	3.95
III.5	45.58 (9.45)	0.505 (0.124)		0.90	3, 11	42.1**	6.82
III.6	8.45 (35.09)		1.182 (0.314)	0.62	3, 11	8.7**	4.13

2.3. Benelux

For the Netherlands, a sample of 43 three- or four-digit indus-tries could be collected, the four-digit products belonging to the textile industry. There are no data on wages and salaries separately for a sufficient number of industries.

The regressions give results which confirm those obtained for Belgium. Equation (III.2) (from table 2.3) may be compared with the following result for the Netherlands:

$$\frac{P64}{P58} = \underset{(10.85)}{36.99} - \underset{(0.060)}{0.090C} + \underset{(0.080)}{0.467} \frac{MC64}{MC58} \bigg/ \frac{Q64}{Q58}$$

$$+ \underset{(0.079)}{0.211} \frac{SW64}{SW58} \bigg/ \frac{Q64}{Q58} \qquad\qquad\qquad \text{(IV.1)}$$

$$\bar{R}^2 = 0.57 \text{ (D.F.} = 3, 39) \qquad F\text{-ratio} = 19.91**$$

$$\chi^2(3) = 9.11$$

with F-statistics of 3.98, 2.83 and 4.03 for each independent vari-able respectively.

A natural question is to ask whether Belgium and the Nether-lands are homogeneous insofar as their slope coefficients are con-cerned and to set up a "within" analysis of covariance using a "combined" regression. [13]

Covariance analysis proceeds in the following way. [14] From the separate (here "national") regressions, one derives a combined re-gression using a moment matrix which is the sum of the national matrices. Let the normal equations of the national regressions be in the usual matrix notation,

---

[13] For similar applications of analysis of covariance, see e.g. H.Houthakker, New evidence on demand elasticities, *Econometrica* 33 (April 1955), or E.Kuh, *Capital Stock Growth: A Micro-Econometric Approach*, chap. 5 (North-Holland Publ. Co., Amster-dam, 1963).

[14] See e.g. G.W.Snedecor and W.C.Cochran, *Statistical Methods,* 6th ed., chap. 14 (Iowa, 1967), or E.J.Williams, *Regression Analysis* (Wiley, New York, 1959).

$(X_i' X_i) \beta_i = X_i' Y_i$,

where $i = 1, \ldots, s$ indicates the different countries involved. The normal equations of the combined regression are

$(X' X) = X' Y$

where

$$(X' X) \beta_c = \sum_{i=1}^{s} (X_i' X_i)$$

$$(X' Y) = \sum_{i=1}^{s} (X_i' Y_i)$$

and β_c is a vector of weighted coefficients.

The slope coefficients of the national regressions are then compared with the slope coefficients of the combined regression. To decide whether the national coefficients are homogeneous (equal among countries), one computes the following F-ratio:

$$F = \frac{\sum_{j=1}^{N} (y_j - \hat{y}_j)^2 - \sum_{i=1}^{s} \sum_{j=1}^{n_i} (y_{ij} - \hat{y}_{ij})^2 \;\; /t(s-1)}{\sum_{i=1}^{s} \sum_{j=1}^{n_i} (y_{ij} - \hat{y}_{ij})^2 /N - s(t+1)},$$

where t = number of independent variables, s = number of countries, $N = \Sigma_i n_i$, n_i = number of observations in country i, y_{ij} = jth observation on the dependent variable in country i, $\hat{y}_j$ = estimated values by the combined regression, $\hat{y}_{ij}$ = estimated values by the national regression for country i.

The number of degrees of freedom of the combined regression is $N-s-t$ (there being no intercept). The number of degrees of freedom of the numerator of F is therefore $N-s-t-N+s(t+1) = t(s-1)$. If the coefficients are very different, from country to country, the difference in the numerator is big, and the F-value is large. If the coefficients were identical, F would be zero.

The use of an F-table allows to decide whether observed differences among the slope coefficients of different countries are due to sampling errors or whether one has structures differing from country to country.

Combining equation (III.2) (for Belgium) with equation (IV.1) (for the Netherlands), we obtain the following weighted coefficients:

$$-0.113C + 0.484 \frac{MC64}{MC58} / \frac{Q64}{Q58} + 0.228 \frac{SW64}{SW58} / \frac{Q64}{Q58}.$$
$$(0.047) \quad (0.069) \qquad\qquad\qquad (0.074)$$

The computations leading to the F-ratio are summarized, as usual in this type of analysis, in the following table:

Source	SS	D.F.	M.S.	F-ratio
Combined regression	6,012.91	3	2,004.30	33.48
Difference of regressions	52.69	3	17.56	0.29
Residual	2,993.40	50	59.87	
Total within	9,059.00	56	161.77	

The first value in the column of the sums of squares (SS) is the sum of squares explained by the combined regression. The second figure in this column is the difference between the sum of squares explained by the national regressions and that explained by the combined regression. The third is the sum of the residual sums of squares of the national regressions and the fourth is the total variation to be explained (for all countries involved).

The M.S. column gives the mean squares. The first F-ratio refers to the combined regression. The second is the F-ratio defined above and is obtained simply by dividing the mean square for the "difference of regressions" by the residual M.S., exploiting the fact that the difference between the residual SS of the combined regression and the sum of the residual sums of squares of the national regression is equal to the difference between the corresponding explained sums of squares.

The number of degrees of freedom for the total SS to be explained is $N - s$. (Here $N = 58, s = 2, t = 3$).

Belgium and the Netherlands are clearly homogeneous, as the F-ratio of 0.29 lies in the acceptance region of the null hypothesis that the differences between the "national" regression coefficients are zero. Notice that for both countries combined, the regression coefficient for C appears as significantly different from zero. But it still remains to verify how this coefficient behaves when SW is weighted by its percentage in the value of shipments.

For the Netherlands alone, we get:

$$\frac{P64}{P58} = 39.56 + 0.020C + 0.504 \frac{MC64}{MC58} / \frac{Q64}{Q58}$$
$$\quad\quad (9.04) \quad (0.053) \quad (0.071)$$

$$+ 0.592 \frac{SW64}{SW58} \cdot \frac{SW64}{S64} / \frac{Q64}{Q58} \quad\quad\quad (IV.2)$$
$$\quad (0.153)$$

$$\bar{R}^2 = 0.63 \quad\quad F\text{-ratio} = 25.54** \quad\quad \chi^2(3) = 9.81$$

and F-statistics of 2.36, 1.06 and 1.84.

A combination of regressions (III.5) (for Belgium) and (IV.2) (for the Netherlands) gives the slope coefficients

$$0.001C + 0.511 \frac{MC64}{MC58} / \frac{Q64}{Q58} + 0.574 \frac{SW64}{SW58} \cdot \frac{SW64}{S64} / \frac{Q64}{Q58}$$
$$(0.042) \quad (0.058) \quad\quad\quad\quad\quad (0.110)$$

and an F-ratio of 0.21, which is again non-significant. Indeed, we can set up the table

Source	SS	D.F.	M.S.	F-ratio
Combined regression	6,701.56	3	2,233.85	47.99
Difference of regressions	29.86	3	9.95	0.21
Residual	2,327.58	50	46.55	
Total within	9,059.00	56	161.77	

We conclude that the administrative inflation hypothesis definitely does not derive any support from Benelux data.

At this point, we have to pause a moment and face an important objection. Are the results reported thus far relevant to the hypothesis to be tested? An implicit assumption is that concentration ratios measure monopoly power. It is reasonable to admit that national concentration ratios bear any relation to market power in economies as open as those of Belgium and the Netherlands? In such countries, they certainly do not measure market shares: Belgium, for example, exports 40% (if not more) of its production while imports represent a substantial part of consumption.

We do not think the objection is very damaging. Case studies show that in concentrated industries prices are determined in a national framework, in the sense that national producers fix prices in their national market, while importers adjust as price-followers, taking over the same price for comparable products. International agreements on sales conditions (such as basing-point systems, exclusive dealing, etc.) give these *ententes* an operational character, separating the markets while allowing for substantial imports – even in Benelux. [15] Although many more case studies would be needed, I do believe that national concentration ratios are good proxy's for the control national producers have over prices in their domestic market. In this sense, they may be used to test the administrative inflation hypothesis.

This is only a statement of belief, however. It is important, therefore, to provide evidence for economies as "closed" as the American. Fortunately enough, the analysis could be carried out for France, which can be considered as sufficiently "closed" to allow comparisons with the U.S.: if American concentration ratios measure any such thing as monopoly power, then French concentration ratios also do.

---

[15] Three cases were analysed in some detail in my dissertation *De l'intégration des marchés* (Nauwelaerts, Louvain, 1962). Of course, the enforcement of art. 85 and 86 of the Roman Treaty may change all this.

2.4. France

The findings for France are very similar indeed to the results reported above. The following regression

$$\frac{P65}{P59} = \underset{(11.50)}{37.28} + \underset{(0.067)}{0.069C} + \underset{(0.072)}{0.465} \frac{MC65}{MC59} / \frac{Q65}{Q59}$$

$$+ \underset{(0.082)}{0.203} \frac{SW65}{SW59} / \frac{Q65}{Q59} \qquad \text{(V.1)}$$

$$\bar{R}^2 = 0.60 \text{ (D.F.} = 3, 36) \qquad F\text{-ratio} = 69.89**$$

$$\chi^2(3) = 9.81$$

can be combined with regressions (III.2) (for Belgium) and (IV.1) (for the Netherlands) to give

$$\underset{(0.039)}{-0.045C} + \underset{(0.049)}{0.460} \frac{MC65}{MC59} / \frac{Q65}{Q59} + \underset{(0.054)}{0.210} \frac{SW65}{SW59} / \frac{Q65}{Q59} .$$

This combined regression is gratified with a significant F-ratio of 51.70. Belgium, the Netherlands and France appear as homogeneous, as far as the national regression coefficients are concerned, for we obtain an F-ratio of 1.22, with 6 and 86 degrees of freedom, indicating that differences between these coefficients are not significantly different from zero. When we weight salaries and wages, the fit is somewhat inferior, however, and the coefficient of SW is not significant [16]

$$\frac{P65}{P59} = \underset{(10.37)}{50.12} + \underset{(0.070)}{0.084C} + \underset{(0.075)}{0.516} \frac{MC65}{MC59} / \frac{Q65}{Q59}$$

$$+ \underset{(0.215)}{0.259} \frac{SW65}{SW59} \cdot \frac{SW65}{S65} / \frac{Q65}{Q59} , \qquad \text{(V.2)}$$

[16] Our guess is that this result might be due to political interference within the framework of the *Plan*.

$$\bar{R}^2 = 0.56 \text{ (D.F.} = 3, 36)} \qquad F\text{-ratio} = 17.07**$$

$$\chi^2(3) = 8.27.$$

But the combination of (V.2) with (III.5) (Belgium) and (IV.2) (the Netherlands) gives

$$0.024C + 0.512 \frac{MC65}{MC59} / \frac{Q65}{Q59} + 0.508 \frac{SW65}{SW59} \cdot \frac{SW65}{S65} / \frac{Q65}{Q59}$$
$$(0.037) \quad (0.045) \qquad\qquad\qquad (0.100)$$

with an F-ratio of 58.58. As for the differences between the national regression coefficients, an F-ratio of 0.66 with 6 and 86 degrees of freedom indicates that they can be considered as negligible.

2.5. Conclusions

The absence of comparable and systematic production statistics (such as annual surveys of manufactures) for the six E.E.C. countries places a heavy burden on empirical work in the field of business pricing policies. One of the aims of the present chapter was to show that quantitative analysis is nevertheless possible.

Analysis of covariance appeared as a useful tool to compensate for the losses in information due to the heterogeneity of national price and production statistics. It also allowed interesting comparisons.

For our problem, the comparison of France with Benelux countries played a crucial role. If the results for France had been different, it would have been difficult indeed to interpret our findings for economies as open as those of Belgium and the Netherlands, because of the dubious significance of national concentration ratios in these countries. The striking homogeneity of all three countries analyzed suggests that our calculations are relevant to the administrative inflation hypothesis and leads to the conclusion that this hypothesis does not derive any support from the European evidence collected. Again, one might object that similarity of results does not imply the action of similar causes and continue to believe that results for Benelux are irrelevant. We will delay our answer to this objection until the final conclusions, where it will be possible to take the findings of the following chapters into account.

Concentrated industries appear to behave in the same way as unconcentrated industries, as far as upward price flexibility is concerned. Prices tend to follow increases in unit costs, while market structure does not appear to have any particular influence.

Of course, the reader should not infer from this that concentrated industries adopt competitive prices: the *level* of prices might still be "too high", leading to "excessive" profits. But that is another matter, to be examined in the following chapter.

APPENDIX TO CHAPTER 2

Table 2.4. Belgium

No concentration ratios are available for Belgium, except for two-digit industries, where they seem meaningless when unweighted. We had to calculate them from the 1961 Industrial Census [1], utilizing frequency distributions of firms by number of employees. Frequency distributions by shipments are not available. Except for the very few cases where one or several classes happened to include exactly the four largest firms, we had to interpolate following the method explained in detail in the statistical appendix of part II. The industries, as defined in the Belgian Census, are "three-digit": some correspond to the American "four-digit" industries, others are somewhat larger but generally smaller than "two-digit".

Official wholesale price indexes are available for only a very limited number of corresponding industries. Fortunately, we had access to the files of the Centre de Recherches Economiques (University of Louvain) which constructs its own indexes for a much larger number of industries. These indexes were used here. They have the advantage of being based on effective market prices, not list prices.

Data on shipments, production worker payroll, salaries and materials cost were taken from the annual surveys of manufactures which the Institut National de Statistique started in the 1950's — but only for a limited number of industries. [2] Each year, a number of industries were added to the list.

---

[1] *Recensement de l'industrie et du commerce,* 31 décembre 1961, tome 4 (Institut National de Statistique, Brussels, 1967).

[2] See the annual issue of *Annuaire Statistique de la Belgique.*

Table 2.5. Netherlands

Wholesale price indexes were furnished by the Centraal Bureau voor de Statistiek. Concentration ratios were calculated by inter-polation from the (unpublished) Industrial Census of 15 October 1963, using again frequency distributions of firms by number of employees. The other data were taken from the *Produktiestatistieken* which are published each year for a number of particular industries.

Table 2.6. France

Fourty wholesale price indexes for 1965 (1959=100), for in-dustries corresponding to the N.A.E. classification (Nomenclature des activités économiques), were provided by I.N.S.E.E. The classi-fication is also used in the 1962 Industrial Census [3] and in the B.I.C. statistics (Bénéfices industriels et commerciaux). We could thus proceed as above, utilizing these three sources.

After this study was completed, concentration ratios for ship-ments were published [4] for an impressive list of products, based on the classification used in the French national accounts. This classification being different from N.A.E., we would have got into troubles if we had tried to aggregate these ratios instead of com-puting our own concentration ratios directly from the Census.

Other countries

Several reasons prevented us from analyzing the other E.E.C. countries.

At the time this manuscript was completed, it was still impos-sible to compute concentration measures for three-digit industries in Germany. The frequency distributions from the 1963 census

[3] *Recensement de l'industrie en France en 1962*, vol. III (Paris, 1968).

[4] J.Loup, La concentration dans l'industrie francaise, d'après le recensement de 1963: la structure des marchés, *Etudes et conjoncture* (February 1969, no. 2) 17–237.

were not published in the German classification and were not available in N.I.C.E. The only data source available was the 1964 German annual industrial survey [5], But this covers only companies employing more than 10 persons: concentration ratios computed from this survey would have been worthless. Furthermore, it was impossible to find comparable data on salaries and wages over a sufficiently long period and for a sufficient number of industries.

For Italy, we encountered the opposite situation. Whereas value data (on shipments, wages, raw materials) were available and comparable (at least between 1961 and 1965 [6] and for large companies), together with the Italian industrial census of 16 October 1961, suitable price indexes were not to be found. The existing price indexes are based on other classifications.

Luxemburg was left out for lack of a sufficient number of observations.

[5] *Industrie und Handwerk*, Reihe I, Betriebe und Unternehmen der Industrie, II. Unternehmen, Beschäftigte und Umsatz, 1964 (April 1966).

[6] See *Note e Relazione*, no. 34, November 1967.

Table 2.4
Data on administrative inflation in Belgium, 1958–64.

Industry	$\frac{P64}{P58}$	C	$\frac{Q64}{Q58}$	$\frac{W64}{W58} \Big/ \frac{Q64}{Q58}$	$\frac{MC64}{MC58} \Big/ \frac{Q64}{Q58}$	$\frac{SW64}{SW58} \Big/ \frac{Q64}{Q58}$	$\dfrac{W64 \cdot W64}{W58 \cdot S64} \Big/ \dfrac{Q64}{Q58}$	$\dfrac{SW64 \cdot SW64}{SW58 \cdot S64} \Big/ \dfrac{Q64}{Q58}$	$\dfrac{MC64 \cdot MC64}{MC58 \cdot S64} \Big/ \dfrac{Q64}{Q58}$
1 Sugar	105	72	107	106	107	109	8.1	11.4	79.4
2 Tobacco	109	32	136	117	114	124	14.6	22.3	62.8
3 Shoes	135	15	112	136	133	134	32.0	36.9	68.1
4 Pulp and paper	95	51	150	109	68	106	15.5	20.4	29.8
5 Paper and paperboard products	102	20	171	104	97	105	12.5	18.7	55.0
6 Leather tanning	136	36	106	132	141	128	17.4	23.0	90.1
7 Rubber	107	67	129	112	109	111	18.8	28.6	56.7
8 Cleaning and toilet goods	96	48	148	105	96	108	5.9	15.6	49.3
9 Clay products	132	15	137	115	113	115	41.8	45.4	23.0
10 Iron and steel	99	53	136	107	95	109	6.7	8.6	77.3
11 Pottery	123	53	119	112	115	114	30.3	40.1	36.9
12 Yarn mills	113	21	136	119	111	117	14.4	17.2	76.4
13 Weaving mills	111	12	142	108	111	107	13.7	16.9	65.7
14 Fats and oils	102	78	135	105	104	114	3.3	5.5	90.5
15 Cokeries	95	100	101	116	93	115	5.8	7.6	78.2
16 Nonferrous metals	134	16	163	105	–	105	15.3	24.7	–
17 Glass	97	58	173	–	91	107	–	32.4	37.8

Table 2.5
Data on administrative inflation in the Netherlands, 1958–64

Industry	$\dfrac{P64}{P58}$	C	$\dfrac{Q64}{Q58}$	$\dfrac{SW64}{SW58}\Big/\dfrac{Q64}{Q58}$	$\dfrac{MC64}{MC58}\Big/\dfrac{Q64}{Q58}$	$\dfrac{\dfrac{SW64}{SW58}\cdot\dfrac{SW64}{S64}}{\dfrac{Q64}{Q58}}$
1 Margarine	99	75.4	120	142.27	110.99	8.10
2 Dairies	ı25	28.6	126	158.76	144.56	13.65
3 Canned vegetables and fruit	106	35.7	152	139.74	99.44	22.92
4 Chocolate	88	47.6	124	126.09	83.35	15.38
5 Cigars	122	42.7	111	122.59	124.17	31.95
6 Cigarettes	122	91.7	120	135.74	108.11	14.13
7 Tobacco	101	80.6	161	110.75	98.45	13.49
8 Yarn/wool	116	59.6	132	124.52	104.52	19.33
9 Woven wool	111	24.7	128	133.68	102.86	28.22
10 Yarn/cotton	97	62.5	118	121.07	92.16	22.01
11 Woven cotton	102	33.7	92	98.63	106.07	21.39
12 Wool carpets	111	49.0	204	81.31	110.89	10.90
13 Coir carpets	132	53.9	119	143.67	156.99	26.44
14 Knitted wear and stockings	100	49.0	167	102.93	105.69	21.16
15 Trimmings	102	40.7	124	107.89	98.18	34.34
16 Footwear	107	31.6	111	120.59	102.50	33.83
17 Work clothing	106	28.8	125	134.86	105.04	27.85
18 Waterproof outergarments	105	44.3	99	125.21	106.95	32.89
19 Shirts	95	36.2	200	99.39	108.47	19.56
20 Men's wear	107	29.0	211	113.28	110.24	23.68
21 Coats	113	33.3	122	123.52	110.63	21.63
22 Women's wear	104	11.2	181	99.23	100.86	18.58
23 Corsets	108	48.1	285	100.45	142.34	21.86
24 Underwear and night wear	102	24.4	221	108.60	103.60	19.39
25 Furniture	103	4.8	180	93.90	101.38	23.62
26 Wood packings	117	37.2	90	115.72	109.86	23.23
27 Strawboard	116	35.4	128	142.21	100.97	27.25
28 Paper	98	90.7	200	138.76	83.58	21.79
29 Paper products	105	50.3	164	134.17	95.23	19.60

Table 2.5 (cont.)

Industry	$\dfrac{P64}{P58}$	C	$\dfrac{Q64}{Q58}$	$\dfrac{SW64}{SW58}\Big/\dfrac{Q64}{Q58}$	$\dfrac{MC64}{MC58}\Big/\dfrac{Q64}{Q58}$	$\dfrac{\dfrac{SW64}{SW58}\cdot\dfrac{SW64}{S64}}{\dfrac{Q64}{Q58}}$
30 Cardboard	101	67.8	245	112.44	109.92	14.65
31 Cardboard boxes	103	18.2	229	98.40	109.23	17.80
32 Leather products	125	24.2	104	126.78	129.87	28.51
33 Leather	83	28.0	132	98.98	80.80	16.57
34 Rubber	102	70.3	156	143.78	91.97	37.38
35 Fertilizers	96	100.0	126	137.97	98.07	20.23
36 Paints, varnishes	99	76.2	158	112.40	87.96	19.76
37 Soap and other detergents	103	63.9	211	124.47	88.46	16.87
38 Medical chemicals and insecticides	86	63.8	281	102.93	73.14	20.23
39 Bricks	137	8.9	106	122.92	110.09	39.69
40 Tiles	139	53.7	117	134.83	129.22	44.21
41 Limestones	111	50.4	160	104.75	107.44	25.42
42 Metal furniture	107	36.1	177	112.30	92.98	30.48
43 Bicycles	108	42.9	138	118.75	108.04	19.14

Table 2.6

Data on administrative inflation in France, 1959–65

No. N.A.E.		Industry	$\frac{P65}{P59}$	C	$\frac{Q65}{Q59}$	$\frac{SW65}{SW59} / \frac{Q65}{Q59}$	$\frac{MC65}{MC59} / \frac{Q65}{Q59}$	$\frac{SW65}{SW59} \cdot \frac{SW65}{S65} / \frac{Q65}{Q59}$
454	1	Coffee	99.1	15.7	133	119.17	97.59	7.09
543	2	Paper and cardboard	110.7	19.5	165	107.70	110.17	15.42
540–41	3	Pulp and paper	109.3	48.3	170	109.56	113.09	13.09
532	4	Flooring and veneering	137.0	10.3	159	127.89	143.11	20.27
531	5	Saw-mills	134.0	2.8	97	121.61	134.88	16.61
517	6	Leather belting	96.9	39.8	171	97.87	89.27	19.25
475	7	Wool/yarn and woven	116.2	14.4	134	110.93	110.30	14.38
474	8	Cotton/yarn and woven	111.5	15.0	146	96.22	115.78	13.56
473	9	Jute/thread and cloth	117.5	56.5	164	109.73	106.62	16.49
472	10	Linen/yarn and woven	133.5	31.4	88	136.70	118.64	22.91
471	11	Linen/steeping, stripping	125.1	22.5	120	116.58	130.73	15.87
470	12	Textile industry	116.3	79.5	11	108.55	113.09	13.06
456	13	Animal feeds	121.8	16.8	306	117.79	121.10	6.78
444	14	Canned fish	128.9	13.5	118	129.16	135.00	13.48
442	15	Canned meat	118.3	28.6	173	116.61	119.86	10.05
441	16	Canned vegetables	111.0	19.2	136	134.28	109.67	15.72
433	17	Cheese	122.5	35.2	139	133.22	124.20	9.41
432	18	Butter	112.8	36.2	148	102.72	115.14	3.82
431	19	Milk	122.8	22.2	193	119.58	126.68	8.86
428	20	Liquors, appetizers	111.6	27.9	178	93.28	100.21	7.66
427	21	Wines	102.9	20.0	265	102.67	108.00	7.58
425	22	Brewery	120.5	22.3	130	127.48	107.25	16.20
403	23	Bakery products	110.5	45.9	126	94.40	105.71	8.45

Table 2.6 (cont.)

No. N.A.E.		Industry	$\dfrac{P65}{P59}$	C	$\dfrac{Q65}{Q59}$	$\dfrac{SW65}{SW59} \Big/ \dfrac{Q65}{Q59}$	$\dfrac{MC65}{MC59} \Big/ \dfrac{Q65}{Q59}$	$\dfrac{SW65}{SW59} \cdot \dfrac{SW65}{S65} \Big/ \dfrac{Q65}{Q59}$
393	24	Soaps	116.1	79.6	115	130.25	95.72	13.45
392	25	Animal fats	122.7	30.5	39	100.59	143.54	9.64
391	26	Vegetal fats	94.0	61.9	116	103.90	85.96	6.16
375	27	Asbestos	86.1	23.0	145	141.81	100.56	32.63
372	28	Tires and inner tubes	109.0	76.5	169	109.35	98.85	21.12
358	29	Industrial explosives	111.9	63.0	131	125.28	69.32	23.72
356	30	Coal tar and benzol	94.5	47.5	256	72.30	54.01	7.06
354	31	Organic chemistry	78.9	32.1	613	74.55	77.76	9.25
351	32	Mineral chemistry	108.1	69.5	93	112.35	84.16	17.01
350	33	Total of chemistry	103.0	86.0	45	139.02	74.13	30.85
325	34	Lime, cement	114.0	41.0	147	99.59	96.71	11.46
324	35	Plaster	124.0	41.8	406	85.04	152.48	10.96
311	36	Bricks and tiles	132.6	11.0	156	113.35	123.73	26.32
201	37	Foundries	95.0	16.5	180	85.93	108.94	16.29
193	38	Steel tubes	110.9	59.4	137	108.39	114.95	12.16
191	39	Nonferrous metals (semi-products)	132.5	67.4	135	122.91	138.76	12.59
30	40	Sheet glass	112.5	30.7	161	106.01	101.90	22.17

CHAPTER 3

PROFITS

3.1. Introduction

Chapter 2 has shown that the administrative inflation hypothesis is not verified in the countries analysed. If it is true, then, that price increases followed increases in unit costs in concentrated as well as unconcentrated industries, it does not necessarily follow that prices were not "too high" in concentrated industries.

As it is very difficult to obtain direct evidence on price and unit cost *levels*, the problem is generally restated in terms of realized *profits*. These profits are measured as rates of return (profits as a percentage of total assets, of net worth, of value of shipments, of market values, . . .). Another approach tries to compute, from aggregate data, average price-cost margins. [1] This approach will not be pursued here.

A strong tradition in the literature suggests that there exists a positive relationship between profit rates, more precisely profit rates averaged over some period, and concentration ratios, both variables being measured industry by industry. If anything, concentration measures should indicate the extent of oligopolistic

[1] See D.Schwartzman, The effect of monopoly on price, *J. of Political Economy* (August 1959); K.Sato, Price-cost structure and behavior of profit margins, *Yale Economic Essays* (1961); L.Telser, Cutthroat competition and the long purse, *J. of Law and Economics* (October 1966); N.R.Collins and L.E.Preston, *Concentration and Price-cost Margins in Manufacturing Industries* (University of California Press, Berkely, 1968); N.R.Collins and L.E.Preston, Price-cost margins and industry structure, *Rev. of Economics and Statistics* (August 1969); L.Telser, *Some Determinants of the Returns to Manufacturing Industries*, Report No. 6935, Center for Mathematical Studies in Business and Economics (University of Chicago, 1969).

market structure. If one then accepts the hypothesis that oligopolists tend to collude to maximize their joint profits, the positive relationship becomes plausible.

It remains then to be seen how this relationship should be specified and whether it is confirmed by hard facts. A survey of the available empirical literature might be useful to start with.

3.2. Survey of the empirical literature on rates of return

The discussion centers around the pioneering contributions by J.S.Bain, the work of G.J.Stigler and a group of rather diversified contributions on related problems.

3.2.1. Bain's contribution

The first empirical study relating return and concentration was published by Bain [2]. His sample was formed of 335 companies belonging to 42 industries. He used annual rates of return defined as the ratios of the profit net of depreciation and after tax to the net worth at the beginning of the year, for the period 1936–40. He then averaged the rates of return for each company and calculated a weighted average of rates of return by industry, using net worth of companies as weight. We must notice that the rates of return so defined refer only to the leading companies of each industry.

As a measure of concentration, Bain took the share of sales of the 8 biggest companies, given, for each industry, by the 1935 Census of manufactures. To calculate those concentration ratios, the authors of the Census divide, for each four-digit industry, the amount of sales due to the plants belonging to the largest companies of the industry by the sales of all plants of the industry.

Bain's sample is not representative of American manufacturing

[2] Relation of profit rate to industry concentration . . ., *Quarterly J. of Economics* (May 1951).

industry, as a consequence of lack of data on rates of return. In fact it is biased towards oligopolistic sectors. Out of the 42 industries of the sample, 38 had at least 30% of their output supplied by the 8 largest firms. [3]

The average profit rate is 11.8 for industries with a concentration ratio above 70% and 7.5 when the concentration ratio is below 70%. The application of a *t*-test on equality of means shows that, under assumption of normality, this difference is significant at 2%. Nevertheless, N.Collins and L.Preston, computing a simple correlation coefficient from Bain's data, found $r = 0.28$ that is significant at 10% only. [4] Those results might lead us to consider that a relation between profitability and concentration would be more easily detected by the use of some threshold than with the help of a continuous regression model.

In his *Barriers to New Competition*, Professor Bain suggests that concentration by itself does not allow to expect profits above the competitive level. Such profits can build up only if firms of an industry are protected by barriers to entry. He defines four barriers of this kind: scale economies and large scale sales promotion, product differentiation which results in brand loyalty and requires sales promotion outlays, cost barriers arising from patents or secret techniques used by established firms and from the control of these firms on the supply of scarce resources, and finally capital requirement barriers resulting from the financial charges entailed by the costs evocated hereabove. As this last barrier is strictly dependent on the first three, Bain drops it in his empirical work.

According to his theory and previous results, Bain might have tested the following hypothesis. Among concentrated industries, there is a significant difference between the profit rates enjoyed by industries protected by high barriers to entry and those of industries with unsufficient barriers. On the other hand, there is no difference in profitability between the industries of this last group and the unconcentrated ones.

[3] J.S.Bain, *Industrial Organization*, 2nd ed. (Wiley, New York, 1968) p. 447.

[4] In: *Concentration and Price-Cost Margins in Manufacturing Industries* (University of California Press, Berkeley, 1968) p. 23.

With respect to barriers to entry, Bain divided American industries into 3 groups. In the very high barrier class, firms could raise their profits by 10% above costs without causing new entries, companies of the substantial barrier class could raise their own profits by 7% and those belonging to industries with moderate to low barriers by 1 to 4%. For 20 industries, he published the concentration ratio for the four largest firms in 1947, the average rate of return of the leading firms for 1947—51 and a division into the three barriers to entry-classes given hereabove. We may consider that a four-firm concentration ratio of 50% is equivalent to an eight-firm concentration ratio of 70%.

The difference in average rate of return between industries with concentration ratio above and below 50% is significant at 1 per mill. The same result holds, among concentrated industries, for those with very high barriers to entry versus the other ones and for the difference in average rate of return between concentrated industries without very high barriers to entry and unconcentrated ones. This last result contradicts our hypothesis. Nevertheless the sample of industries is small and biased towards oligopoly: further studies are required to support even tentative conclusions. [5]

A first opportunity to verify Bain's results is provided by a paper by H.Mann . [6] This author examined the effect on rates of return of concentration ratios and of barriers to entry, for 30 four-digit American industries. The rates of return referred to leading companies and were averaged over the period 1950—1960. Eight-firm concentration ratios were taken from the 1958 Census of manufactures. According to Bain's criteria, Mann had to decide which kind of barrier to entry protected the firms of each industry. The eight industries with very high barriers to entry belonged to the group of 21 the eight-firm concentration ratio of which was larger than 70%.

[5] Only two concentrated industries had moderate to low barriers to entry. Their average rate of return is significantly greater than the rate of the unconcentrated industries at the 5% level.

[6] Seller concentration, barriers to entry and rates of return in thirty industries 1950—1960, *Rev. of Economics and Statistics* (August 1966).

Leading firms of concentrated industries had an average profit rate of 13.3 while this rate was only 9.0 for the unconcentrated ones. The difference is significant at 1 per mill level. Among the industries with eight-firm concentration ratios greater than 70%, he found that the ones with very high barriers to entry had an average profit rate of 16.4 while the rate was 11.1 for the industries with substantial barriers and 11.9 when barriers were moderate to low. The difference between the last two figures is not significant.

We therefore aggregated the rates of return of the two corresponding classes to compare them on the one hand with the rates of return of the concentrated industries protected by very high barriers and on the other hand with the rates of the unconcentrated industries.

The test of difference of means for concentrated and highly protected industries and concentrated industries with substantial to low barriers is significant at 1 per mill level. On the contrary, the difference between the average profit rate of concentrated but not highly protected industries and unconcentrated industries is not significant even at 10% level. This second result contradicts the findings of Bain who performed the same test on his sample and obtained a difference significant at 1 per mill. It is in accordance with the hypothesis that very high barriers to entry are a necessary condition of the existence of monopolistic profits.

Mann's data were reexamined by D.Kammerschen.[7] On the whole sample, he essentially performed a multiple regression, using a dummy variable to take into account the threshold of 70% for concentration ratios and another one to distinguish between industries with very high barriers to entry and industries less protected. The coefficient of the first dummy variable was not significant at 5% but the second one was significant at 1%. When Kammerschen uses the concentration ratios instead of dummies, the corresponding coefficient is not significant any more but the

---

[7] The determination of profit rates in oligopolistic industries, *J. of Business* (July 1969).

coefficient referring to barriers to entry remains significant at 1%. No test of multicollinearity was performed but we may notice that the simple correlation coefficients between the variables referring to barriers to entry and the ones related to concentration are not significant at 5% level.

Kammerschen also induced in his regressions the number of firms as another proxy of competition and the value of shipments to check the possibility of a specific relationship between the rate of return and the size of the industry which somehow might have been the result of the profitability of this industry. These two variables were not significant. [8]

K.George developed Mann's study in another direction. [9] He used four-firm concentration ratios and included growth of net assets. Barriers to entry were introduced first by means of two dummies, one for very high and another for substantial barriers and then by multiplying the values of concentration ratios by the values taken by these dummies. George kept 28 industries in his sample while Kammerschen had discarded 5 of the 30 industries selected by Mann.

Perhaps thanks to this or because he used four-firm concentration ratios, George obtained a coefficient for the concentration ratio significant at 5% but low: 5×10^{-2}. Growth and the first dummy variable were significant at 1%. In the second regression, growth and the combined variable retaining only concentration ratios of industries with very high barriers to entry were significant at 1%; the value of the second coefficient was 7×10^{-2}.

In a general study, Weiss inserts three equations respectively referring to the 20 industries studied by Bain on the periods 1936–40 and 1947–51 and to the 30 industries of Mann. He

---

[8] In the *Rev. of Economics and Statistics* (August 1967), M.Hall and L.W.Weiss published a study on Firm size and profitability, of which the main achievement was to show that, for the largest companies and after having taken into account economic fluctuations and heteroskedasticity, both concentration and firm size have a significant impact on rates of return. These significant results were obtained when the values of concentration ratios were introduced (but not when they were replaced by dummies).

[9] In: A note on concentration, barriers to entry and rates of return, *Rev. of Economics and Statistics* (May 1968).

correlates the rates of return with concentration ratios multiplied by three dummies, one for each class of barriers to entry. [10] What is striking in his study is the relatively high value of his significant coefficients. But for the first study of Bain, concentration is significant only with very high barriers to entry.

Before leaving Bain's tradition, we must examine the work of H.Levinson. [11] This author defines his measure of concentration as follows: the ratio of the value of shipments from four-digit industries with concentration ratio greater than 50% and belonging to the same two-digit industry to the total value of shipments of this industry.

By definition, this index may take any value between 0 and 1. The extreme values are taken when the four-digit industries are respectively all under or all above what may be considered as Bain's threshold of concentration. To see how both approaches are comparable let us consider that both test the same hypothesis, "for a typical industry, if the concentration ratio passes some level, the rate of return must be expected to grow by a definite amount". For individual observations, this move may be offset by random errors. In order to get rid of these we may compare average rates of return. That is the way suggested by Bain and followed by Mann. On the other hand, we may aggregate, e.g. at the two-digit level. Levinson chose this device.

The various correlation coefficients he found scaled from 0.45 to 0.76 for the years 1951–52 to 1957–58 and profits before and after taxes (correlated with concentration ratios of 1954). [12] The highest values of r are obtained for correlation with profits after taxes. Averaging the rates of return over the period 1952–56

[10] In: *Econometric Studies of Industrial Organization* (unpublished), p. 22.

[11] We could only get hold of the summary of Levinson's study written by Collins and Preston in *Concentration and Price-Cost Margins* . . ., Op. cit., p. 23 onwards.

[12] We must remember that the level of significance of a correlation coefficient heavily depends upon the size of the studied sample. The t-test of significance refers indeed to the distribution of $r\sqrt{n-2}/\sqrt{1-r^2}$ and the increasing number of degrees of freedom is far from compensating the scale effect appearing in this formula. If we believe that the increase of studied samples does not change their characteristics, the absolute value of r is more important than the level of significance, for comparison purposes.

does not improve the fit. The correlation coefficients are definitely higher than the ones obtained as a result of studies at the four-digit level, for the same years.

From these American studies, we must retain that high barriers to entry increase the power of concentrated industries and their possibilities of raising monopolistic profits. In addition, we may notice that the influence of concentration upon profits may be tested in two alternative ways, by means of a linear relationship between concentration ratios and rates of return or by assuming that rates of return are significantly larger above a certain level of concentration.

3.2.2. Stigler's contribution

In his first contribution, G.Stigler is concerned with a sample of 99 three-digit American industries for various dates between 1938 and 1957. [13]

In accordance with Bain's hypothesis of a relevant threshold in the study of concentration related to profitability, he first divides his sample into three classes. Industries with four-firm concentration ratios above 60% are considered as concentrated. Those with a national market and a concentration ratio smaller than 50% or with a regional market and a concentration ratio below 20% are called unconcentrated. The remaining industries are classified as ambiguous.

Data for rates of return of corporations are on a three-digit basis. As usual, four-digit concentration ratios (arithmetic averages of those published for 1947 and for 1954) are weighted by shipments. In order to improve the accuracy of his data for rates of return, Stigler estimates the rates of return of firms that do not publish balance-sheets, takes into account special regulations for depreciation and increases the returns of small companies by including as profits parts of the salary of the owners.

---

[13] G.Stigler, *Capital and rates of return in manufacturing industries,* chap. 3 (Princeton University Press, 1963).

In opposition to Bain, Stigler takes loans and interests paid into account to calculate profitability. Theoretically, this way of calculating the rate of return may seem more valid than the one used by Bain who considered net worth only as relevant for his calculation. Stigler's rate of return shows indeed what is the profitability of all funds at management disposal, without disregarding some of them for ownership reasons (which might seem meaningless as far as performances of the entreprise are concerned). Despite its theoretical merits, Stigler's rate of return may be empirically disappointing. It is likely that it will not vary as sensitively with concentration as the rate defined by Bain because interest paid on loans might not differ according to the level of concentration of the industry emitting bonds.

Consider the results Stigler found most characteristic. The differences between average rates of return enjoyed in concentrated and unconcentrated industries were significant at 5% for 1951–54 and at 2% for 1955–57. Averaging the rates of return on a longer period (1947–54), Stigler did not find any significant difference of means. This result was confirmed by regression analysis after correction for excessive salaries in small companies (both when data referring to industries with regional markets were included into the regression and when they were not).

Stigler tried to test Bain's idea that monopolistic profits are to be expected only in those industries that can prevent new entries by erecting "very high" barriers, while the existence of "substantial" or lower barriers does not allow colluding oligopolists to fix prices above the competitive level. This hypothesis implies that the variance of rates of return among concentrated industries is greater than amongst unconcentrated ones. An F-test on the ratio of variances was not significant for the period 1947–54, but was significant at 1% for 1938–47. Similarly, for this last period, Stigler noticed that concentrated industries were significantly abler to maintain their rate of profit from year to year.

Collins and Preston reexamined Stigler's data. [14] They classified

---

[14] In: *Concentration and price-cost margins*, p. 37–39.

the industries, among the three classes of concentration, separately for 1947 and 1954 and moved from "unconcentrated" to "ambiguous" industries those referring to miscellanous products.

They took rates of return for 1947, 1947–48, 1954 and 1953–55, and found a significant difference of means of rates of return between concentrated and unconcentrated industries in the two last cases only but then at 1% level. The regression of coefficients of rates of return on concentration ratios of national industries were significant at 1% for the two same cases but quite small: 0.04 each. The values of r were 0.36 and 0.39 respectively, significant at 1% for a sample of 75 industries.

Stigler's second study is an interesting attempt to support empirical measurement of concentration by a theoretical model. [15]

Assume that the probability of attracting a new customer is, for a firm, proportional to its share of output in the industry. Each firm will have a mathematical expectation and a variance of the share of sales to new customers it can enjoy. For a given number of customers, the sum of these variances will vary in the direction opposite to an index of concentration called H-index and equal to the sum of squares of market shares. The importance of this theoretical result comes from the fact that collusion usually tends to maintain the shares of sales over time and so collusion will be reflected in a high H while a situation of competitive oligopoly will be likely to persist for an industry with a lower H.

For 17 four-digit concentrated industries, Stigler calculated Spearman rank correlation coefficients of four-firm concentration ratios given by the 1954 census and of H-indexes, with the average rate of return of dominant firms of those industries, over the period 1953–57. The H-index gave more significant coefficients than the concentration ratio. For the first index, the coefficient was significant at 5% with rates of return calculated on all assets and at 1% when computed on net worth. The corresponding coefficients with the concentration ratio were nonsignificant and significant at 5% level, respectively. We may notice that the

[15] A theory of oligopoly, *J. of political economy* (February 1964).

correlation is higher with rates of return calculated on net worth, as expected.

A final point to be noticed is that, for both measures of concentration, the highest Spearman coefficient is obtained when these measures are compared with the ratio of the market value of the leading companies over their book value. This is quite important with respect to an argument [16] which says that a positive relationship between concentration and profitability cannot be verified with data taken from balance-sheets because assets of firms exerting monopoly power would be reevaluated to take this power into account. If the argument were correct, and given that market value reflects monopoly power, the ratio market value over book value could not vary significantly with concentration.

In their survey, Collins and Preston computed linear correlation coefficients between concentration ratios and rates of return calculated on all assets and on net worth, from the data Stigler had used for his second study. [17] The correlation coefficients were significant at 10% and 5% level, respectively. The absolute values of r were 0.46 and 0.53 versus 0.36 and 0.39 for Stigler's first study. The loss of significance may partially be imputed to a sharp diminution in the size of the sample. We must remember that a change in the size of a sample that does not change the variances of the correlated variables does not affect the value of r, but does affect the value of t computed to test the significance of r.

The way Stigler corrected rates of return of small companies was criticized by R.Kilpatrick. [18] According to this author, Stigler might have overestimated the share of salaries of the owners of small companies that was in fact return on capital. By doing this, he might have unduly wiped out the positive relationship between rate of return and concentration.

The author tried other methods to separate the influence of concentration on profitability from disturbances caused by small com-

---

[16] Evocated by Stigler in: *Capital and Rates of Return*, p. 69.

[17] In: *Concentration and Price-Cost Margins*, pp. 41–42.

[18] Stigler on the Relationship between industry profit rates and market concentration, *J. of Political Economy* (May-June 1968).

panies. By the same token, he tried to isolate the effect of concentration from whatever influence variations in demand might have.

Before coming to his results, we may notice that Kilpatrick corrected concentration ratios to take imports into account. They were added to sales in the computation of four-digit concentration ratios and in the weights used to aggregate concentration ratios.

For 1950, 1956 and 1963, Kilpatrick regressed rates of return, calculated by using net worth, and four-firm concentration ratios, on the pourcentage of output produced by corporations smaller than $ 250,000 or $ 500,000 of assets and on change in output with respect to some preceding year. [19] Alternatively he used rates of return computed without taking small companies into account. This method is similar to the one followed by Stigler in his second study when he considered rates of return of leading firms only.

For 1953 and 1956, the inclusion of a variable for small corporations lessens the coefficient of the concentration ratio. For 1956 this coefficient remains significant at 5% at least. For 1963, the introduction of small corporations in the analysis has a doubtful effect.

Notice also that Kilpatrick obtained 0.09 and 0.15, as values of the coefficient of the concentration ratio, in a regression of the rate of return on the concentration ratio and the variation of output, for 1950 and 1956 respectively. Data on change in output were not available for 1963. The coefficient of the concentration ratio in the simple regression was 0.13. These results are quite tentative, though, because the corresponding confidence intervals are wide.

In a footnote, Kilpatrick mentions that a quadratic relationship between rates of return and concentration ratios was fitted but that the coefficient of the quadratic term was non significant, generally speaking. He also worked with dummies instead of concentration ratios. The result obtained led to the conclusion that the use of concentration ratios is rather more convincing.

---

[19] In his estimate, Stigler had taken into account all small firms and not only the corporated ones.

On this last point, Weiss makes the following remark in his survey. [20] The use of dummies rests on the hypothesis that, passed a certain level of concentration, the rate of return jumps while the precise value of the concentration ratio in the range above or below this level is not relevant to determine an expected rate of return. Alternatively, he proposes to test the hypothesis according to which there would be a linear relationship relating concentration ratios and rates of return below a certain level and another one above this level. These two relationships would differ by their slope. In such a case, it is possible, writes Weiss, that the existence of a threshold would not prevent a simple regression model to be more realistic than a model including dummy variables.

In the same paper, Weiss suggests that the relatively poor results obtained by Stigler might be due to the years chosen. During most of these, the U.S. had open or repressed inflation. The influence of concentration on profitability might be clearer in recession years.

3.2.3. Further studies on profitability, concentration and other explanatory variables

In the two last sections, we came across a few empirical studies centered on the relationship between profit, concentration and barriers to entry. We now return to pieces of research which are somewhat outside this main line of attack.

A first study to be mentioned was written by V. Fuchs. [21] His sample was composed of 38 three-digit industries. Rates of return after taxes for corporate assets, including loans as in Stigler's book, were averaged over 1953–54. The four-digit concentration ratios, weighted by value added, were taken from the 1954 census.

Fuchs obtained a simple correlation coefficient between profits and concentration of 0.28, significant at 10% level. This rather

---

[20] *Econometric Studies of Industrial Organization*, p. 16.

[21] Integration, concentration and profits in manufacturing industries, *Quarterly J. of Economics* (May 1961).

low value of r might be partly due to the fact that concentration ratios are calculated on a national basis. If the markets were regional, the concentration ratio would underestimate monopoly power.

The author introduced a coefficient of scatter defined as the least number of states required to account for 75% of value added, in each industry. When the value of this coefficient is high, the true markets can be expected to be regional. A regression of rate of return on concentration ratio and this coefficient gives a partial correlation coefficient between the first two variables of 0.42 significant at 1% level. This would be the correlation coefficient to be expected if the same value of the coefficient of scatter were observed for all industries. Broadly speaking, this would be the case if all markets were national and thus if concentration ratios were defined for true markets.

W.Comanor and T.Wilson focussed their attention on 46 consumer goods industries. [22] They used profit rates calculated as a percentage of stockholders equity. The companies with assets worth less than $ 500,000 were not considered. As a result, Comanor and Wilson had not to bother about the bias due to excessive salaries of owners of small firms, noticed by Stigler. The rates of return were averaged for the years 1954–57, considered as a business cycle.

Simple correlation between concentration ratios of 1954 and profit rates computed as above was 0.36, significant at 5%. (With rates of return calculated on all assets, including loans, $r = 0.33$, also significant at 5%.)

In a multiple regression analysis, Comanor and Wilson took into account, besides concentration ratios, high and moderate technical barriers to entry, high and moderate advertising intensities, defined as the ratio of advertising expenditures to total revenue, and regional markets. They also included the log of growth of sales. Only high advertising intensity and growth were

---

[22] Advertising, market structures and performances, *Rev. of Economics and Statistics* (November 1967).

significant at 5%, despite the fact that $\overline{R}^2 = 0.36$ was significant at 1%. Concentration ratios were significant at 10% only and the value of their coefficient was very small: 6×10^{-4}.

When a new variable called capital requirements is introduced and defined as the amount of capital required for entry at the scale of a single efficient plant, concentration ratios have no significant coefficient any more. This may be explained by a regression of concentration ratios on capital requirements, economies of scale and the regional industry dummy variable. The t-ratio corresponding to the coefficient of capital requirements is 3.9 significant at 1 per mill level.

Another author related concentration to advertising intensity. [23] His study is a continuation of an article in the *Southern Economic Journal*. [24] Miller had found there that weighted averages of concentration ratios of 1958 were positively correlated with the rates of return, alternatively defined as in Stigler's and in Bain's work, and that marginal concentration ratios i.e. shares of the 5th to the 8th largest firm were negatively correlated with the same rates of return.

In his second study, Miller introduced as new variables advertising intensity, defined as the ratio of advertising expenditures to total revenue, and corporate diversity. This last variable is defined as the ratio of employment of plants classified in an industry to total employment of firms having plants in this industry. The more firms of an industry operate in other industries, the smaller is the value taken by the variable "corporate diversity". Diversification may be explained e.g. by the appeal of vertical integration or by the advantages of a greater dimension. It is sometimes understood as a specific barrier to entry because it could give more power to established firms on all markets in which they operate.

All four regression coefficients on both kinds of rates of return

[23] R.A.Miller, Market structure and industrial performance: relation of profit rates to concentration, advertising intensity and diversity, *J. of Industrial Economics* (April 1969).

[24] R.A.Miller, Marginal concentration ratios and industrial profit rates: some empirical results of oligopoly behavior, *Southern Economic J.* (October 1967).

were highly significant. This result is different from the one obtained by Comanor and Wilson as far as concentration ratios are concerned. Nevertheless we must remember that neither growth nor capital requirements or economics of scale were introduced in Miller's study and that all these variables are likely to be correlated with concentration ratios. We must also notice that if the positive coefficient of concentration ratios is about 4×10^{-2} when four variables explain the rate of return, the negative one of marginal concentration ratios is about 0.2.

The three last studies to be mentioned here have a basic feature in common. They are concerned with two-digit industries, We can thus expect that the significance of a relationship between rate of return and concentration ratio will be enhanced, as a consequence of aggregation.

Minhas correlated the rate of return on net worth after tax, averaged over the period 1949–58, with the four-firm concentration ratio of 1947 and the average annual rate of growth during the period 1949–58, for the 20 two-digit manufacturing industries. [25] He obtained a regression coefficient of 0.12 for the concentration ratio, significant at 1% and higher than the value obtained with three-digit industries. The magnitude of this coefficient is stable whether growth is or is not introduced in the regression. Growth has a coefficient significant at 5% and, when it is introduced, $\bar{R}^2$ goes up from 0.34 to 0.44. The inclusion of an index of research and development expenditure does not improve the fit.

Weiss amended the two-digit classification by splitting two industries [26] to obtain 22 observations. He used weighted averages of four-firms concentration ratios of 1954. The rates of return were calculated on equity for 1949–58. The simple correlation is 0.73. [27] When growth is added, $\bar{R}^2$ goes up to 0.83!

[25] B.Minhas, *An International Comparison of Factor Costs and Factor Use* (North-Holland Publ. Co., Amsterdam, 1963), pp. 82–84.

[26] L.Weiss, Average concentration ratios and industry performance, *J. of Industrial Economics* (July 1963).

[27] This value is especially high. Sherman, correlating the rates of return on equity

Collins and Preston made a comparative study of the relationship between the concentration ratio and various rates of return.
Leaving aside the price-cost margin, we shall concentrate on rates
of return as a percentage of sales, assets and shareholders equity
before and after taxes. [28]

Eight-firm concentration ratios for 1958 were weighted by shipments. The various rates of return were taken for 1958 and for the
period 1956–60.

Some general results are to be retained. The slope coefficients
of the concentration ratio are twice as big for profits before taxes
than for profits after taxes. Rates on shareholders equity also give
a much higher coefficient than the two other rates of return, while
rates on all assets give a coefficient of 0.06, in line with the results
obtained by other authors. The rates averaged over 1956–60 do
not give more significant results than the rates for 1958. Finally,
the rate of return on value of sales always yields the less significant
slope coefficient for the concentration ratio.

3.2.4. *British studies*

P.Hart made the first attempt to find a relationship between
concentration ratios and rates of return of British industries. [29]
T.Barna provided him with rates of return defined as the ratio of
value added minus employee compensation to total assets. [30]
The estimates of total assets were based "on the fire insurance value of a sample of firms in each industry". Concentration ratios

---

with the eight-firm concentration ratios of 1954, had obtained 0.66 only. The difference
between these two results may be due to the fact that Sherman, by using eight-firm concentration ratios, combined the positive effect of four-firm concentration ratios and the
negative influence of marginal concentration ratios. Cf. H.Sherman, *Macrodynamic
Economics*, chap. 8 (Appleton Century Crofts, New York, 1964).

[28] N.Collins and L.Preston, *Concentration and Price-Cost Margins in Manufacturing
Industries*, chap. 3 (University of California Press, Berkeley, 1968).

[29] *Studies in Profit, Business Saving and Investment in the United-Kingdom 1920–
1962*, ed. P.Hart (Allen and Unwin, London, 1968), vol. 2, pp. 258–264.

[30] T.Barna in: *The Theory of Capital*, ed. F.Lutz and D.Hague (MacMillan, London,
1964), p. 83.

on value added were taken from Evely and Little's book and averaged with value added as weight. [31] In a simple regression the coefficient of concentration ratios was much smaller than its standard deviation.

We performed two other tests on Hart's data. We first compared average rates of return of industries having concentration ratios larger or smaller than 40%. This threshold was chosen because Evely and Little usually calculated three-firm concentration ratios. The t-value obtained was smaller than one. We then tested the hypothesis that the variance of rates of return would be greater for concentrated industries as a consequence of various entrepreneur's behaviours in those industries in accordance with different heights of barriers to entry. The F-test did not give a value significantly greater than 1.

Those results, quite different from the American ones taken as a whole, might be due partly to the estimate of assets via fire insurances. It may be thought that monopoly rents are taken into account when companies evaluate their assets for insurance purposes.

J.Samuels and D.Smyth tested the hypothesis that, in concentrated industries, rates of return are more stable from year to year than in unconcentrated industries. [32]

They also used Evely and Little's concentration ratios but rates of return were defined as ratios of profit after depreciation and before tax to net worth and taken over the period 1954–63 for 116 companies.

Samuels and Smyth computed the trend of rates of return for each company. In order to test their hypothesis on the link between concentration and the stability of rates of return, they plotted residual variances of profit rates about those trends against concentration ratios. The graph showed that residual variances were smaller for concentrated industries. That was confirmed with

---

[31] R.Evely and I.Little, *Concentration in British Industries*, National Institute of Social and Economic Researches (Cambridge University Press, Cambridge, 1960) pp. 296–312.
[32] Profits, variability of profits and firm size, *Economica* (May 1968).

a *t*-test on the means of residual variances for industries with concentration ratios larger or smaller than 30%. The difference between means was significant at 1% level.

3.2.5. *Final comment*

Most American studies have shown that there exists a positive relationship between rates of return and concentration ratios in manufacturing industries in the U.S. The shape of this relationship is not clear and the level of concentration is far from explaining the rate of return satisfactorily. When transitory factors and barriers to entry are introduced, the influence of concentration ratios on return remains in general statistically significant.

There is very little information on other countries. [33] British studies do not tend to confirm the American results, except for the greater stability over time of rates of return in more concentrated industries. Before concluding at a genuine opposition, we must remember that assets used in Hart's study might include monopoly rents.

3.3. Measures of the rate of return

In the Bain tradition, rates of returns are obtained by dividing net profits by "net worth" i.e. "equity", i.e. "invested capital" (of some companies in an industry). In the Stigler tradition, one takes the ratio of net profits plus interests paid over total assets (of some or all companies in an industry).

We are going to follow the Bain tradition and to measure equity by capital plus reserves (i.e. *fonds propres* in French). One reason is that the available statistical sources do not allow to compute with precision the amounts borrowed. Furthermore, it can be argued that the rate of return on equity is the correct concept on

---

[33] For an analysis of economic performance and size of the largest firms in the Common Market, see A.Jacquemin, Dimension, stabilité et performance des 40 plus grandes entreprises européennes 1956–1967, *Rev. d'économie politique* (1970) 221–36.

theoretical grounds. [34] It is what managers acting in the owners' best interests would seek to maximize, using more or less foreign capital. These borrowed funds can be treated as inputs, whose relative importance varies from industry to industry according to factors such as growth prospects and stability. Rates of return on total assets should thus differ between industries, even in perfectly competition long run equilibrium. The hypothesis to be tested here clearly implies that rates of return should be equal between industries in long run competition equilibrium, which would be the case for rates of return on equity.

For one country (France) we were unable to find reliable data on equity and had to use the value of sales instead. It should be clear that the resulting profit-sales ratios are different from rates of return on equity. Interindustry differences in profit-sales ratios reflect differences in rates of return on equity only if the sales-equity ratio is constant from industry to industry. Indeed we have

$$\frac{\text{profits}}{\text{equity}} = \frac{\text{profits}}{\text{sales}} \cdot \frac{\text{sales}}{\text{equity}} .$$

On the other hand, profit-sales ratios measure price-cost margins, which are not to be equalized in competitive long-run equilibrium.

"Equity" ("invested capital") will be measured from its book value. Some economists object to this, arguing that equity should be measured from the current market value of equity shares on a stock exchange. In the context of an analysis of the effects of market structure, this procedure would be wrong. The market value includes the present value of the monopoly return, with the result that rates of return on market values could not show any relation with concentration ratios.

The next problem is to eliminate short-run variations in demand and costs over the business cycle, to obtain a kind of "structural" rate of return, typical for each industry. We decided to use the

[32] See M.Hall and L.Weiss, Firm size and profitability, *Rev. of Economics and Statistics* (August 1967) 321.

simple average of yearly rates of return over the period 1958–64 for Belgium. To what extent are these averages typical for each industry?

One way to answer this question is to look at the Spearman rank correlation between these averages for two successive time periods covering different business cycles. If the correlation is significantly different from zero, there is an indication that the ranking of the industries, in terms of their rates of return, remains unchanged from one business cycle to another.

For 33 Belgian industries, the rank correlation between the averages for the periods 1958–64 and 1951–57 is 0.569. It is significant at the 0.01 level. This gives a clear positive answer to our problem. However, when the 33 industries are partitioned into three groups, according to the level of concentration, important differences appear. The highly concentrated group ($C > 50$), including 9 industries, gets a rank correlation of 0.833, which is again highly significant. The two other groups ($25 < C < 50$ and $C < 25$), with 9 and 15 industries respectively, obtain only 0.55 and 0.45 which are not or barely significant. In other words, the ranking of industries according to average rates of return persists only in the group of highly concentrated industries.

Let us now stick to one period and see how the annual rates of return behave. Following Stigler's example, simple correlations between rates of return for two successive years, and then for the pairs of years T and $T-2$, T and $T-3$, etc. were computed. The averages of the correlation coefficients obtained for each type of lag are reported in tables 3.1 and 3.2.

For Belgium (table 3.1), there is a partition in three concentration classes. Relative positions are seen to be much more volatile in the classes with moderate and low concentration than in the highly concentrated group. In the latter, correlation is still 0.75 after 6 years (between 1958 and 1964). Interindustry differences clearly persist longer in the highly concentrated group.

Similar comments can be made for Italy (table 3.2) for the period 1959–65, where we admit a partition in two groups: a highly concentrated group ($C \geqslant 30$) including 11 industries, and

Table 3.1
Correlations of current and lagged profit rates in Belgium for the years 1958 to 1964

Concentration level	Number of comparisons	Average of correlations
		$T, T-1$
High (100–51)	6	0.871
Medium (50–26)	6	0.820
Low (25–0)	6	0.733
		$T, T-2$
High	5	0.833
Medium	5	0.778
Low	5	0.542
		$T, T-3$
High	4	0.790
Medium	4	0.655
Low	4	0.417
		$T, T-4$
High	3	0.739
Medium	3	0.585
Low	3	0.294
		$T, T-5$
High	2	0.732
Medium	2	0.594
Low	2	0.106
		$T, T-6$
High	1	0.746
Medium	1	0.447
Low	1	-0.035

Table 3.2
Correlations of current and lagged profit rates in Italy for the years 1959 to 1965

Concentration level	Number of comparisons	Average of correlations
		$T, T-1$
High (100–30)	6	0.768
Low (29–0)	6	0.687
		$T, T-2$
High	5	0.656
Low	5	0.380
		$T, T-3$
High	4	0.566
Low	4	0.319
		$T, T-4$
High	3	0.498
Low	3	0.378
		$T, T-5$
High	2	0.490
Low	2	0.415
		$T, T-6$
High	1	0.517
Low	1	0.277

group with low concentration ($C < 30$) including 19 industries. Notice, however, that the average correlations are lower than in Belgium for the first group, because of very low correlations of the terminal year (1965) with the years 1960, 1961, 1962 and 1963, which affect the averages considerably. However, 1965 is highly correlated with both 1964 *and* 1959. Indeed, we have (for the highly concentrated group):

1959 and 1965 = 0.517
1960 and 1965 = 0.197
1961 and 1965 = 0.139
1962 and 1965 = 0.168
1963 and 1965 = 0.159
1964 and 1965 = 0.566

Now, 1964 and 1965 are two recession years, [35] following a period of expansion. As for 1959, this is also a year of recession, more exactly the end of a downswing of the business cycle. [36] The fact that years of recession behave in a particular way is to be remembered in view of the hypothesis that the positive profit-concentration relationship may be typical for certain phases of the business cycle only.

To conclude, highly concentrated industries seem to realize rates of return that are more stable over time. The averages of these rates over a number of years have a good chance to reflect "structural" position. For the other industries, we can only express the hope that the short-run variations average out around some typical level, as is suggested by the rank correlation over the Belgian sample (between 1958–64 and 1951–57) reported earlier. In any case, it would be wise to test the profit-concentration relationship year by year, and to pay special attention to the recession years.

Before proceeding, we have to face an objection that is very often raised with respect to the profit data published by European firms. Do these profit accounts reproduce "true" profits? More precisely, do interindustry differences in aggregate profit data represent true differences?

At first sight, one is tempted to make the simple comment that there seems to be no reason why European accounting practices should lead to larger biases than, say, American practices. And it is well known that these practices do tend to bias profit rates

[35] See *Rev. of the Economic Conditions in Italy,* Banco di Roma, XIX (1965) 218, and XX (1966) 217.

[36] See G.Miconi, Recessions in Italy during the last fifteen years, *Rev. of the Economic Conditions in Italy* XIV, 6 (1960).

towards equality. To quote L.Weiss [37], "accounting procedures probably bias reported profit rates toward equality because large and profitable firms have the most to gain in tax avoidance and public relations by the understatement of profits, because some corporate assets are revalued when they change hands or are written down to reflect the capitalization of their profit prospects, and because original cost asset evaluation plus inflation leads to the relative overstatement of rates of return in slowly growing firms (which are usually relatively unprofitable)". This argumentation is quite general and should apply to European as well as to American firms. There is one practice, however, which seems to be typical for the countries analyzed here: it is equalization of reported profits between firms belonging to the same financial holding. To the extent that these member firms belong to different industries, there is a direct impact on interindustry differences in profit rates. If this is a generalized practice, and given the importance of financial holdings in the Common Market, our chances to find a relation between profits and concentration are seriously reduced.

A further obvious difficulty is related to the openness of countries such as Belgium and the Netherlands. In some industries, most reported profits are realized on sales abroad, i.e. on markets which may have a structure very different from the national market. Add to this the doubts one might have about the significance of a concentration ratio in such countries, and one comes very close to the conclusion that an analysis of the profit-concentration problem in such a context is doomed to lead to negative or inconclusive results. As discouraging as these thoughts may be, we decided nevertheless to look at the data by ourselves.

3.4. Belgium [38]

Economic theory has nothing particularly precise to say about

---

[37] L.Weiss, *Econometric Studies of Industrial Organization* (unpublished, 1969), p. 13.
[38] See the explanation given on the data sources in the appendix to this chapter.

the shape of the relationship between profits and concentration. Theory simply suggests that higher concentration leads to higher profits, because of greater collusion or market power. These higher profits will be maintained if high barriers to entry protect the existing market structure or the existing agreements. It seems reasonable, then, to adopt a research strategy in which one first divides the available observations into subsets according to the level of concentration, the level of profits and the height of the barriers (or some combination of these criteria) and verifies the existence of significant differences or correlations between these subsets. In a second stage, one tries to find out whether there is a continuous relationship. If there is such a relationship, one finally tries to determine its shape.

A natural starting point is to compare the average values of the rates of return [39] in highly concentrated industries (with $C > 50$) and in industries with $C \leqslant 50$, where C is the four-firm concentration ratio. These averages turn out to be practically equal in Belgium (a t-test of differences of means give $t = 1.45$). Variances turn also out to be equal ($F = 1.06$). This is not an encouraging result to start with.

The next thing to do is to set up a contingency table, [40] classifying rates of return in higher and lower than some critical level, which is taken to be 7%. As table 3.3 shows, the contingency coefficient is practivally zero (0.022) and non-significant, χ^2 being 0.021. This means that the number of industries in our four classes is not significantly different from the number we might expect to find by chance.

But what if we classify industries according to barriers to entry? Barriers to entry are generally seen to result from scale economies, sales promotion (or product differentiation) and patents. We are able to provide a (very rough) measure of the first type of barriers only. Data on patents by industry seem to be lacking. As for ad-

---

[39] These rates being time averages over 1958–64.

[40] See S.Siegel, *Nonparametric Statistics for the Behavioral Sciences* (Wiley, New York, 1956), pp. 196–202.

vertising expenditures, which probably influence both profits and concentration, [41] we examined very closely the existing statistical material, which is published by private organizations. [42] Unfortunately, these sometimes very detailed data refer to particular products and cannot be aggregated as there is no way of finding a link with any of the existing national or international industrial classifications.

Barriers due to scale economies are measured as the "minimum capital required", i.e. the number of Belgian Francs invested per person employed, mulitplied by the minimal efficient size of establishments in an industry. Minimal efficient size is measured by the average number of persons employed in the largest establishments which, together, represent 50% of total employment in an industry. This procedure has the advantage of eliminating small establishments, the idea being that entry of small new firms on the one hand, and the survival of older small establishments, on the other hand, might be responsible in most cases for the existence of suboptimal units.

We define barriers as being "high" when the minimum capital required is higher than 100 million Belgian Francs. This criteria leads to the second contingency table [43] in table 3.3. We now find a contingency coefficient of 0.252, χ^2 being equal to 3.04 (with one degree of freedom). This is significant only at the 10% level.

We can go one step further and combine high concentration with high barriers. Given the American experience, one would expect higher profits to show up in industries that are both concentrated and difficult to enter. To set up a third contingency table, we define a dummy variable D_1 equal to 1 in industries with "high" barriers and zero elsewhere. Multiplying the concentration ratio

---

[41] See e.g., W.S.Comanor and T.A.Wilson, Advertising, market structure and performance, *Rev. of Economics and Statistics* (November 1967), and the Symposium on Advertising and Concentration in the *J. of Industrial Economics* (November 1969).

[42] P.Kende's help is gratefully acknowledged. The interested reader should consult his monograph *Les statistiques européennes en matière de publicité*, Cahiers de la Fédération Internationale pour la Recherche dans le Domaine de la Publicité, No. 1.

[43] The match industry was classified as having "high" and the miscellaneous food industries as having "low" barriers. See table 3.7 in the appendix to this chapter.

Table 3.3
Contingency tables for Belgium, profits-concentration-barriers to entry

C \ RR	<7	≥7	N_i
≤50	17 — 17.22	14 — 13.78	31
>50	8 — 7.78	6 — 6.22	14
N_j	25	20	$N = 45$

Contingency = 0.022; $\chi^2(1) = 0.021$.

barriers \ RR	<7	≥7	N_i
low	14 — 11.11	6 — 8.89	20
high	11 — 13.89	14 — 11.11	25
N_j	25	20	$N = 45$

Contingency = 0.252; $\chi^2(1) = 3.042$.

by D_1, for each industry, we obtain the classification we wanted. However, the contingency coefficient is again non-significant (see bottom of table 3.3).

How does one rationalize these results? One way out is to admit that something is wrong, indeed, with the Belgian concentration ratios, in the sense that they do not measure market power. This would be in contradiction with the suggestion we made in the

Table 3.3 (cont.)

RR CD₁	<7	≥7	N_i
≤50	19 / 18.33	14 / 14.67	33
>50	6 / 6.67	6 / 5.33	12
N_j	25	20	N = 45

Contingency = 0.070; χ^2 (1) = 0.204.

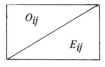

C = concentration ratio
RR = (average) rate of return
O_{ij} = number of industries observed in class ij

$$E_{ij} = \frac{(N_i)\,(N_j)}{N} = \text{expected number in class } ij$$

$$\chi^2\,[(k-1)\,(r-1)] = \sum_i \sum_j \frac{(C_{ij}-E_{ij})^2}{E_{ij}}$$

contingency coefficient = $\sqrt{\chi^2/(N+\chi^2)}$.

previous chapter (sections 2.3 and 2.5). Another explanation is to say that something is wrong with Belgian rates of return. These rates may reflect for a very large part profits realized on foreign markets. But it is possible also that the partition of rates of return or concentration ratios in classes is not appropriate or, more fundamentally that the level of aggregation over time or over industries is wrong. To these verifications we now turn.

Let us report first that a breakdown of rates of return and concentration ratios in three classes ($RR < 5, 5 \leqslant RR \leqslant 10, RR > 10$ and $C < 25, 25 \leqslant C \leqslant 50$ and $C > 50$) does not lead to any improvement. On the other hand, a Spearman correlation coefficient (between rates of return and concentration ratios) of −0.07 has nothing to be proud of.

To make sure that the process of averaging over seven years did not lead to a loss of relevant information, a simple regression was performed separately for each year. One should, indeed, recognize the possibility that the positive relationship found in the U.S. is typical for certain phases of the business cycle. After all, Bain used data covering a period of which most years were late depression (1936–40) while Stigler covered periods characterized by inflation (or price controls). The regression results for each year and also for average rates of return (the concentration ratios referring always to December 1961) are as follows:

$$RR_{58} = 5.93 + 0.01C \qquad R^2 = 0.002 \qquad (3.1)$$
$$\phantom{RR_{58} = }(1.53) \quad (0.03)$$

$$RR_{59} = 4.88 - 0.01C \qquad R^2 = 0.0004 \qquad (3.2)$$
$$\phantom{RR_{59} = }(1.72) \quad (0.04)$$

$$RR_{60} = 7.27 - 0.02C \qquad R^2 = 0.007 \qquad (3.3)$$
$$\phantom{RR_{60} = }(1.54) \quad (0.03)$$

$$RR_{61} = 8.17 - 0.03C \qquad R^2 = 0.016 \qquad (3.4)$$
$$\phantom{RR_{61} = }(1.62) \quad (0.04)$$

$$RR_{62} = 8.95 - 0.02C \qquad R^2 = 0.012 \qquad (3.5)$$
$$\phantom{RR_{62} = }(1.54) \quad (0.03)$$

$$RR_{63} = 8.54 - 0.02C \qquad R^2 = 0.012 \qquad (3.6)$$
$$\phantom{RR_{63} = }(1.55) \quad (0.03)$$

$$RR_{64} = 8.21 - 0.03C \qquad R^2 = 0.021 \qquad (3.7)$$
$$\phantom{RR_{64} = }(1.53) \quad (0.03)$$

$$RR = 7.42 - 0.02C \qquad R^2 = 0.009 . \qquad (3.8)$$
$$(1.29) \quad (0.03)$$

No single year behaves better than the average (RR) over the whole period 1958–64, while all give non-significant results.

The introduction of the dummy variable (D_1) for industries with high technological barriers leads to

$$RR = 7.10 - 0.06C + 3.81D_1 \qquad R^2 = 0.14 . \qquad (3.9)$$
$$(1.23) \quad (0.03) \quad (1.52)$$

This is a surprising result. While D_1 is gratified with a significant positive coefficient (confirming the indication given by the second contingency table in table 3.3), the concentration ratio now appears with a significant negative coefficient. Profits are higher on the average in high barrier industries but decrease with the level of concentration. Furthermore

$$RR = 8.80 - 0.03CD_1 - 0.12CD_2 \qquad R^2 = 0.12 \quad (3.10)$$
$$(1.37) \quad (0.03) \quad (0.05)$$

where D_2 is a dummy variable equal to 1 in the industries where D_1 is zero. Regression (3.10) allows the group of high barrier industries to have a slope coefficient (for C) different from the slope coefficient of low barrier industries, and tends to show that the negative profit-concentration relationship is typical only for low barrier industries. [44]

Again, something may be wrong with the concentration ratios. Alternatively, rates of return may reflect for a large part profits realized abroad while technological barriers to entry, being similar from country to country, may measure the opportunities that exist to protect profits both on the national market and abroad. It might be wise not to try to make a choice among these two explanations for the moment — admitting that something may be wrong with both rates of return and concentration ratios — and to look first at the results of the coming chapter.

In a final (and desperate) attempt, the Belgian data were aggregated into 17 two-digit industries, [45] in the hope to overcome pos-

---

[44] Attempts to introduce (as additional variables) annual rates of growth of assets (G), production increases, marginal concentration ratios and export ratios lead to inconclusive results. However, when industries with negative growth rates (G) are eliminated, G does obtain a significant positive coefficient.

[45] See table 3.8 in the appendix to this chapter.

Table 3.4
Contingency tables for France, profits-concentration-barriers to entry.

C \ RR	<4		≥4		N_i
≤50	89	85.12	48	51.88	137
>50	16	19.88	16	12.12	32
N_j	105		64		N=169

Contingency = 0.120; χ^2 (1) = 2.47

barriers \ RR	<4		≥4		N_i
low	53	52.19	31	31.81	84
high	52	52.81	34	32.19	85
N_j	105		64		N=169

Contingency = 0.020; χ^2 (1) = 0.07.

sible redistributions of profits among firms belonging to different three-digit industries. Industries with $C > 30$ now have an average rate of return of 8.65, while the other industries get only 5.77, the difference being significant at 10% ($t = 1.99$). However, the following regression results (obtained from these 17 observations)

$$RR = 6.66 + 0.02C \qquad R^2 = 0.02 \qquad (3.11)$$
$$\quad\;\; (1.58) \quad (0.04)$$

Table 3.4 (cont.)

RR CD_1	< 4	≥ 4	N_i
≤ 50	91 86.98	49 53.02	140
> 50	14 18.02	15 10.98	29
N_j	105	64	$N=169$

Contingency = 0.130; χ^2 (1) = 2.86.

$$RR = 7.07 - 0.07C + 4.95R_1 \qquad R^2 = 0.30 \qquad (3.12)$$
$$\quad\;\;(1.39)\quad(0.05)\quad(2.07)$$

(where R_1 is a dummy equal to 1 for $C > 30$) tend to prevent any cry of victory.

3.5. France

For reasons given in the appendix to this chapter, rates of return on equity could not be computed for France. It was decided to compute rates of return on shipments (value of sales), remembering that these are quite different. For profit-sales ratios to be equal to profit-equity ratios, sales-equity ratios would have to be equal from industry to industry! Economic theory therefore does *not* suggest that profit-sales ratios should be equalized under competitive conditions. Our only excuse to use these is a desire to know whether any correlation might show up (which would be rather annoying).

In fact, the classification of French industries according to level

of profits and of concentration appears to be entirely random
(table 3.4).

The same is true when concentration is replaced by barriers to
entry. To avoid the cumbersome and very time consuming computation of minimal efficient scale as defined in the previous section, also to avoid the temptation of deciding on an intuitive basis
in which industries barriers are high, the following device was
used. We computed the average size of the companies in the class
with the largest number of persons employed, and decided that
barriers are high when this average is larger than 350. The procedure is partly arbitrary. But it is better to have an imperfect rule
of thumb than to have no criterion at all.

Anyway, the resulting classification, given in the second contingency table in table 3.4, is exactly the one we would have obtained if industries had been assigned to the four cases by chance.
A combination of concentration and barriers, as in the third contingency table, gives somewhat better although still entirely un-
convincing results.

It is better then to abandon France: these data are really irrelevant. [46]

3.6. Italy

Italian rates of return (on equity) appearing as relatively very
low (possibly because of particular accounting practices), a rather
low critical value of 2% was selected after some trials. On the
other hand, Italy also has, on the average, the lowest concentration
ratios of the countries analyzed here, for reasons explained in
chapter 6. As the critical value of 50 for the concentration ratio
has certainly no magic or intrinsic value, it seems worthwhile to try
lower values. A quick look at table 3.10 (in the appendix to this
chapter) suggests that a value of 30 is a good candidate. Are we

---

[46] An aggregation of the French data into 33 two-digit industries (as defined in the
French census) did not lead to any better results.

Table 3.5
Contingency tables for Italy, profits-concentration

C \ RR	< 2		≥ 2		N_i
≤ 50	13	11.20	11	12.80	24
> 50	1	2.80	5	3.20	6
N_j	14		16		N = 30

Contingency = (0.288); $\chi^2(1)$ = (2.712).

C \ RR	< 2		≥ 2		N_i
≤ 30	13	8.87	6	10.13	19
> 30	1	5.13	10	5.87	11
N_j	14		16		N = 30

Contingency = 0.497; $\chi^2(1)$ = 9.841.

cheating by choosing critical values that lead to the results we are looking for? No. What we are doing is to try to find the relevant critical value, if any. Theory suggests there should be such values, but leaves the determination of their precise values entirely open.

The reader may wonder, though, whether a value of 30 can reasonably be considered as a borderline between "monopolistic" and "competitive" industries. The answer is yes: the Italian con-

Table 3.6
Contingency tables for Italy, profits-barriers-concentration

barriers \ RR	<2	≥2	N_i
low	10 / 7	5 / 8	15
high	4 / 7	11 / 8	15
N_j	14	16	$N = 30$

Contingency = 0.372; $\chi^2(1) = 4.82$.

CD_1 \ RR	<2	≥2	N_i
≤30	13 / 8.87	6 / 10.13	19
>30	1 / 5.13	10 / 5.87	11
N_j	14	16	$N = 30$

Contingency = 0.497; $\chi^2(1) = 9.841$.

centration ratios used here are weighted averages (of something like three-digit ratios) and tend therefore to take rather low values, while the basic ratios are already on the low side, as noticed in the previous paragraph.

Let us be entirely honest and report first that, when a critical value for the concentration ratio of 50 is used, we get a contingency coefficient whose significance is not clear and probably very low. Two of the four expected frequencies E_{ij} (see table 3.5) being less than 5, the χ^2 test cannot properly be used. But what if we use $C \geq 30$?

Now we obtain a splendid contingency coefficient of 0.50, as can be seen from table 3.5. The significance of this result is beyond question, the more as the means of the two groups of industries ($C \leq 30$ and $C > 30$) are different ($t = 2.05^*$) while the variances are not ($F = 1.21$).

Let us hasten then to make a classification according to barriers to entry. A dummy variable D_1 is given the value 1 when barriers are high, and zero otherwise. To determine D_1, we use the same rule as for France: when the average size of companies in the class with the highest employment is greater than 350, barriers are supposed to be high.

Table 3.6 shows that the degree of association of profits and barriers is significant. When barriers and concentration are combined, we get exactly the same picture as when we consider concentration only, because all industries with $C > 30$ also have $D_1 = 1$.

A Spearman rank coefficient of 0.41^* is an indication that a regression analysis is in order. Here are the year by year regression results:

$$RR_{59} = 2.66 + 0.04C \qquad R^2 = 0.02 \qquad (3.13)$$
$$\phantom{RR_{59} =} (1.51) \quad (0.04)$$

$$RR_{60} = 4.10 - 0.004C \qquad R^2 = 0.001 \qquad (3.14)$$
$$\phantom{RR_{60} =} (0.76) \quad (0.022)$$

$$RR_{61} = 3.92 - 0.002C \qquad R^2 = 0.000 \qquad (3.15)$$
$$\phantom{RR_{61} =} (0.88) \quad (0.026)$$

$$RR_{62} = 2.35 + 0.02C \qquad R^2 = 0.04 \qquad (3.16)$$
$$\phantom{RR_{62} =} (0.69) \quad (0.02)$$

$$RR_{63} = 0.74 + 0.03C \qquad R^2 = 0.08 \qquad (3.17)$$
$$\phantom{RR_{63} =} (0.71) \quad (0.02)$$

$$RR_{64} = -2.23 + 0.07C \qquad R^2 = 0.26 \qquad (3.18)$$
$$\phantom{RR_{64} = }(0.78) \quad (0.02)$$

$$RR_{65} = -2.75 + 0.09C \qquad R^2 = 0.31 \ . \qquad (3.19)$$
$$\phantom{RR_{65} = }(0.81) \quad (0.02)$$

For the averages of RR over the period 1959–65, the regression gives

$$RR = 1.25 + 0.03C \qquad R^2 = 0.10 \ . \qquad (3.20)$$
$$(0.65) \quad (0.02)$$

While (3.20) is not too convincing, (3.18) and (3.19) present a particular interest. It was noticed before that 1964 and 1965 were recession years in Italy. It now appears that these are the only years for which the positive profit-concentration relationship is clearly and unambiguously verified.

Given that high barriers and high concentration ratios coincide in Italian manufacturing industry, the dummy D_1 should not be expected to add much to the explanation. Indeed

$$RR_{64} = -2.23 + 0.07C + 0.04D_1 \qquad R^2 = 0.26 \qquad (3.21)$$
$$\phantom{RR_{64} = }(0.79) \quad (0.03) \quad (1.31)$$

$$RR_{65} = -2.77 + 0.10C - 0.87D_1 \qquad R^2 = 0.32 \qquad (3.22)$$
$$\phantom{RR_{65} = }(0.82) \quad (0.03) \quad (1.36)$$

$$RR = 1.26 + 0.03C + 0.17D_1 \qquad R^2 = 0.11 \ . \qquad (3.23)$$
$$(0.66) \quad (0.03) \quad (1.09)$$

Most interestingly, the positive profit-concentration relationship turns out to be typical for high barrier industries, according to

$$RR_{64} = -1.99 + 0.07CD_1 + 0.05CD_2 \qquad R^2 = 0.26$$
$$\phantom{RR_{64} = }(1.06) \quad (0.03) \quad\quad (0.07) \qquad\qquad\quad (3.24)$$

$$RR_{65} = -2.73 + 0.09CD_1 + 0.08CD_2 \qquad R^2 = 0.31$$
$$\phantom{RR_{65} = }(1.11) \quad (0.03) \quad\quad (0.08) \qquad\qquad\quad (3.25)$$

$$RR = 1.26 + 0.03CD_1 + 0.03CD_2 \qquad R^2 = 0.10$$
$$(0.89) \quad (0.02) \quad\quad (0.06) \qquad\qquad\quad (3.26)$$

where D_2 is a dummy equal to one when D_1 is equal to zero. An analogous result is obtained when the subsets of industries with $C_1 = C > 30$ and $C_2 = C < 30$ are allowed to have different slopes. We find

$$RR_{64} = -1.08 + 0.06C_1 - 0.02C_2 \qquad R^2 = 0.31 \qquad (3.27)$$
$$\phantom{RR_{64} = } (1.12) \quad (0.03) \quad (0.07)$$

$$RR_{65} = -1.44 + 0.07C_1 - 0.01C_2 \qquad R^2 = 0.37 \qquad (3.28)$$
$$\phantom{RR_{65} = } (1.16) \quad (0.03) \quad (0.07)$$

$$RR \; = \; 1.70 + 0.03C_1 + 0.00C_2 \qquad R^2 = 0.12 \; . \qquad (3.29)$$
$$ (0.96) \quad (0.02) \quad (0.06)$$

3.7. Conclusions

We had a very hard time to derive interesting results on the profit-concentration problem. A lot of experimenting was needed to find the right thresholds above which concentration, barriers and profits can be said to be high and also to find the appropriate levels of aggregation over time and over industries.

It turns out that the thresholds have to be put the lower, the larger the country, as far as concentration is concerned. Barriers to entry can be treated the same way, whatever the size of the country, while the separation of profits into "high" and "low" has to take account of national accounting practices.

Averaging rates of return over a period of several years is dangerous, in the sense that nothing seems to be gained while losses in information might be important. When averages are used, one should be careful to stay within the same phase of the business cycle. This conclusion is in contradiction with our initial intention to use the averaging process in order to eliminate fluctuations over the business cycle, based on the finding that the inter industry pattern of rates of return is more stable over the business cycle in highly concentrated industries.

Rather than justifying the use of time averages of rates of return, this greater stability may help to explain why, for Italy at least, a positive profit-concentration relationship shows up only, but then very clearly, in recession years. The more as this positive relationship appears to be typical for industries that are highly concentrated and highly protected by technological barriers to entry.

For Belgium, no significant results could be obtained, except for a negative (sic!) relationship between profits and concentration in industries with low barriers and a higher average level of profits in high barrier industries. It is not clear whether these surprising results are due to the fact that concentration ratios do not measure market power in small and "open" economies or rather to the fact that rates of return are too much affected by profits realized on foreign markets.

The computations for Italy and Belgium are based on rates of return on equity after taxes. For Belgium, all joint-stock companies are included, while for Italy the data include only larger companies (with a capital of more than 100 million lire). This may be part of the explanation why orthodox results are obtained for Italy, as small companies may overstate rates of return relatively more than larger companies.

For France, only rates of return on value of shipments are available, and these do not seem to be relevant to the problem at hand.

Table 3.7. Belgium

The structural data are obtained using the 1961 industrial census. When necessary, weighted average concentration ratios are given, the weights being value added, when possible, and otherwise the number of persons employed.

Rates of return on equity after taxes and after depreciation are computed from the tables *Rendement des sociétés belges par action en 19 . .* published annually in the *Bulletin de statistique de l'I.N.S.*, for the years 1958 to 1964. These tables give aggregates of book values published by all Belgian joint-stock companies for the preceding year.

To these data were added 16 industries of the sector *fabrications métalliques* for which the *Caisse Générale d'Epargne et de Retraite* keeps detailed records. It should be noticed that, for these 16 industries, (a) the data include only joint-stock companies that were still in operation in 1967 and (b) cover book values published between June 30 of the preceding and June 29 of the current year. The loss in homogeneity, resulting from the inclusion of these 16 industries, is probably compensated by the gain in degrees of freedom.

Table 3.7 gives the simple averages of the rates of return of the years 1958 to 1964.

The computation of the other variables is explained in the text.

Table 3.8. Belgium

Two-digit rates of return are obtained after aggregating the book values given in *Bulletin de statistique.*

Two-digit concentration ratios are weighted averages of three-digit concentration ratios, the weight being the number of persons employed.

Table 3.9. France

Concentration ratios are computed (by interpolation as explained in the statistical appendix of part II) from the frequency distributions in terms of persons employed published in *Recensement de l'industrie en France en 1962*. [1] Rates of return are computed from *Bénéfices industriels et commerciaux* [2] and are *before* taxes. These rates are on value of shipment (*chiffre d'affaires*), not on equity.

Rates of returns could not be based on equity, as more than half of the firms that operate under the *régime de l'imposition d'après le bénéfice réel* are not obliged to declare their capital and reserves. As a consequence, the data on equity given in the B.I.C. did not seem to give the relevant information. Table 3.9 gives simple averages over the period 1958 to 1964.

The determination of barriers to entry is explained in section 3.5.

Table 3.10. Italy

This table gives 30 averages, over the period 1959–65, of yearly rates of return on equity by *sottoclassi di attività economica* computed from the *Statistiche sulle società italiane per azioni* [3]. Equity is defined as *capitale versato* plus *riserve e fondo conguaglio monetario* plus *accantonamenti vari*. Returns are after taxes and after depreciation and refer to companies with a capital larger than 100 million lire.

The thirty corresponding concentration ratios are weighted aver-

---

[1] Vol. III (Paris, 1968).

[2] Published in *Statistiques et études financières*, Tableau III.

[3] Published by the *Associazione fra le Società per Azioni*.

ages of concentration ratios for *categoria di attività economica* computed from frequency distributions by number of *addetti* referring to the 16th October 1961. [4] The weights are based on the number of *addetti* per *categoria*. The "categoria" correspond to a five-digit classification.

Other countries

Germany being absent for the reasons given in chapter 2, we might add simply that Dutch statistics on profits [5] refer to financial holding companies and not to industrial firms. These statistics include only 13 industrial sectors, and this number will be reduced to 8 because of increased financial concentration. Given the results reported for Belgium and the comments made at the end of section 3.3, this might be a very sensible way of presenting statistics on profits in small countries. It implies in any case that the standard statistical techniques cannot be used for the Netherlands.

---

[4] *4° Censimento generale dell'industria e del commercio*, vol. III, Industrie, Tomo 1, Imprese, tav. 3 (Istituto Centrale di Statistica, Roma, 1966).

[5] *Winststatistiek der grotere naamloze vennootschappen* (Centraal Bureau voor de Statistiek, The Hague).

Table 3.7
Data on rates of return, concentration and barriers to entry in Belgium

	Industry	RR (1958– 64)	C	Min. capital required in 1,000 B.F.	D_1	G
1	Wire-drawing, etc.	5.89	56.8	361,140	1	–
2	Forging, punching, etc.	6.67	42.2	167,232	1	–
3	Sheet metal works	8.11	21.0	233,732	1	–
4	Fabricated steel for buildings	7.93	20.6	298,683	1	–
5	Metal bridges, frames, boilers	5.11	31.1	166,088	1	–
6	Shipbuilding	9.10	55.7	344,228	1	–
7	Railroad and street cars	4.72	55.2	283.220	1	–
8	Motor cars, cycles and areonautics	24.47	29.6	131,917	1	–
9	Pneumatic and hydraulic machines	11.16	27.9	122,640	1	–
10	Machine tools	5.07	36.7	879,186	1	–
11	Miscellaneous mechanical constructions	2.64	28.4	40,448	0	–
12	Lifting, handling and weighing equipment	7.85	42.9	128,850	1	–
13	Machines and equipment for mis- cellaneous indus- tries	11.43	27.8	251,603	1	–
14	Electrical machinery	11.50	40.7	543.634	1	–
15	Arms and ammunition	– 1.32	56.5	16,502	0	–
16	Mechanical preci- sion instruments	2.93	51.2	64,260	0	–
17	Dairy products	12.37	12.8	5,700	0	9.08
18	Glass	11.13	58.1	215,760	1	5.91
19	Cement	9.38	79.9	1,073,358	1	9.66
20	Nonferrous metals	8.68	46.2	727,168	1	6.84
21	Wearing apparel	7.54	5.5	1,292	0	2.93

Table 3.7 (cont.)

	Industry	RR (1958–64)	C	Min. capital required in 1,000 B.F.	D_1	G
22	Sawing	7.07	7.9	1,551	0	6.79
23	Printing and publishing	7.03	11.8	6,004	0	4.52
24	Petroleum	7.01	90.6	1,046,896	1	5.46
25	Paper and board	6.45	44.4	99,064	0	4.75
26	Tobacco	6.35	32.4	82,400	0	4.28
27	Baked clay products	6.34	15.2	22,989	0	6.13
28	Breweries	5.89	22.1	134,397	1	5.76
29	Diamonds	5.85	13.0	825	0	1.93
30	Furniture	5.56	8.4	1,632	0	8.04
31	Sugar	5.34	71.9	485,460	1	0.70
32	Steel mills	4.80	49.4	2,003,042	1	5.80
33	Footwear	4.42	12.6	1,560	0	2.42
34	Ceramics	2.81	53.2	127,890	1	3.31
35	Hosiery	2.76	12.0	10,488	0	3.06
36	Milling	1.23	17.2	24,640	0	2.58
37	Leather	0.88	36.4	25,992	0	−2.91
38	Nitrogen	−0.17	84.9	559,000	1	−0.90
39	Distillery and organic chemistry	−2.00	64.1	180,144	1	17.34
40	Phamaceutical products	10.73	31.5	37,576	0	11.38
41	Mineral chemistry	7.96	70.2	205,020	1	−0.13
42	Pigments and paints	6.72	20.3	31,265	0	6.28
43	Fats	4.69	48.0	83,439	0	−3.16
44	Miscellenaous food industries	10.62	24.9	−	0	5.57
45	Matches	11.72	100.0	−	1	6.11

Table 3.8
Two-digit data on profits and concentration in Belgium

Industry	RR (1958–64)	C
Food	8.43	22.1
Breweries	5.89	22.1
Tobacco	6.35	32.4
Textiles	2.98	23.2
Apparel	6.75	6.8
Lumber	6.30	11.3
Paper	6.45	44.4
Graphic industries	7.03	11.8
Leather	1.46	26.0
Chemical industries	7.06	60.6
Petroleum	7.01	90.6
Non-metallic mineral products	9.02	46.6
Primary metals	5.78	50.1
Metal construction	7.35	23.9
Machines	8.16	30.7
Electrical construction	11.50	40.7
Transportation equipment	16.50	34.5

Table 3.9
Data on rates of return, concentration ratios and barriers to entry in France (N.A.E. classification)

No. of N.A.E.	Industry	RR (1958–64)	C	Average size in class with largest employment	D_1
191	Nonferrous metals	2.98	67.40	6,213	1
192	Wire-drawing and cold-rolled steel	3.02	37.25	1,310	1
193/194	Steel tubes, forgings, stampings	4.49	59.30	1,787	1
200	Boilers and railroad machinery	1.23	68.60	4,091	1
201	Foundry	2.98	16.50	2,491	1
202	Boilers, plate work, welding	4.27	14.95	2,568	1

Table 3.9 (cont.)

No. of N.A.E.	Industry	RR (1958–64)	C	Average size in class with largest employment	D_1
203	Valves, pipes and lubricating	5.42	22.30	837	1
204	Industrial combustion equipment	6.32	32.80	1,719	1
205	Refrigeration equipment	2.77	41.60	1,212	1
206/207	Engines, compressors	4.89	49.20	1,000	1
208	Pumps, hydraulic turbines	3.82	45.05	1,183	1
209	Fire extinguishing equipment	4.53	53.10	336	0
211	Lifting and handling equipment	3.19	12.75	339	0
212	Railroad equipment	1.89	38.65	1,000	1
213	Machine tools	4.36	12.70	296	0
214	Farm machinery	2.01	34.80	3,240	1
215	Machinery for food and chemical industry	3.84	14.40	381	1
216	Sawing machines	2.88	67.10	503	1
217	Textile machinery	4.81	26.30	982	1
218	Machines for paper and printing industry	4.62	32.75	398	1
220	General workshops	4.46	3.60	31	0
221	Rural mechanics	6.02	1.40	1	0
222	Metal processing	2.96	8.70	30	0
223	Precision instruments	3.71	17.20	32	0
224/225	Model making	1.30	74.70	1,522	1
226/228	Arms, ammunition, small repair	6.45	74.75	753	1
231	Metal cutting, stamping, sawing, etc.	3.95	11.80	364	1
232	Screw cutting	4.77	9.30	31	0
233	Bolts, nuts, etc.	3.13	15.70	337	0
234/235	Springs, metal chains	5.33	35.30	672	1
236	Hand tools	4.11	20.05	596	1
237	Hardware	4.49	8.90	387	1
241	Tinplate	5.37	34.50	278	0
242	Household items	3.36	18.50	753	1
243	Cutlery	10.43	22.60	253	0
244	Metal furniture	2.53	15.40	138	0

Table 3.9 (cont.)

No. of N.A.E.	Industry	RR (1958–64)	C	Average size in class with largest employment	D_1
245	Metal wrapping	2.23	41.40	2,749	1
252/253	Shipbuilding (iron and wood)	1.20	50.90	1,585	1
254	Barges (iron and wood)	1.49	33.35	104	0
255	Ship repairing and demolition	1.84	27.00	450	1
261/262	Automobile construction	2.07	59.20	17,626	1
263	Automobile parts	4.79	27.80	1,758	1
264	Automobile repair	3.85	1.20	1	0
265	Parts for cycles and motorcycles	2.06	30.35	545	1
266	Cycles and motorcycles	0.88	77.35	1,000	1
267	Repair of cycles and motorcycles	5.77	3.70	1	0
27	Aircraft	1.71	45.05	4,875	1
280	Electrical equipment for industrial use	3.04	71.50	4,049	1
281	Heavy electrical machinery, etc.	2.64	38.40	5,182	1
282	Isolated wires and cables	4.57	52.40	1,592	1
283	Radioelectric and electronic equipment	3.69	34.05	3,902	1
284	Telegr., tel., small electric appliances	4.80	29.35	2,667	1
285	Meters, transformers, control instruments	5.41	36.25	916	1
286	Miscellaneous electrical equipment	2.02	24.60	1,606	1
287/288	Batteries, lamps	5.52	55.95	1,000	1
289	Repair of electrical equipment	4.46	7.49	1	0
290	Clocks	3.40	22.55	971	1
291	Mechanical meters and control instruments	4.14	53.75	2,363	1
292	Weighting equipment	3.12	36.60	500	1
293	Optical instruments	4.75	28.55	1,100	1
294	Photographic equipment	2.64	30.20	347	0
296	Precision instruments	6.76	69.25	1,562	1

Table 3.9 (cont.)

No. of N.A.E.	Industry	RR (1958– 64)	C	Average size in class with largest employment	D_1
298	Surgical and mechanical instruments	5.37	10.30	1	0
30	Glass	4.61	30.70	2,896	1
311	Bricks, tiles, pottery, etc.	3.39	11.00	136	0
313	Clay refractories	4.54	53.55	655	1
314	Sandstone, industrial ceramics	4.82	61.90	1,000	1
315/317	China, kitchen articles	2.65	31.80	1,074	1
318	Art ceramics	5.01	20.45	1	0
321	Cut stone, stone products	3.45	19.90	1	0
322	Building marble	4.02	28.40	2	0
323	Funeral marble	8.35	47.10	2	0
324	Plaster	4.36	41.80	162	0
325	Cement, lime	5.14	41.00	1,307	1
326	Miscellaneous agglomerates	5.06	25.20	1,887	1
327	Miscellaneous building materials, n.e.c.	3.46	56.90	372	1
350	Chemical industry	5.42	86.00	4,100	1
351	Mineral chemical industry	4.82	69.50	2,786	1
352	Miscellaneous mineral products	3.27	43.20	578	1
353	Fertilizers. Nitrogen	3.50	45.00	2,713	1
354	Synthetic organic chemicals	2.89	32.10	1,228	1
355/356	Animal and vegetable products, Coal tar, benzol	3.78	47.50	1,465	1
358	Industrial explosives. Fireworks	7.29	63.00	484	1
359	Pharmaceutical products	5.02	20.50	312	0
361	Abrasive products	6.81	59.00	401	1
362	Artificial coal	2.83	98.30	1,049	1
363	Whitening products, cleaning, etc.	3.25	45.50	1,234	1
364	Paints, varnishes, inks	3.11	16.80	140	0
366	Insecticides	5.64	56.50	515	1
367	Photographic products	10.88	82.10	1,092	1
368	Chemicals for industr. use	5.69	46.90	78	0

Table 3.9 (cont.)

No. of N.A.E.	Industry	RR (1958–64)	C	Average size in class with largest employment	D_1
369	Perfumes	4.67	20.00	344	0
371/373	Tires and inner tubes	4.10	76.50	8,590	1
374/375	Asbestos	3.60	23.00	247	0
391	Vegetable fats, oils	1.18	61.90	682	1
392	Animal fats	2.29	30.50	32	0
393	Soap	3.41	79.60	323	0
401	Milling	1.41	13.90	1	0
403	Pastes	1.76	45.90	478	1
425	Brewery	2.86	22.30	897	1
426	Cider	2.13	28.00	92	0
427	Distilled alcohol	1.67	20.00	126	0
428	Liquors and appetizers	4.10	27.90	770	1
429	Beverages, cold drinks	2.92	15.60	2	0
431	Milk	2.75	22.20	31	0
432	Butter	1.20	36.20	258	0
433	Cheese	2.60	24.20	2	0
440	Assorted canned goods	1.93	35.20	850	1
441	Canned fruits and vegetables	1.57	19.20	252	0
442	Canned meat, liverpaste, dinners	2.04	28.60	1,833	1
443	Jam	2.88	46.60	256	0
444	Canned fish	1.88	13.50	275	0
451	Sweets	1.91	16.70	376	1
452	Chocolate	3.07	33.40	791	1
454	Coffee, thea, chicory	2.14	15.70	182	0
456	Animal feeds	2.62	16.80	29	0
470	Textile industries	2.42	79.50	845	1
471	Retting and dycing of linen, hemp, broom	2.49	22.50	28	0
472	Linen, hemp	1.39	31.40	518	1
473	Twine, cordage, hard fibres textures	1.14	56.50	1,620	1
474	Cotton	6.94	15.00	2,746	1
475	Wool	1.09	14.40	2,054	1
481	Hosiery	1,83	7.30	296	0
482	Rubberized fabrics	2.91	33.00	149	0
483	Lace and net products	5.72	10.90	30	0

Table 3.9 (cont.)

No. of N.A.E.	Industry	RR (1958–64)	C	Average size in class with largest employment	D_1
484	Ribbons and trimmings	3.16	11.20	30	0
485	Netting, fishing nets	5.47	37.90	98	0
486	Dyeing and cleaning	2.88	36.50	2,301	1
491	Tailormade garment and underwear	4.21	9.00	1	0
492	Ready-made garment and underwear	2.22	3.10	31	0
493	Woman's hats	3.62	10.00	1	0
494	Miscellaneous clothing	3.21	9.60	1	0
495	Misc. ready-made fabrics	2.52	17.90	32	0
503	Fur goods	3.48	11.10	1	0
513	Gloves	1.33	29.20	263	0
514	Morocco-dressing	3.29	11.50	32	0
515	Militairy leather goods	1.63	42.10	106	0
516	Saddlery	10.04	12.70	1	0
517	Industrial leather, belts	2.11	39.80	121	0
521	Footwear	2.47	16.00	290	0
522	Slippers	1.32	15.50	71	0
523	Sabots, wood soles	4.92	18.40	1	0
524	Shoe leather	3.47	50.80	308	0
525	Custom-made shoes	3.75	20.20	1	0
527	Galoshes and clogs	3.08	49.00	1	0
531	Sawing	1.94	2.80	2	0
532	Mechanic word preparation	2.70	10.30	32	0
533	Wood furniture and seats	3.76	3.80	1	0
543/544	Paper manufacturing	3.92	19.50	1,692	1
545	Paper transformation	3.27	45.30	291	0
551	Printing, advertising, magazines	4.39	10.20	31	0
552	Typesetting, photo-engraving, etc.	5.13	19.70	346	0
553	Books, cards	4.19	39.30	955	1
554	Bookbinding	6.80	17.80	66	0
555	Newspapers	1.10	11.20	667	1
556	Photography	7.41	16.70	2	0
562	Jewelry and lapidary work	4.90	21.90	153	0
571	Games and toys	3.19	24.40	28	0
572	Sporting and camping goods	4.22	19.00	149	0

Table 3.9 (cont.)

No. of N.A.E.	Industry	RR (1958– 64)	C	Average size in class with largest employment	D_1
573	Children's vehicles	1.03	41.20	326	0
581	Musical instruments	4.92	33.30	203	0
582	Tape-recorders, records	3.89	53.40	374	1
591	Brushes	3.18	20.40	30	0
592	Mantel-pieces, tablets	3.38	18.70	1	0
593	Stationery	3.58	44.10	635	1
594	Products for smokers	3.97	41.90	544	1
601	Art industries	4.27	11.50	2	0
602/603	Wrought straw	3.96	18.50	1	0
605	Catgut	2.74	23.00	80	0

Table 3.10

Data on rates of return, concentration ratios and barriers to entry in Italy (Italian classification)

No.	Industry	RR	C	Average size in class with largest employment	D_1
3.01A	Milling	1.98	5.28	4	0
3.01B	Confectionery	3.24	35.39	3,677	1
3.01C	Canned food	0.32	19.30	152	0
3.01.18	Sugar	2.37	64.12	4,406	1
3.01G	Alcoholized drinks	6.54	19.19	31	0
3.01H	Non-alcoholized drinks	4.77	18.69	4	0
3.03A	Silk	1.53	26.35	155	0
3.03B	Cotton	0.04	25.75	3,455	1
3.03C	Transformation of artificial and synthetic fibres	3.42	31.41	367	1
3.04	Wool	1.36	28.54	6,995	1

Table 3.10 (cont.)

No.	Industry	RR	C	Average size in class with largest employment	D_1
3.05	Other textile industries	0.80	15.95	154	0
3.06	Clothing	−0.92	3.46	4	0
3.07	Footwear	2.13	2.45	1	0
3.08	Furs and leather	1.41	11.21	31	0
3.09, 3.10	Wood and furniture	1.90	3.53	4	0
3.11	Metallurgy	3.26	47.03	7,640	1
3.12	Machinery, except electrical	2.12	12.49	152	0
3.13	Electrical machinery	2.92	20.50	3,893	1
3.16	Transportation equipment	2.71	31.20	725	1
3.17.04	Cement	6.97	35.70	3,550	1
3.17B	Glass and ceramics	1.51	15.70	152	0
3.18	Chemistry	4.00	52.78	5,664	1
3.19	Petroleum and coal derivatives	−1.68	50.03	1,592	1
3.20	Rubber	3.33	53.50	13,915	1
3.21	Synthetic fibres, cellulose	5.44	84.17	7,719	1
3.22	Paper and cardboard	1.65	15.04	350	1
3.23	Graphics industry	2.89	14.69	31	0
3.24	Photo-, phono-, cinematography	−2.59	15.48	3	0
3.25	Manufactured plastic products	2.22	53.86	6,227	1
3.26.01−2	Electrical equipment	1.01	23.76	31	0

CHAPTER 4

WAGES

4.1. Survey of the literature

The best way to introduce the subject of this chapter is perhaps to describe a few prominent contributions to the analysis of the wage-concentration problem. [1]

Garbarino's work is a convenient starting point. Nobody will object to its basic idea that the firm is an entity that is organized to make profits by selling goods (on the product market) which are the result of the use of services bought on the market for factors of production. The wage rate is the price paid for one of these services.

This wage rate will thus be influenced by two types of elements, some internal to the firm, others external. The external elements are the product and the factor markets, characterized respectively by more or less concentration and unionization, while the internal elements are mostly of a technological nature, such as increases in productivity. Concentration and unionization are described as "positive variables" which influence wages within the constraints set by the internal or "permissive" variables.

Garbarino offers several rationalizations of a positive wage-concentration relationship, all based on the idea that oligopolistic market structures allow firms to protect cost reductions (due to

[1] See J.W.Garbarino, A theory of interindustry wage variation, *Quarterly J. of Economics* (May 1950); H.G.Lewis, *Unionism and Relative Wages* (Chicago, 1963); M.Segal, The relation between union wage impact and market structure, *Quarterly J. of Economics* (February, 1964); L.W.Weiss, Concentration and labor earnings, *Am. Economic Rev.* (March, 1966).

increases in productivity) and the resulting profits against competition from other firms in the industry. People employed in the
industry would then receive their share of these profits either because of unionistic pressure, or because entrepreneurs want to be
"wage leaders" or simply because of governmental intervention.

In this empirical work, Garbarino found a positive correlation
between wages on the one hand and concentration, unionization
and productivity on the other hand. He did not, however, try to
estimate the impact of each variable on wages. We will try to do
this in the framework of the following regression model

$$W = a_0 + a_1 C + a_2 TU + a_3 GE , \qquad (4.1)$$

where W = hourly wage, C = four-firm concentration ratio, TU =
index of unionization (power of trade unions), and GE = growth
of employment.

The variable GE will replace the productivity variable suggested
by Garbarino. One can indeed imagine, following Dunlop[2], that
industries with increasing productivity are also industries with ex-
panding employment. Growth of employment might thus serve as
a proxy for productivity growth.

One should notice that the three "independent" variables in
(4.1) might be related to each other, and in particular that concentration might influence unionization or vice-versa. This point was
made by M.Segal in his "market structure proposition", who em-
phasizes that the market structure of an industry has a significant
influence on the possibility for trade unions to build up a strong
position.

Weiss and Lewis also analyze this concentration-unionization
relationship in an attempt to incorporate it in the wage-concentration framework. There might be a positive interaction between
C and TU in their influence on W. It might also be that interaction
reduces the sum of the separate effects. Mathematically speaking,
these possibilities are allowed for by introducing the product

[2] J.T.Dunlop, Productivity and the wage structure, in: *Income, Employment and
Public Policy* (N.W.Norton, New York, 1948).

of C and TU as an additional variable in the regression equation.
Thus

$$W = a_0 + a_1 C + a_2 TU + a_3 C(TU) , \qquad (4.2)$$

where a_3 may take a positive or negative sign. The reasoning starts
from the idea that unionization certainly leads to higher wages in
non-concentrated industries. When C gets larger, a larger TU might
have a smaller effect on W because of a sort of "countervailing
power" and as a result a_3 would turn up with a negative sign. If
however the effect of TU is the larger, the larger is C, then a_3 has a
positive sign.

With specification (4.2), Weiss obtains a positive a_0 and a positive a_1 but a negative a_3. By way of illustration, he shows that a
given increase in concentration leads to a rise in wages of 33%
when trade unions are weak, but only by 13% when trade unions
are strong. When other variables such as employment growth,
establishment size, durability of goods produced, percentage of
men employed and qualification of the workers, are added, the
coefficients are reduced but remain statistically significant. However, once personal characteristics are introduced, the partial regression coefficient of C ceases to be significant.

These findings are important and were obtained from a sample
of observations of *individual* wage-earners. With this sample,
Weiss was in fact able to test two quite different hypotheses. The
first hypothesis states that *for a given job* more concentrated industries pay higher wages: this hypothesis was verified. The second
hypothesis says that these high wages are higher, even if one takes
into account the personal characteristics of the wage earner (in particular his training, age, etc.). It is this second hypothesis that turns
out to be wrong. Individual workers do not receive, in more concentrated industries, a higher wage than they would elsewhere,
given their qualification, with the implication that if more concentrated industries pay more, they also get a better quality in
return.

With the aggregate data (*average* wages per industry) used here,
it will not be possible to test the second hypothesis. If a positive

wage-concentration relationship turns up, it will not be possible to disentangle the two ideas and to make sure that the positive sign does not simply reflect the fact that concentrated industries hire superior personnel.

Lewis's book, which focuses on the wage-unionism issue, presents a model that comes very close to equation (4.2). It may be written as

$$\log W = a_0 + a_1 \log (PR) + a_2 \log (RR)$$

$$+ a_3 C + a_4 TU + a_5 C(TU) , \tag{4.3}$$

where PR represents productivity and RR rates of return.

This short survey of the literature gives an idea of how to tackle the problem and of the nature of the variables to look for. Let us try, then, to set up a similar analysis for Belgium, before turning to other countries.

4.2. Belgium

To begin with, a closer look at the definition of the variables to be used is in order.

4.2.1. *The variables*

Wages (dependent variable W). W is measured by average gross hourly earnings by industry, as given in the Belgian wage survey (of October 1961) published by the Institut National de Statistique (I.N.S.). Gross earnings include any payments in cash made by the employer to the employee for work done during the period considered.

Concentration ratio (C). C again measures four-firm concentration ratios computed by interpolation from the frequency distributions of persons employed published in the 1961 Belgian Industrial Census.

Percentage of male employment (M). It is a well established fact that female wages are generally lower than male wages and many rather obvious explanations of the inequality are available. One particularly important aspect of the problem is that the principle "equal work, equal pay" is not always adhered to. Women often consider their wage as an additional income for the family, its standard of living being determined by the husband's pay. Furthermore, women are often in a minority position on the labour market and display a smaller propensity to unionize.

For these reasons, industries with a majority of male employment probably pay higher average wages and it is an elementary precaution to include M, the percent of male employment, among the independent variables in a regression analysis.

Size of establishment divisions (SD). It seems reasonable to introduce also a variable characterizing the industries according to the size of their production units. In an empirical study of French industrial and commercial establishments, J.Meraud [3] observed that average earnings are practically independent of size in establishments employing 10 to 200 workers, whereas they increase rapidly with size at higher levels. In Belgium, an analogous phenomenon has been observed, [4] in particular for wages of males. These earnings increase with the size of the production unit because of a higher productivity, which allows to satisfy claims for higher wages. And these claims are probably more forceful in larger units: in financial and organizational terms, unionization is easier in larger units, the more as workers have a higher propensity to unionize when the gap between managers and employees is larger.

To characterize each industry, we compute SD as the percentage of persons employed in establishment divisions of 200 persons or more.

---

[3] J.Meraud, Les salaires français suivant la taille des établissements, *Etudes et conjoncture* (1958).

[4] See, e.g., I.N.S., *Bulletin de statistique* (1962), p. 1848, and D.Crespi, *Les salaires belges, Faits et théories* (A.Colin, Paris, 1960).

Power of the trade unions (TU). How does one express the power of trade unions, given that no data are available on the rate of unionization? It is worthwhile to try to construct an index which combines the different elements that jointly determine [5] the power of a trade union in an industry. We retain the following elements:

(1) the percentage of male employment (*M*)
(2) the size of the production units (*SD*)
(3) the geographical dispersion of these units (*GD*)
(4) the degree of unemployment (*U*).

The two first elements have been briefly discussed above. As for the third, it is admitted that group solidarity works better when production units are geographically close. *GD* is going to be measured by the smallest number of *arrondissements* (counties) necessary to obtain 75% of total employment in the industry.

The variable *U* is of course a must. When unemployment is low, total demand is high, employers have to compete on the labour market and do not hesitate to offer wages that are above the conventional levels. For the same reason, employers are ready to make concessions during wage negociations, while trade unions are much aware of this fact. Finally, the supply of labour is inelastic.

Our index should thus increase with *M*, *SD* and *GD* and decrease when *U* rises. It is defined as the geometric mean

$$TU = \sqrt[4]{\frac{M \cdot (SD) \cdot (GD)}{U}}$$

For lack of more detailed data, the index could be computed only for two-digit industries, as can be seen in the appendix to this chapter.

Employment growth (GE). Industries with rapidly growing employment probably offer higher wages, given the facts that there is imperfect foresight of job opportunities and that the supply of

[5] We will follow suggestions made by J.Debelle in *Disparité géographique des salaires en Belgique*, Mémoire de Licence (Louvain, 1962).

labour is not perfectly elastic. This is a first and a sufficient reason to try GE. [6] Dunlop offers an additional reason, arguing that industries with growing employment are also industries with improving productivity. [7]

To this already long list, several other possible variables, such as the durability of the goods produced, the percentage of foreign workers, etc. could be added. But one has to stop somewhere, if only for statistical reasons.

4.2.2. Empirical results

Two sets of results, following two different approaches, are going to be presented.

Approach I first verifies the Garbarino model and follows specification (4.1). Here, concentration, the power of the trade unions and employment growth are considered to be the relevant variables. In a second stage, the interaction between concentration and unionization as formalized in equation (4.2) is examined more closely.

Unfortunately, the multicollinearity tests (described in section 2.2.2.) reveal a strong multicollinearity which makes it difficult to evaluate the regression coefficient of C. Approach II tries to circumvent this difficulty by respecifying the regression equation. Instead of TU, two of its components, namely M, the percentage of male employment and SD, the size of production units, are used: this ad hoc procedure clarifies things a lot, at least as far as multicollinearity is concerned.

Approach I. Table 4.1 gives the regression results for equation (4.1), with standard-errors between brackets as usual.

The concentration ratio is gratified with a positive and significant coefficient, which is entirely as expected. Unfortunately, the other variables get high standard-errors because of an important

[6] See L.Weiss, Concentration and labor earnings, *Am. Economic Rev.* (March 1966).
[7] See Garbarino, op. cit.

Table 4.1
Wages and concentration in Belgium. Regression coefficients for equation (4.1)

No.	C	TU	GE	$\bar{R}^2$	D.F.	F-ratio	χ^2
I.1	24.92 (1.26)	0.16 (0.03)		0.40	1, 41	28.8**	
I.2	21.59 (2.24)	0.11 (0.04)	1.52 (0.86)	0.43	2, 40	16.7**	23.5**
I.3	20.47 (2.39)	0.13 (0.04)	1.04 (0.93)	2.13 (1.68)	0.44	3, 39	11.9**	30.6**

multicollinearity between C and TU as indicated by the values of χ^2 and also by the t-tests (which give $t = 5.7$ in (I.2) and $t = 6.1$ in (I.3) for the pair C and TU). On the other hand, it is reassuring to find that the coefficient of C is nevertheless significant. One should also remember that TU could be computed only for two-digit industries, with the result that its value had to be taken as identical for all three-digit branches within the same two-digit industry. We feel entitled therefore to consider these results as reliable and to use equation (I.2) in table 4.1 for the following illustration, which comes very close to findings reported by H.G.Lewis. [8]

Let us take rather extreme values for C and TU and compute the average hourly wage rate (in Belgian francs) using the estimated values of a_0, a_1 and a_2 given in table 4.1, equation (I.2). This leads to table 4.2.

The positive effect of an increase in concentration is smaller in industries where unions have a strong position. This is due, no doubt, to the fact that the average level of wages is already higher. Conversely, in highly concentrated industries, the impact of unionization is somewhat reduced, again because wages are already higher. Needless to say that the conjunction of high concentration and high unionization leads to the highest wages.

[8] H.G.Lewis reports in *Unionism and Relative Wages* (Chicago, 1963) that unionization has increased the earnings of unionized workers by 15% as compared to earnings of non-unionized workers.

Table 4.2
Impact of concentration and unionization on wages in Belgium

TU C	2.0	4.5	%Δ
10	25.73	29.53	15
60	31.23	35.03	12
%Δ	21	19	

Table 4.3 was meant to show the effect of the interaction of C and TU as formalized in (4.2) (with the possible addition of employment growth). Unfortunately, multicollinearity is most impressive and affects all variables: most coefficients are nonsignificant. This line of attack has to be abandoned.

Table 4.3
Interaction of concentration and unionization in Belgium. Regression coefficients for equation (4.2)

No.	C	TU	$C \cdot (TU)$	G	$\bar{R}^2$	D.F.	F-ratio	χ^2
III.1	24.46	0.02	0.66	0.02		0.43	3, 39	11.6**	136.0**
	(3.54)	(0.09)	(1.19)	(0.02)					
III.2	23.27	0.04	0.21	(0.02)	2.08	0.44	4, 38	9.2**	142.1**
	(3.64)	(0.09)	(1.23)	(0.02)	(1.68)				

Approach II. Let us redefine (4.1), replacing TU by M and SD and adding E, as

$$W = a_0 + a_1 C + a_2 M + a_3 GE + a_4 E + a_5 SD . \tag{4.5}$$

The rationale for adding E, total employment, is that in industries with a large labour force unions are probably in a stronger position. By splitting up TU in that way, and trying different combinations in turn, we hope to be able to isolate the combination that

Table 4.4
Wages and concentration in Belgium. Regression coefficients for equation (4.4)

No.		C	M	GE	$E(10^{-4})$	SD
IV.1	13.96 (1.93)	0.12 (0.02)	0.16 (0.02)			
IV.2	8.75 (2.00)	0.12 (0.02)	0.17 (0.02)	4.13 (0.95)		
IV.3	12.67 (1.99)	0.13 (0.02)	0.16 (0.02)		0.54 (0.28)	
IV.4	8.48 (2.02)	0.12 (0.02)	0.17 (0.02)	3.83 (0.98)	0.27 (0.25)	
IV.5	8.67 (1.95)	0.07 (0.03)	0.17 (0.02)	3.91 (0.93)		0.05 (0.03)

No.		$\bar{R}^2$	D.F.	F-ratio	χ^2
IV.1	13.96 (1.93)	0.70	2, 40	48.9**	3.1
IV.2	8.75 (2.00)	0.78	3, 39	53.6**	4.1
IV.3	12.67 (1.99)	0.71	3, 39	36.0**	5.9
IV.4	8.48 (2.02)	0.79	4, 38	40.6**	10.1
IV.5	8.67 (1.95)	0.80	4, 38	43.2**	50.5**

avoids the multicollinearity problem without loosing too much in economic content. An additional objective is to find a suitable specification introducing only variables that are easy to measure and thus facilitate international comparisons.

Table 4.4 suggests that efforts along these lines are rewarding. Most coefficients are significant, $\bar{R}^2$'s are markedly higher and multicollinearity is no longer a problem.

Comparing equations (IV.1) to (IV.4) (in table 4.4), one is impressed by the remarkable stability of the coefficient of C around 0.12. (The introduction of other variables simply increases $\bar{R}^2$.) This value is also very close to the ones found in table 4.1 and in particular to the 0.11 value used in table 4.2. The stability of the coefficients of M and G should also be noticed, and is entirely in line with the low values of χ^2.

The economic interpretation of these results is clear. Concentration characterizes the product market as a measure of monopoly power. An increase of the concentration ratio by 10 points, other things being equal, leads to an increase in average earnings of 1.20 Belgian francs. M and E are "proxies" for unionization, while M also introduces an important personal characteristic. (Remember that W is an average of wages for males *and* females). The variable GE gives an idea of the internal evolution of the companies, and possibly of their productivity. We have thus the three variables that play a key role in Garbarino's argumentation as explained in the introductory section.

The preceding comments refer to equations (IV.1) to (IV.4). As for (IV.5), it is interesting to notice that the introduction of the size of production units (SD) reduces the coefficient of C markedly while increasing multicollinearity. Concentration is related to size, and that is probably the reason why C and TU were multicollinear in table 4.1.

All in all, then, we find a stable, significant and positive coefficient for C. This coefficient has the value of 0.12: in Belgium, an increase in the concentration ratio by 10 points leads to an increase of average hourly earnings by 1.20 Belgian francs. We are well equipped by now to try an international comparison.

4.3. Some Common Market countries

It so happens that the subject of this chapter is the only one, in part I, that can be treated with the help of the Common Market industrial census, and thus of the data classified according to N.I.C.E. and gathered in the statistical appendix (to be found at

Table 4.5
General informations on data for Belgium, France and Italy

	Belgium	France	Italy
Total employment (sum of E)	1,044,100	5,185,100	4,522,400
Total production worker employment ($\Sigma\ E_W$)	738,380	3,047,000	2,403,300
Average of M	77	71	70
Average of W	38,89 B.F.	3.22 F.F.	282.5 lires
Number of N.I.C.E. industries included	83	96	98

the end of this book). This is an heartening fact and a sufficient reason to redefine some variables such as to be able to exploit the possibilities offered by the census, in particular its homogeneity and comparability. [9]

W is redefined as earnings of production workers (only) divided by the number of hours worked (by production workers). Accordingly, M is going to be the percentage of male production workers, and E_W the total number of production workers employed.

SD, our previous measure of size of divisions (production units), is replaced by $\bar{S}$, the average size of establishments, because the Common Market census ignores the concept of a "division".

Concentration ratios C, total employment E and average size of establishments are to be found in tables A.1 and A.4 of the statistical appendix. Employment growth G has to be abandoned for lack of comparable data.

Table 4.5 gives some general informations on the data used in the analysis that follows.

4.3.1. Belgium, France and Italy

To begin with, it is necessary to verify whether the shift from

---

[9] One drawback is that very many frequency distributions were still missing for the Netherlands when this chapter was completed, with the result that this country was dropped to get the benefits of a perfect comparability of the data.

Table 4.6
Wages and concentration in Belgium. Regression results with N.I.C.E. data

No.		C	M	$E(10^{-4})$	$E_W(10^{-4})$	$\bar{S}$
VI.1	29.43 (1.10)	0.12 (0.02)				
VI.2	16.31 (1.75)	0.10 (0.02)	0.18 (0.02)			
VI.3	14.33 (1.79)	0.11 (0.02)	0.19 (0.02)	0.94 (0.30)		
VI.4	14.75 (1.77)	0.10 (0.02)	0.19 (0.02)		1.26 (0.45)	
VI.5	16.49 (1.70)	0.08 (0.02)	0.18 (0.02)			0.005 (0.002)

No.		$\bar{R}^2$	D.F.	F-ratio	χ^2
VI.1	29.42 (1.10)	0.21	1, 81	24.14**	
VI.2	16.31 (1.75)	0.58	2, 80	57.7**	1.41
VI.3	14.33 (1.79)	0.62	3, 79	45.8**	3.67
VI.4	14.75 (1.77)	0.62	3, 79	44.4**	2.31
VI.5	16.49 (1.70)	0.61	3, 79	43.39**	18.80**

the U.N. to the N.I.C.E. classification and the changes in the definitions of some variables affect the regression results. Table 4.6 shows that this is not the case.

Compare this table with tables 4.1 and 4.4: the results are very similar indeed, at least as far as C and M are concerned. Their coefficients display the same stability and are in the same ballpark. The size of establishments is again collinear with concentration and reduces the latter's coefficient.

Table 4.7
Wages and concentration in France. Regression results with N.I.C.E. data

No.		C	M	$E(10^{-5})$	$E_W(10^{-5})$	χ^2
VII.1	2.78 (0.09)	0.016 (0.003)				
VII.2	2.12 (0.16)	0.015 (0.002)	0.010 (0.002)			
VII.3	2.00 (0.17)	0.016 (0.002)	0.010 (0.002)	0.21 (0.09)		
VII.4	2.03 (0.17)	0.015 (0.002)	0.010 (0.002)		0.28 (0.14)	
VII.5	2.12 (0.17)	0.015 (0.002)	0.010 (0.002)			−0.13 (2.16)

No.		$\bar{R}^2$	D.F.	F-ratio	χ^2
VII.1	2.78 (0.09)	0.30	1, 94	39.8**	
VII.2	2.12 (0.16)	0.41	2, 93	33.8**	1.47
VII.3	2.00 (0.17)	0.43	3, 92	25.1**	4.37
VII.4	2.03 (0.17)	0.43	3, 91	24.4**	1.80
VII.5	2.12 (0.17)	0.40	3, 91	22.1**	10.03**

The economic implications are therefore roughly the same. To illustrate, let us take the coefficients of (VI.4) and choose values of C of 10 and 60. Other things being equal (with $\bar{M}$ = 77 and $\bar{E}_W$ = 8,896), the increase of C from 10 to 60 leads to an increase of average wages, in Belgium, of 16%. This figure compares favorably with the impact of 19 to 21% found in section 4.2.2.

We may proceed and take up France (see table 4.7).

The dependent variable is now measured in French francs,

Table 4.8
Wages and concentration in Italy. Regression results with N.I.C.E. data

No.		C	M	$E(10^{-3})$	$E_W(10^{-3})$	$\bar{S}$
VIII.1	225.17 (8.46)	2.11 (0.24)				
VIII.2	151.58 (15.37)	2.00 (0.22)	1.10 (0.20)			
VIII.3	140.43 (16.80)	2.09 (0.22)	1.11 (0.20)	0.17 (0.11)		
VIII.4	133.34 (16.58)	2.05 (0.21)	1.16 (0.20)		0.52 (0.20)	
VIII.5	152.81 (15.36)	2.18 (0.24)	1.12 (0.20)			−0.06 (0.04)

No.		$\bar{R}^2$	D.F.	F-ratio	χ^2
VIII.1	225.17 (8.46)	0.44	1, 96	74.9**	
VIII.2	151.58 (15.37)	0.57	2, 95	63.7**	0.83
VIII.3	140.43 (16.80)	0.57	3, 94	44.0**	7.33
VIII.4	133.34 (16.58)	0.59	3, 93	46.7**	3.00
VIII.5	152.81 (15.36)	0.59	3, 93	43.7**	23.19**

which were worth about 10 Belgian francs. Multiplying all results (in table 4.7) by 10, we get the impression that the influence of C (very stable around 0.15) is somewhat stronger than in Belgium, while the impact of M is smaller and again absolutely stable. The average size of establishments seems to play only one role: to create a lot of multicollinearity with concentration.

That the impact of concentration on wages is rather on the high side, at least when compared with Belgium, is confirmed by the following (by now usual) illustration: *ceteris paribus* ($\overline{M} = 71$, $\overline{E}_W = 31{,}740$) an increase of C from 10 to 60 leads to a rise in wages of 27% according to equation (VII.4).

What is the situation in Italy? See table 4.8.

Given that wages are in lires, these Italian results have the same properties as the Belgian and the French, except that the impact of C is even stronger (1 B.F. = 12.5 lires). With $\overline{M} = 70$ and $\overline{E}_W = 24{,}523$ in equation (VIII.4), an increase of C from 10 to 60 now leads to a wage increase of *43%*!

It is nice to find that in all three countries concentration has a highly significant positive influence. But it is puzzling that this influence seems to be so much stronger in some countries. (As will be shown in the next section, these differences are indeed significant.) We have therefore to offer an explanation.

The basic philosophy of this chapter is that firms with a greater market power are able, with equal productivity, to pay higher wages because they realize higher rates of return. Part of labour earnings are thus monopoly rents which workers share with employers. [10] One way of explaining the divergence between the 16% increase in Belgium, the 27% in France and the 43% in Italy would be to refer to the previous chapter on profits and to say that highly concentrated industries are less competitive and therefore get higher profits in France and Italy. A possible stronger profit-concentration relationship would thus be reflected in a stronger wage-concentration relationship.

This can be but half of the story, however. At least in the case of Italy, the probability is high that the regression coefficient of C also measures other influences, among which there must be a geographical factor. Average wages per industry are certainly affected by the location of the industry: if concentrated industries have their plants located mainly in the north of Italy, and unconcentrated in the south, as is often the case, then the typical wage differentials between the north and the south of Italy account for a good deal of the impact of C.

---

[10] It is not impossible that this conclusion would be weakened, if not reversed, if the qualification of the labour force could be given proper treatment.

It would be easy to verify this second argument by adding a variable measuring geographical concentration of the industries in the north and the south. Most unfortunately, regional data were not tabulated in the Common Market census!

On the other hand, one should recognize the possibility that a change of C from 10 to 60 may not mean the same thing for a small country as for a larger one. We will see, in chapter 6, that because of the influence of market size concentration ratios tend to stick at lower values in larger countries. On a diagram relating W and C, with C measured on the horizontal axis, this amounts to a change in the units of measurement on the horizontal axis. In larger countries, the consequence is a steeper slope. There might be an effect of this sort in the difference in wage increases between Belgium on the one hand and Italy and France on the other.

4.3.2. Covariance analysis

This section opens a parenthesis in order to verify that the impact of the independent variables on W is indeed different. A natural way to do this is to set up a covariance analysis in the way explained in chapter 2 (section 2.3).

We want to test the homogeneity of the slope coefficients of the regression equation

$$W = a_0 + a_1 C + a_2 M + a_3 E_W$$

in Belgium, France and Italy. The number of observations may be different from country to country, but the dependent variable should be expressed in the same units. All average wages are therefore expressed in U.S. dollars ("unités de compte" = 50 B.F. = 4.937 F.F. = 625 lires). The regression results are given in table 4.9. Regression coefficients appearing in the same column are expressed in the same units of measurement and the problem is to determine whether they are significantly different from one country to another.

The F-ratio of $0.024/0.007: 3.26$, with 6 and 263 degrees of

Table 4.9
Regression results for Belgium, France and Italy. Wages in U.S. dollars

No.	Country		C	M	$E_W(10^{-6})$	$\bar{R}^2$
IX.1	Belgium	0.29	0.0020 (0.0004)	0.0037 (0.0004)	2.52 (0.90)	0.62
IX.2	France	0.41	0.0031 (0.0005)	0.0020 (0.0004)	0.57 (0.29)	0.43
IX.3	Italy	0.21	0.0033 (0.0003)	0.0019 (0.0003)	0.82 (0.33)	0.59

No.	Country		D.F.	F-ratio	χ^2
IX.1	Belgium	0.29	3, 79	44.4**	2.31
IX.2	France	0.41	3, 91	24.4**	1.75
IX.3	Italy	0.21	3, 93	46.7**	3.15

freedom, is significant at the 1% level. The null hypothesis of homogeneity of the slope coefficients has to be rejected.

On statistical grounds, the conclusion is clear. It is much less on economic grounds. We have already recognized the fact that smaller countries have larger concentration ratios and that this circumstance might explain part of the difference among the slope coefficients of C and reduce their significance from an economic point of view. Looking back at table 4.9, a similar comment seems in order with respect to the coefficients of E_W: given that the

Table 4.10
Covariance analysis Belgium–France–Italy

Source	SS	D.F.	M.S.	F-ratio
Combined regression	2.205	3	0.735	100.50**
Difference of regressions	0.143	6	0.024	3.26**
Residual	1.923	263	0.007	
Total within	4.271	272	0.016	

range of the values taken by total employment is much smaller in smaller countries, because of their small market size, part of the difference might simply reflect difference in market size, i.e. in units of measurement. There might be a stretching of the x-axis, to speak in diagrammatic terms, with a corresponding reduction in slope in larger countries.

All in all, then, the non-homogeneity of the results should not be dramatized.

4.3.3. Zellner's model

Up to now, we ran regressions for each country separately, and applied the method of ordinary least-squares. Covariance analysis was then used as a first step towards combining all data. It is possible to go one step further and to estimate all parameters (for all three countries) simultaneously using a method proposed by A.Zellner [11] for the case of "seemingly unrelated regressions". This method has the advantage of leading to estimators that are at least asymptotically more efficient.

The basic idea is to consider our three regression equations (one for each country) as forming one single "big" regression and to apply to it Aitken's method of generalized least-squares. To do this, one has first to estimate the variance-covariance matrix of the error terms from the residuals of the individual regressions.

The variance-covariance matrix is meant to take account of inter-country correlations between disturbances relating to a particular industry. It implies constant variances and covariances from industry to industry as well as the absence of any auto-correlation of the disturbance terms. Inter-country correlations between disturbances in a particular industry are meant to arise because our basic equation neglects some factors. If this neglect leads to a large disturbance for a particular industry in country A, it is possible that it also leads to a large disturbance for the same

[11] A.Zellner, An efficient method of estimating seemingly unrelated regressions and tests for aggregation bias, *J. Am. Statistical Association* (June 1962).

industry in country B. It is of course difficult, in principle, to identify the factors under discussion (otherwise they would have been included explicitly in the model). In our case, it might be that they include employment growth and/or geographical concentration, both variables having been deleted for lack of appropriate data. However these influences could show up in the variance-covariance matrix only to the extent that they work in the same direction (in the same industries) in different countries.

The approach is thus more powerful than covariance analysis, the more as it also allows to test the equality of regression coefficient vectors and the absence of (one type of) aggregation bias. Indeed, if the null hypothesis of equality is valid, our countries may be aggregated in a simple linear way. The only (minor) drawback is that the *same* industries and the same number of industries have to be used for each country (*micro-unit*), which implies a possible loss of information. This will be the case here, the number of industries for which matching observations are available in all three countries being 82 (to be compared with the initial numbers of 83, 96 and 98 in Belgium, France and Italy respectively).

For each country, we had the equation

$$W = a_0 + a_1 C + a_2 M + a_3 E_W + u ,$$

which we will write now in matrix notation as

$$Y_i = X_i \beta_i + u_i , \qquad (4.6)$$

where $i = 1, 2, 3$ designates the countries to be analysed. The equation is considered to be the i-th equation in a system written as

$$\begin{bmatrix} Y_1 \\ Y_2 \\ Y_3 \end{bmatrix} = \begin{bmatrix} X_1 & 0 & 0 \\ 0 & X_2 & 0 \\ 0 & 0 & X_3 \end{bmatrix} \begin{bmatrix} \beta_1 \\ \beta_2 \\ \beta_3 \end{bmatrix} + \begin{bmatrix} u_1 \\ u_2 \\ u_3 \end{bmatrix} , \qquad (4.7)$$

where Y_i represents 82×1 vectors of observations on W, X_i represents 82×4 matrices of observations on the independent variables, u_i is a 82×1 vector of disturbances and β_i a 4×1 vector of regression coefficients. The system (4.7) may be written in compact notation as

$$Y = X\beta + u \, . \tag{4.8}$$

The vector u is supposed to have the variance-covariance matrix

$$\Sigma = V(u) = \begin{bmatrix} \sigma_{11} & \sigma_{12} & \sigma_{13} \\ \sigma_{21} & \sigma_{22} & \sigma_{23} \\ \sigma_{31} & \sigma_{32} & \sigma_{33} \end{bmatrix} \otimes I \, , \tag{4.9}$$

where I is a unit matrix of order 82×82. The Aitken estimator is then

$$\tilde{\beta} = (X'\Sigma^{-1}X)^{-1} X'\Sigma^{-1}Y \, . \tag{4.10}$$

To estimate Σ, the residuals obtained from an equation-by-equation application of ordinary least-squares are used.

Table 4.11 presents, country by country, the results obtained by ordinary least-squares (equation-by-equation) and Zellner's generalized least squares, using 82 observations. Wages are expressed in U.S. dollars as in table 4.9. Comparing the ordinary least-square results in table 4.11 and table 4.9, we find that France and Italy still have the highest coefficients for the variable C. However, the order is reversed as between France and Italy: the impact of C is now the highest in France! This is due to the loss of 14 observations for France and 16 observations for Italy. The two sets of results are thus not comparable: this is the price one has to pay for using more powerful techniques.

Comparing ordinary and generalized least-squares results, we can verify that the latter indeed lead to a gain in efficiency. Inevitably, the estimated coefficients are different from the ordinary least-squares estimates.

In fact, the estimated impact of concentration on wages is seen to be lower in the Zellner model than in the equation-by-equation approach. Furthermore – and this is particularly interesting here – the difference in impact between Belgium and France is reduced (with the result that Italy again appears with the highest slope

Table 4.11
Ordinary and generalized least-squares, Belgium–France–Italy

No.	Country	Method		C	M
XI.1	Belgium	Ordinary least-squares	0.29 (0.04)	0.00195 (0.00035)	0.00379 (0.00041)
XI.2	Belgium	Generalized least-squares (Zellner)	0.31 (0.03)	0.00139 (0.00031)	0.00394 (0.00039)
XI.3	France	Ordinary least-squares	0.41 (0.04)	0.00346 (0.00056)	0.00221 (0.00046)
XI.4	France	Generalized least-squares (Zellner)	0.44 (0.03)	0.00252 (0.00050)	0.00217 (0.00044)
XI.5	Italy	Ordinary least-squares	0.23 (0.03)	0.00325 (0.00041)	0.00172 (0.00033)
XI.6	Italy	Generalized least-squares (Zellner)	0.25 (0.03)	0.00287 (0.00036)	0.00155 (0.00032)

No.	Country	$E_W(10^{-6})$	$\bar{R}^2$	D.F.	F-ratio
XI.1	Belgium	2.409 (0.889)	0.62	3, 78	45.4**
XI.2	Belgium	2.000 (0.765)			
XI.3	France	−0.010 (0.002)	0.44	3, 78	22.7**
XI.4	France	−0.007 (0.002)			
XI.5	Italy	0.762 (0.333)	0.54	3, 78	33.1**
.XI.6	Italy	0.606 (0.283)			

coefficient for C). Indeed, instead of the ordinary least-squares estimates 0.0019, 0.0035 and 0.0032, we now have 0.0014, 0.0025 and 0.0029 for Belgium, France and Italy respectively. By taking the contemporaneous covariance structure into account (the data are weighted by elements of the covariance matrix's inverse), we apparently succeeded in eliminating some of the forces that were neglected in the separate regressions.

Statistically speaking, the national coefficient vectors (β_1, β_2 and β_3) are not equal, as Zellner's F-test leads to $F = 183.43$ (with 12 and 70 degrees of freedom). One wonders again to what extent the remaining inter-country difference correspond to different economic structures (see the comments at the end of section 4.3.1 above).

Table 4.12 gives the values (in U.S. dollars) that W takes in the Zellner model for different values of C, with M and E_W equal to their national averages.

Table 4.12
Impact of concentration on wages in Belgium, France and Italy (generalized least-squares)

Concentration	10	50	60
W in Belgium	$ 0.643	$ 0.698	$ 0.712
$\bar{E}_W$ = 8,896 $\bar{M}$ = 77			
W in France	$ 0.616	$ 0.717	$ 0.742
$\bar{E}_W$ = 31,740 $\bar{M}$ = 71			
W in Italy	$ 0.403	$ 0.518	$ 0.547
$\bar{E}_W$ = 24,523 $\bar{M}$ = 70			

In percentage terms, an increase of C from 10 to 60 leads, according to table 4.12, to an increase in W of the order of 11% in Belgium, 20% in France and 36% in Italy (to be compared with figures of 16%, 27% and 43% obtained by ordinary equation-by-equation least-squares).

4.4. Conclusions

There is clear evidence in favour of a positive wage-concentration relationship, in Belgium as well as in France and in Italy.

A country-by-country approach leads to the conclusion that an increase of the concentration ratio from a value of 10 to a value of 60 leads to wage increases of 16% in Belgium, 27% in France and 43% in Italy.

These impacts seem to be overevaluated, however, mainly because of the absence in our regressions of variables measuring geographical concentration.

We therefore turned to the Zellner model, which allows to estimate the national coefficient vectors simultaneously and to take into account "contemporaneous" correlations between disturbance terms, i.e. correlations between countries (for the same industries). The different nations are thus treated as "micro-units" with the Common Market (or part of it) as the macro-unit.

Relations at the micro-level appear as statistically different, as was already suggested by a covariance analysis. Furthermore, the country-by-country approach seems indeed to be biased upwards. The Zellner model gives, for a *ceteris paribus* change in the concentration ratio from 10 to 60, wage increases of 11% in Belgium, 20% in France and 36% in Italy.

In absolute terms, these percentages correspond to a wage increase of $ 0.014 or 0.70 B.F. in Belgium, $ 0.025 or 1.26 B.F. in France and $ 0.029 or 1.44 B.F. in Italy, as the result of an increase by 10 points of the concentration ratio.

One cannot exclude, without further evidence on personal characteristics of the labour force, the possibility that the positive wage-concentration relationship reflects the use of higher quality labour in more concentrated industries. At first sight, however, our results point towards a sharing of the workers in higher profits realized by employers. To the extent that this is true, these findings would strengthen the conclusions of the previous chapter as to a positive profit-concentration relationship.

Intercountry differences in slope coefficients could be partly explained away by two considerations. First, regional wage differ-ences could account for a large part. Secondly, the smaller range of the concentration ratio in larger countries might turn slopes upwards (and conversely for smaller countries). Clearly, here is an area that is open to further research.

APPENDIX TO CHAPTER 4

Table 4.13. Belgium

W, average gross hourly earnings in Belgian francs (male plus female) by industry, are taken from I.N.S., *Bulletin de statistique* (July-August 1962). They refer to October 1961 and follow the U.N. international classification of industries (to complicate matters).

M, the percentage of male employment, is computed from *Recensement de l'industrie et du commerce 1961*, tome 2, tableau IV.

SD, the percentage of persons employed in establishment divisions of 200 persons or more, by industry, is computed from the same source, tome 2, tableau III.

In the definition of TU, index of the power of trade unions, appear M and SD, defined above, and also GD and U. GD is an index of geographical dispersion, namely the smallest number of "arrondissements" (counties) necessary to obtain 75% of total employment in an industry, and is based on data given in *Recensement de l'industrie et du commerce 1961*, tome 1, tableau XV. Unemployment U is to be found in *Bulletin de statistique* (february 1962).

To compute employment growth GE, which is simply total employment (E) in 1961 divided by total employment in 1947, per industry, we had to use the *Recensement de la Population 1961*, tome 8 and the *Recensement industriel 1947*, tome 10.

Needless to say that all data had to be adapted to the U.N. classification of industries, which fortunately is rather close to the classification used in the Belgian 1961 census.

Table 4.13
Data on wages, concentration and industrial structure in Belgium, 1961

No.	U.N.	Industry	W	C	M	SD	GE	TU	C·(TU)	E
1	201	Meat slaughtering and processing	27.01	13.7	89	9.6	0.50	2.20	30.14	6,533
2	202	Milk	27.65	12.8	87	9.1	1.56	2.20	28.16	7,354
3	203	Canned fruits and vegetables	24.08	40.5	52	28.8	1.03	2.20	89.10	4,323
4	205.1, 205.2	Corn milling Other cereals	28.84	17.2	90	16.9	0.69	2.20	37.84	4,363
5	206.1. 206.2	Bread Biscuits, pastries	27.80	9.4	74	16.3	1.21	2.20	20.68	23,219
6	207	Sugar	33.25	71.9	91	57.8	0.85	2.20	158.18	5,206
7	208	Cocoa, chocolate, confectionery	24.85	30.1	51	34.1	0.81	2.20	66.22	8,000
8	204, 209	Other food	28.00	26.1	79	21.0	0.88	2.20	57.42	13,691
9	213	Beer and malt	30.63	22.1	95	44.4	0.74	2.98	65.85	14,886
10	211, 214	Other drinks	27.50	31.3	84	22.7	1.23	2.98	93.27	7,240
11	22	Tobacco	22.94	32.4	34	63.6	0.96	2.91	94.28	8,392
12	232.1, 232.2	Hosiery Stockings	22.54	12.0	20	19.0	1.53	2.84	34.08	16,440
13	241	Foot-wear	25.96	14.6	50	26.6	0.87	1.70	24.82	15,756
14	243.1,	Men's and women's wear	19.83	3.8	20	12.4	1.07	1.70	6.46	59,112
	243.2	Work clothing, underwear								
15	251.1	Sawmills and planing mills	27.65	7.9	96	5.4	0.75	1.76	13.90	7,711

Table 4.13 (cont.)

No.	U.N.	Industry	W	C	M	SD	GE	TU	C·(TU)	E
16	251.2	Carpentry	31.34	10.8	95	0.0	0.26	1.76	19.01	3,308
17	252, 259	Other wood products	28.44	19.9	85	6.5	0.54	1.76	35.02	6,421
18	260	Wood furniture	30.05	8.4	94	12.7	1.30	1.76	14.78	22,925
19	271.1	Pulp, paper and board	34.26	51.0	77	72.5	1.02	3.95	201.45	10,930
20	281–283	Printing and binding	34.97	11.8	80	29.0	1.02	3.74	44.13	28,663
21	272	Paper and board products	27.40	20.3	64	31.7	1.09	3.95	80.19	12,730
22	291	Tannery	28.32	36.4	76	48.4	0.67	2.59	94.28	4,003
23	293	Leather products	21.93	21.9	58	0.0	0.77	2.59	56.72	3,310
24	300	Rubber	31.65	64.0	77	65.0	0.86	5.33	341.12	7,844
25	311.1, 311.2, 311.3	Nitrogen fertilizers, superphosphate, paints	38.00	84.9	93	67.6	0.62	4.34	368.47	3,887
26	313	Lac and varnishes	28.87	20.3	74	17.7	1.25	4.34	88.10	4,895
27	319.1	Soap, cosmetics, detergents	28.40	48.0	49	42.2	1.72	4.34	208.32	5,262
28	319.2	Pharmaceutical products	24.33	31.5	47	23.8	1.40	4.34	136.71	6,780
29	321	Petroleum	51.02	90.6	96	84.7	2.41	5.66	512.80	3,113
30	322	Cokeries	38.40	99.8	98	83.7	0.50	5.66	564.87	2,418
31	331.1, 331.9	Bricks, Baked clay products	32.71	15.2	95	31.4	0.84	3.58	54.42	14,239
32	332	Glass	30.98	58.1	85	83.6	0.94	3.58	208.00	23,222

Table 4.13 (cont.)

No.	U.N.	Industry	W	C	M	SD	GE	TU	$C \cdot (TU)$	E
33	333	China, pottery	25.63	53.2	56	48.9	0.78	3.58	190.46	4,109
34	334	Cement	40.15	79.9	94	71.5	0.63	3.58	286.04	3,662
35	342	Non-ferrous metals	36.05	46.2	95	84.0	1.02	4.58	211.60	18,057
36	350	Metallic construction	32.72	23.4	86	49.0	1.30	3.77	88.22	75,273
37	360	Electric machines	34.92	30.6	94	44.0	1.10	3.55	108.63	58,608
38	370	Electrotechnical industries	30.18	40.4	71	73.0	1.60	4.10	165.64	74,281
39	381	Ship building and repairing	40.51	54.6	98	65.3	0.64	3.69	201.47	13,228
40	382	Railroad and streetcars	33.94	52.4	96	79.8	0.56	3.69	193.36	7,650
41	383	Automobiles and parts	40.25	41.5	94	60.6	2.29	3.69	153.14	15,891
42	384	Repair of automobiles	31.83	17.8	95	4.3	1.66	3.69	65.68	22,713
43	385	Motorcycles and cycles	26.23	33.3	88	36.8	0.65	3.69	122.88	3,689

CHAPTER 5

RESEARCH [1]

5.1. Introduction

There is a strong tradition in economic literature, going back to Schumpeter through Galbraith, which considers firm size as a factor favorable to research. The financial power of larger firms, their wider economic horizon, and their possibilities of diversification are cited to support this view. Reference is also made to the degree of concentration of the markets on which the big firms operate, their market power permitting them to accumulate profits and/or replace price competition by quality competition. Hence an intensification of research. [2]

While the theoretical arguments are numerous, empirical studies have been rather few. [3] The present chapter is intended to make a contribution on the empirical level on the basis of Belgian data. The method adopted was suggested by that developed by F.M. Scherer [4] as the available data lend themselves to comparable statistical treatment.

[1] This chapter reproduces a paper entitled Concentration, dimension et recherche dans l'industrie manufacturière belge, *Recherches Economiques de Louvain*, No. 1, February 1969. A shortened version appeared in *European Economic Rev.* (1970) No. 4.

[2] For a good synthesis of this literature, see e.g. D.Hamberg, Size of firm, oligopoly, and research: the evidence, *Canadian J. of Economics and Political Science* (February 1964) 62–75.

[3] Recent contributions include W.S.Comanor, Market structure, product differentiation, and industrial research, *Quarterly J. of Economics* (November 1967) 639–657, and H.G.Grabowski, The determinants of industrial research and development: a study of the chemical, drug and petroleum industries, *J. of Political Economy* (March/April 1968) 292–306.

[4] F.M.Scherer, Firm size, market structure, opportunity, and the output of patented invention, *Am. Economic Rev.* (December 1965) 1097–1125.

In Belgium we can avail ourselves of surveys carried out every two years by the Conseil National de la Politique Scientifique which cover the private enterprises (with more than 50 persons employed) of the extractive, manufacturing, construction and public works industries. The present study is based on the 1963 survey and is limited to the manufacturing industry. Of 325 enterprises which replied that they did carry out research, 301 could be retained in the sample, whereas 24 which did not furnish indispensable information had to be excluded. [5]

We utilized two types of quantitative data from the survey: (1) the personnel by whom research is carried out (in the following designated RP), defined as the number of persons with a diploma either of higher education or of higher technical education of whom the employers declared that their work was wholly devoted to scientific research in the field of the natural sciences: [6] and (2) the total personnel (TP) of the firms retained in the sample.

With these data, of which it can be assumed that they represent all private enterprises of the manufacturing industry of some importance, we try to determine,

(a) to what extent research is a function of firm size on the one hand and of the technological characteristics of the industries concerned on the other;

(b) to what extent the neo-Schumpeterian thesis that the research effort grows at an increasing rate with firm size is verified; and

(c) to what extent research is favored by an oligopolistic structure of the markets on which the enterprises concerned operate.

Before we start, a few misgivings. Unfortunately, the survey does not furnish information on value of shipments, which would have been a better measure of size because it is neutral in relation

---

[5] We excluded 22 firms of small size (between 50 and 400 workers) which answered that they did carry out research but could not specify the number of workers so employed. This exclusion has important consequences for the interpretation of our results which will be indicated below. The two other firms which were not included were specialized research institutes juridically independent from their mother firms.

[6] An employee who devoted half of his time to research was counted as a half unit.

to the proportions of utilized factors, represents the demand better, and seems to be the determining variable in decisions concerning research budgets. On the other hand, the survey does not permit the construction of an index of diversification (number of industries in which a given enterprise operates). Finally, it should be emphasized that we cannot identify research done to the benefit of other firms of the same or of other industries.

5.2. Size and technological opportunities

That research grows with firm size is easily verified. A simple regression over the whole sample (301 observations) gives

$$RP = 1.40 + 8.02TP \qquad (5.1)$$
$$ (1.49) \quad (0.58)$$

with $r^2 = 0.39$ (the standard error of the coefficients appearing in parentheses). It is to be noted that TP is expressed in 1,000 persons. Thus, on the average an increase of size by 1,000 persons entails the employment of eight more research workers.

Yet, the research effort differs very significantly from one industry to the other. To show this, we first regrouped our observations by industries, following the U.N. two-digit classification. Regressions by industry reveal great differences in the regression coefficients. Since for certain industries there were too few observations, we made a second regrouping into 12 sectors, taking into account the order of magnitude of the coefficients obtained and technological similarities. The results are shown in table 5.1. [7]

Notice first that the fact of giving each sector an intercept and a slope coefficient brings with it a significant complement of information. Let us add up the sums of squared deviations (SSD)

---

[7] The petroleum industry was combined with the "miscellaneous" sector because of its negative coefficient in the preliminary regressions. This result, which may seem surprising, is explained by the exclusion of a certain number of firms of the petroleum industry which specialize in research and are juridically independent from their mother firms, the inclusion of which would have distorted all our computations.

Table 5.1
Simple regressions of research personnel (RP) on total personnel (TP)

U.N.	Industries	Constant	Slope coefficient	N	$\bar{R}^2$	F-ratio
20, 21, 22	Food, beverages, tobacco	1.11 (0.65)	3.31 (0.75)	32	0.37	19.51
23, 24, 29	Textiles, shoes, apparel, leather	1.25 (0.23)	0.84 (0.22)	33	0.30	14.79
25, 27, 28	Paper, wood, cork	0.43 (0.58)	3.98 (0.63)	18	0.70	40.31
30	Rubber	0.40 (0.42)	5.23 (0.54)	7	0.94	92.87
31	Chemical	−0.38 (3.24)	22.38 (1.57)	56	0.79	202.88
33	Cement, glass, baked clay	−0.39 (0.51)	5.43 (0.20)	26	0.97	709.97
34	Basic metals	10.16 (5.07)	1.20 (0.85)	22	0.04	1.96
35	Metallic construction	1.11 (0.44)	2.38 (0.15)	21	0.93	251.96
36	Machinery	2.96 (0.77)	1.88 (1.20)	41	0.03	2.44
37	Electric machines	−2.02 (5.44)	15.26 (1.33)	29	0.83	131.57
38	Transportation equipment	4.25 (11.94)	7.95 (8.58)	10	–	0.86
32, 39	Petroleum and miscellaneous	3.95 (1.38)	0.59 (1.65)	6	–	0.13
	All industries	1.40 (1.49)	8.02 (0.58)	301	0.39	188.93

"explained" by each of the 12 regressions, the deviations being taken with respect to the "grand" mean (the average of the 301 observations on RP). The figure obtained exceeds the SSD of regression (1) by 110.027 and represents a reduction of about

40% of the total variance to be explained, as shown in table 5.3 (stage A.5). Thus, the interindustry differences account for at least as great a part of the variance as the interfirm differences (which explain only 38.72%).

Two sectors clearly dominate over the rest: chemical industry, with 22 research workers per 1,000 supplementary workers, and electrical equipment, with 15. Next, a "moderate" group is discernible, comprising rubber, cement, glass and ceramics, and transportation equipment. Finally, there is a "non-progressive" group (this adjective being used without any sense of opprobrium), which includes the sectors of food, apparel, the metal industries, etc.

The structure of our data is grasped well through this distinction into four groups, since 4 regressions by technological group explain 78% of the variance of RP, as much as the 12 regressions by industry do (see stage A.8 of table 5.3). The F-test indeed shows that the loss of 0.62% is not statistically significant. [8]

How explain these differences, if not by differences of what Scherer calls the peculiar "technological opportunities" which favor the progress of scientific and technical knowledge. We will try later to determine whether these differences are not linked also to other structural elements, such as the degree of concentration.

5.3. Increasing and decreasing returns

While a positive relationship between research and size is generally accepted, there is disagreement in the literature on the question whether research grows with size at an increasing rate. Let us test the idea with the same sample, stressing however at the outset, that the choice of personnel (TP) as size variable favors the thesis of growth at an increasing rate, [9] especially because the large firms

[8] The same can be said for the regressions with a squared or cubic term (stages A.9 and A.10 of table 5.3).

[9] See Scherer, Size of firm, oligopoly and research: comment, *Canadian J. of Economics and Political Science* (may 1965) 258–60.

are proportionally larger in terms of sales volume than in terms of employment.

In a first approach, the cumulative totals of *RP* and *TP* for the 4, 8, 12, 20, etc. largest firms are computed as shown in table 5.2. It is immediately evident that the answer to the question we have posed cannot be simple. The four largest firms employ 22% of the total personnel but only 15% of the research personnel. For the 8 largest, the situation is reversed. A reduction of research effort as we pass from 8 to 12 is followed by an appreciable intensification on the level of the 20 and 30 largest firms, after which the percentage of *RP* (of total *RP*) remains smaller than the percentage of *TP* (of total *TP*). If we look at the differences from figure to preceding figure, we get the impression of "increasing returns" followed by "diminishing returns" on the level of the 10 or 12 largest firms.

In this context, the term "increasing returns" is used to mean that input of research workers grows at an increasing rate with the size of firm. This use of the term, which we adopt to simplify our presentation, should not lead to confusion. It is quite possible that, for instance, diminishing returns in terms of *RP* go with a proportional output in inventions (or patents). [10] Since we have no information other than input in research workers, our conclusions can apply only to the research effort as measured by *RP*. They do not answer the question of returns from this input in terms of output of inventions.

Table 5.2. suggests a rather complex non-linear relationship between *RP* and *TP*. Let us try to determine this relationship more precisely by resorting to regressions involving different functional forms.

It is not very likely that a good fit could be obtained with a double logarithmic form. In fact, the extreme observations risk in this case to impose an upward convexity (slope coefficient smaller

[10] Scherer's study shows, however, that an analysis of patent applications leads to the same conclusions as the analysis in terms of research personnel employed. This leaves open the question whether the number of patent applications is in fact a good measure of research output.

Table 5.2
Concentration of research personnel (*RP*) and of total personnel (*TP*) of 301 firms.

Number of firms classified according to *TP*	Cumulative sums of *RP*	Cumulative sums of *TP*	*RP* in % of total *RP*	*TP* in % of total *TP*
4 largest	424.0	65,260.0	15.1	21.9
8 largest	1,027.0	105,650.0	36.6	35.5
12 largest	1,117.0	128,050.0	39.8	43.1
20 largest	1,597.0	155,870.0	56.9	52.4
30 largest	1,749.0	179,560.0	62.3	60.4
40 largest	1,839.5	197,990.0	65.5	66.6
50 largest	1,949.5	211,570.0	69.4	71.1
75 largest	2,068.5	236.840.0	73.8	79.6
100 largest	2,205.5	253.330.0	78.6	85.2
150 largest	2,421.5	274,500.0	86.3	92.3
200 largest	2,609.5	286,020.0	93.0	96.2
301	2,807.5	297,460.0	100.0	100.0

than one), thus neglecting the increasing returns which seem to characterize the majority of firms. For the same reason, one might expect that a polynomial of the second degree (in *TP*) will get a negative coefficient for the squared term (and that the fit will be bad). Everything indicates that a third degree polynomial will represent the data best: one expects a positive coefficient for $(TP)^2$ and a negative coefficient for $(TP)^3$. Thus, decreasing returns, as here defined, correspond to a negative value of the second derivative. Putting this derivative equal to zero and solving for *TP*, the size from which the returns become diminishing can be determined.

In fact, the third degree polynomial is the winner, since we get [11]

$$\log RP = -2.65 + 0.62 \log TP \qquad \bar{R}^2 = 0.14 \qquad (5.2)$$
$$(0.27) \quad (0.04) \qquad \qquad F\text{-ratio} = 197.27$$

$$RP = -3.17 + 16.01TP - 0.51(TP)^2 \qquad (5.3)$$
$$(1.52) \quad (1.25) \qquad (0.07)$$

$$\bar{R}^2 = 0.47 \qquad F\text{-ratio} = 135.37$$

[11] For the double logarithmic equation, $\bar{R}^2$ was computed from antilogs.

$$RP = 1.89 + 3.93TP + 1.47(TP)^2 - 0.07(TP)^3 \qquad (5.4)$$
$$(1.62) \quad (2.18) \quad (0.31) \quad (0.01)$$

$$\bar{R}^2 = 0.54 \qquad F\text{-ratio} = 425.01.$$

Evidently, equation (5.4) gives the best fit. For the whole Belgian manufacturing industry,

$$2(1.47) - 6(0.07)(TP) = 0 \qquad \text{gives} \qquad TP = 7.$$

The number of research workers grows at an increasing rate up to a size of 7,000 persons employed. Beyond 7,000 there are diminishing returns. However, there are only 9 enterprises with more than 7,000 workers in the sample. This is to say that for the great majority of Belgian firms, an increase in size entails a more than proportional increase in research personnel. In fact the research intensity (RP/TP) grows up to around 10,000, the tangency point between the third degree polynomial and a straight line through the origin (see fig. 5.1), beyond which the elasticity of RP to TP becomes less than 1. [12]

5.4. Returns by industry

It is important to know whether the conclusion of the preceding section applies to particular industries. A regression was run for each of the 12 two-digit industries (and for each of the functional forms discussed above).

The double logarithmic form could be eliminated from the outset because of an obvious inferior fit. It is sufficient to point out that all industries appear with an elasticity smaller than 1 (diminishing returns). This is due to the simple fact that the double logarithmic form cannot account for the inflexion point which probably exists in many cases.

[12] It should be noted that if we had included the small firms which did not state the number of research workers employed, our conclusions would have been strengthened. The curve representing equation (5.4) would then have had a steeper inclination before the point of inflexion.

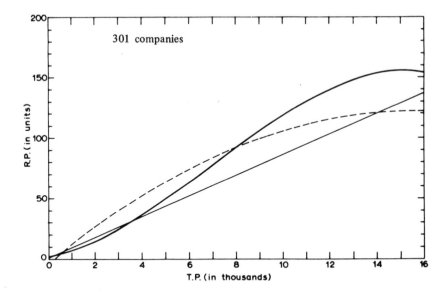

Fig. 5.1. Belgian manufacturing industry, research personnel and total personnel.

The quadratics and cubics show an extraordinary diversity. Of the first (see table 5.4 in the appendix to this chapter), six squared terms $(TP)^2$ have a positive and six a negative sign. The same is true for $(TP)^3$ in the cubic form (table 5.5). A discussion of each sector is thus useful. In what follows, we present the regression results that are selected as giving the best results in terms of $\bar{R}^2$ and of standard-errors (see also figs. 5.2, 5.3 and 5.4).

For the *food, beverages and tobacco* industry, we select

$$RP = 2.43 - 2.55TP + 2.86(TP)^2 \qquad \bar{R}^2 = 0.45 \qquad (5.5)$$
$$(0.84) \quad (2.66) \quad (1.25)$$

indicating increasing returns throughout. However, if the reader were ready to accept the cubic (table 5.5), he would find decreasing returns above a dimension of 1,500 employers. In our sample, only four firms are above this threshold.

The research effort is very small in the *textiles* and *wearing apparel* industry and it is difficult to recognize any significant non-

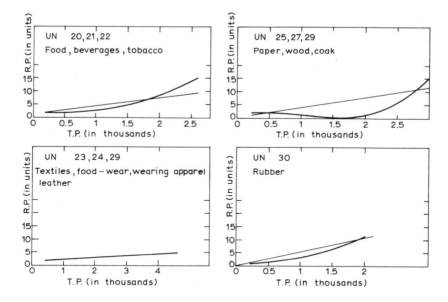

Fig. 5.2. Food, paper, textiles, rubber and other industries.

proportional tendency. The result of table 5.1 may be accepted as representative: an increase in dimension by 1,000 workers leads at most to an increase of *RP* by one research worker.

The *paper* and *wood* industry is very well described, the small number of observations notwithstanding, by the third degree polynomial

$$RP = 0.69 + 5.54TP - 7.14(TP)^2 + 2.34(TP)^3 \qquad (5.6)$$
$$(0.39) \quad (2.02) \qquad (1.76) \qquad (0.40)$$

$$\bar{R}^2 = 0.96.$$

The positive coefficient of $(TP)^3$ indicates increasing returns, with an inflexion point at 1,000 persons.

Rubber is characterized by increasing returns according to

$$RP = 1.47 - 0.81TP + 2.89(TP)^2 \qquad \bar{R}^2 = 0.97 \qquad (5.7)$$
$$(0.45) \quad (2.07) \quad (0.98)$$

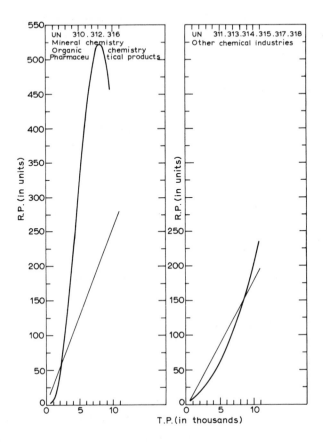

Fig. 5.3. Chemical industry.

The regression with a (negative) cubic term does not contradict this, as it gives an inflexion point at 1,300 above which there is only one producer.

The *chemical industry* merits a special treatment because of its high average research intensity. For the whole sector, the quadratic and cubic regressions lead to contradictory and/or non-significant results, suggesting that a breakdown is in order.

A partition in two groups is suggested, the first including mineral chemistry (U.N. 310), organic chemistry (U.N. 312) and pharmaceutical products (U.N. 316), where research efforts are the highest, while the second group includes all other chemical industries (U.N. 311, 313, 314, 315, 317 and 318). Now the results are very clear (fig. 5.3).

The first group has increasing returns, up to a dimension of 4,300 workers according to

$$RP = 14.33 \quad - \quad 39.88TP + 33.32(TP)^2 \quad - \quad 2.55(TP)^3 \qquad (5.8)$$
$$\quad (5.32) \quad (15.12) \qquad (5.65) \qquad \quad (0.40)$$

$$\overline{R}^2 = 0.95.$$

On the contrary, the second group follows the quadratic

$$RP = \quad 3.01 \quad + \quad 4.28TP + \quad 1.53(TP)^2 \qquad \overline{R}^2 = 0.97. \qquad (5.9)$$
$$\quad (1.40) \quad (2.57) \qquad (0.28)$$

An excellent result can be reported for the *cement, glass* and *baked clay* sector (fig. 5.4):

$$RP = \quad 2.21 \quad - \quad 3.08TP + \quad 3.31(TP)^2 \quad - \quad 0.22(TP)^3 \qquad (5.10)$$
$$\quad (0.56) \quad (1.59) \qquad (0.74) \qquad \quad (0.05)$$

$$\overline{R}^2 = 0.99.$$

Decreasing returns show up only above a size of 5,000 workers.

A very different picture is given by the *basic metals* industry. Not only is the average research intensity very low: it also decreases continually as firms are bigger (and these firms are among the biggest in the sample). Indeed

$$RP = \quad 1.43 \quad + \quad 6.84TP - \quad 0.24(TP)^2 \qquad \overline{R}^2 = 0.21. \qquad (5.11)$$
$$\quad (5.99) \quad (2.59) \qquad (0.11)$$

At first sight, *metallic construction* (without machines and transport equipment) has an increasing research intensity according to

$$RP = \quad 2.34 \quad - \quad 1.59(TP) + \quad 0.30(TP)^2 \qquad \overline{R}^2 = 0.95. \qquad (5.12)$$
$$\quad (0.48) \quad (1.11) \qquad (0.08)$$

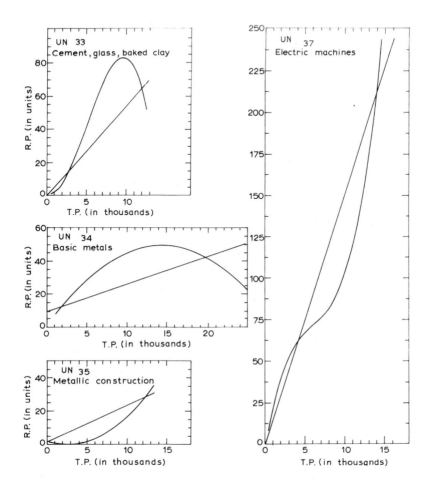

Fig. 5.4. Other industries

However, a more detailed analysis of the sample shows that this result is due to the presence of one highly specialised firm (*not* representative of the industry).

We have nothing to say about *machine construction*, where research efforts are probably very different from one field to the other. On the contrary, a good result is obtained for the construction of *electric machines*, where

$$RP = -5.61 + 29.38TP - 4.07(TP)^2 + 0.22(TP)^3 \quad (5.13)$$
$$ (5.55) \quad (8.92) \quad (1.50) \quad (0.06)$$

$$\overline{R}^2 = 0.90.$$

Returns are decreasing until a dimension of 6,000. Above that level, returns are increasing thanks to the research efforts of one of the three firms that employ more than 6,000 people.

Finally, the *transport equipment* industry seems to be characterized by an important research effort in rather small firms. That is all there is to be said about this industry, given the small number of observations and its diversified production pattern.

All in all, then, there is a striking diversity in these different sectors. In most of them, though (with the exception of paper, "other" chemical industries and electric machines), the largest firms entered a phase of decreasing returns. Together, these ten "big ones" determine the overall shape of the third degree polynomial in fig. 5.1. The visual impression obtained from this graph must not make one forget that for the great majority of Belgian firms research gains from an increase in size.

5.5. Research and concentration

An empirical verification of the neo-Schumpeterian thesis of a positive link between industrial concentration and research meets with considerable practical difficulties. Where find comparable statistics? The industrial censuses do, in general, not give information that permits evaluation of the research effort. The statistics published in this area are not easily compared with concentration ratios (taken from censuses) since they are incomplete or classified according to other criteria. It is therefore necessary to resort to data for individual firms: in an ideal world, it would be possible to identify the four largest firms entering into the calculation of the concentration ratio of a given industry and then to add up the data on research workers employed (or of patent applications, etc.): but down here, in Europe at least, the statistical secret poses a serious obstacle.

Thanks to the C.N.P.S. surveys, we believe to have succeeded in clearing this obstacle, without therefore betraying the statistical secret. But we could do this only at the cost of introducing certain hypotheses, on the strength of which the reader should form his personal opinion.

It seems that three types of data can be utilized.

Since the C.N.P.S. survey identifies the U.N. three-digit industry to which every firm belongs and since the U.N. classification is very close to the classification of the Belgian industrial census, we could (for each of the 301 firms) correlate the number of research workers with the concentration ratio of the industry to which it belongs. [13,14] The idea was that if an industry is strongly concentrated and if concentration causes a greater research intensity, all firms of that industry (and not only the four largest) must have a greater number of research workers (*for a given size*) — a strong assumption, which besides entails certain difficulties. It implies in fact that several observations on *RP* are paired with one identical concentration ratio (*C*) common to all firms of the industry. This results graphically, when *RP* is measured on the vertical and *C* on the horizontal axis, in several superposed points. [15] This means that we hoped to see a cloud of points which in spite of a certain thickness presents a positive inclination. It seems worth trying

[13] To do this well we would have to know which percentage of the production of a firm does in fact belong to the industry under which the firm is classified, so that those firms which belong to too many different industries can be eliminated. But such refinements, which are feasible in the United States, cannot be envisaged with the information available to us.

[14] The concentration ratios were computed from the census of December 31, 1960, following the interpolation method proposed by J.S.Bain in *International Differences in Industrial Structure* (New Haven, 1966), pp. 27–28, and explained in the statistical appendix.

[15] Fortunately, half of the U.N. industries include only four firms or less.

since we have here the same 301 observations as in the preceding sections, which should facilitate comparisons and cross-checking.

The next step was, quite naturally, to add up the number of research workers employed by the four largest firms and to divide the result by the total personnel of these firms. In this manner an index of the research intensity in the four largest firms (RI_4) is obtained, which is to be correlated with C. It need not be said that it was not possible to ascertain whether these firms were the same on the one side and the other, that is, in the C.N.P.S. survey and in the industrial census. The probability is great that it was so.

Finally, we calculated the average research intensity by industries by dividing the total number of research workers of an industry by the total number of persons employed by the firms which participated in the survey. [16] This third type of information is perhaps the most valuable.

What are the results?

For 301 firms, after introducing their size (TP) since the reasoning supposes it constant, we find

$$RP = -2.92 + 0.13C + 7.52TP \qquad \bar{R}^2 = 0.39 \qquad (5.14)$$
$$(2.73) \quad (0.06) \quad (0.59) \qquad F\text{-ratio} = 93.66.$$

Considering the nature of the data, this result is not so bad. Concentration does exert a positive influence: if C rises by 10 points, there will be 1.3 additional research workers. That is not much, but, given the orders of magnitude of PR, perhaps not negligible.

Is the influence of concentration the same from one industry to the next? Does it make itself felt in a less progressive technological context as much as in the chemical and electronic industries? Let us again introduce our four technological groups, of which the first is identified with the chemical and the second with the electronic industry, while the "moderate" group comprises the U.N. sectors 30, 33, and 38, and the last, "non-progressive" group com-

---

[16] This number includes the personnel of those firms which answered that they did not conduct research.

prises all other sectors. When each group is allowed to have its own slope coefficient with regard to C, we find

$$RP = -0.72 + 7.57TP + 0.21C_{(31)} + 0.30C_{(37)}$$
$$\quad\;\; (2.85) \quad (0.58) \quad\;\; (0.07) \quad\quad\; (0.12)$$

$$+ \; 0.02C_{(moderate)} - 0.05C_{(non\text{-}prog.)} \tag{5.15}$$
$$\;\;\; (0.08) \quad\quad\quad\quad (0.09)$$

$$\overline{R}^2 = 0.41 \qquad F\text{-ratio} = 43.05.$$

Concentration does not favor research *except where the technological context is favorable.* [17] This restriction may be of importance, especially from the point of view of antitrust policy.

The four regression coefficients for C in (5.15) could be interpreted as measuring "research propensities on the basis of market control". They appear to be different. Does this difference have any bearing on the explanation of the interfirm variance of RP? In section 5.2 it was suggested that 39% were explained by the interfirm differences of size and that 40% were linked to interindustrial differences. The predominant impression was that these interindustrial differences could be identified as being of a technological type, as representing contexts more or less favorable to research. Now the moment has come to try to decompose this reduction of 40% and to see which part of it is linked to differences in the "propensities" discussed above.

The diversity of the propensities seems to have a very restricted explanatory role. In passing from regression (5.14) to regression (5.15) $\overline{R}^2$ grows only by 2 points. Similarly, when we pass from a simple regression of RP on C to a multiple regression on the C's subdivided in 12 sectors (according to the sector to which the firms belong), $\overline{R}^2$ only rises by 1 point.

---

[17] To account for a possible interaction between C and TP, the following regression was computed:

$$\log (RP) = -0.82 - 0.57\log (TP) + 0.21\log C + 0.15\log C_{(31)} + 0.18\log C_{(37)}.$$
$$\quad\quad\;\; (0.14) \quad\; (0.05) \quad\quad\quad (0.10) \quad\quad (0.04) \quad\quad\quad\; (0.05)$$

It confirms the additive results. Notice that here TP is measured in tens.

Let us now pass to the second type of data defined above. Whereas the simple regression of research intensity in the four largest firms (RI_4) on the concentration ratio (C) does not reveal any significant relationship, the distinction into four technological groups is once more useful. Indeed

$$RI_4 = \underset{(0.16)}{0.64} + \underset{(0.15)}{0.25C_{(37)}} + \underset{(0.04)}{0.16C_{(31)}}$$

$$+ \underset{(0.039)}{0.024C}_{\text{(moderate)}} - \underset{(0.045)}{0.006C}_{\text{(non-prog.)}} \qquad (5.16)$$

$$\bar{R}^2 = 0.19 \qquad F\text{-ratio} = 5.36,$$

where RI_4 is defined in per mill and 71 observations (three-digit industries) are utilized. The influence of concentration is significant only in the chemical (and possibly in the electrical equipment) industry.

The result is the same when we employ the research intensity of the whole industry $(RI_I$, defined per mill) in

$$RI_I = 5.7 + \underset{(0.15)}{0.23C_{(37)}} + \underset{(0.04)}{0.18C_{(31)}}$$

$$+ \underset{(0.040)}{0.032C}_{\text{(moderate)}} + \underset{(0.047)}{0.004C}_{\text{(non-prog.)}} \qquad (5.17)$$

$$\bar{R}^2 = 0.23 \qquad F\text{-ratio} = 6.17.$$

While the order of magnitude of the coefficients of C in (5.16) and (5.17) is the same as in (5.15), it must be noted that they are here expressed not in units but in units per thousand persons employed. They therefore express a much more important influence, which tends to confirm the hypothesis to be tested.

5.6. A comparison with the United States

At this point, the reader will doubtless ask himself the inevitable question: where is Belgium in comparison with the United States?

Let us therefore compare our conclusions with those of F.M. Scherer.

There is agreement insofar as differences in technical investment possibilities, linked to the progress of science, can be said to be the chief factor explaining interindustry differences of research effort. But for the rest, the conclusions are divergent enough, without therefore always being contradictory.

As for the manufacturing industry as a whole, Scherer finds that 450 of the greatest American firms are characterized by the fact that research efforts grow less than proportionally with size. We found a more than proportional growth for the majority of Belgian firms. These two results, however, complement each other very well, since the firms of the American sample are generally larger than those analyzed here. Moreover, we saw that the largest among the Belgian firms had a weaker research intensity. In short, our fig. 5.1 could without difficulty be spliced to the corresponding American graph: beyond a certain threshold, which only a few Belgian firms exceed, the research intensity bends.

Then, Scherer finds a remarkable uniformity from one industry to the next. In Belgium there is a great diversity of situations.

Finally, the American sample shows no systematic link between concentration and research effort, while in Belgium this link exists, though only in the two sectors where research is most intensive.

APPENDIX TO CHAPTER 5

Table 5.3
Covariance analysis

	Description		SSD	In % of A.1 SSD	D.F.	F-ratio
A. 1	Dependent variable RP		275.831	100.00	1	
A. 2	Overall regression of RP on TP	Reduction from A.1 Residual	106.805 169.026	38.72 61.28	1 299	189.00[a]
A. 3	Overall regression of RP on TP and $(TP)^2$	Reduction from A.2 Residual	24.502 144.524	8.88 52.40	1 298	50.45[a]
A. 4	Overall regression of RP on TP, $(TP)^2$ and $(TP)^3$	Reduction from A.3 Residual	18.297 126.227	6.63 45.77	1 297	43.05[a]
A. 5	12 regressions by industry of RP on TP	Reduction from A.2 Residual	110.027 58.999	39.89 21.39	22 277	23.51[a]
A. 6	12 regressions by industry of RP on TP and $(TP)^2$	Reduction from A.5 Residual	9.465 49.534	3.43 17.96	12 265	4.21[a]
A. 7	12 regressions by industry of RP on TP, $(TP)^2$ and $(TP)^3$	Reduction from A.6 Residual	6.432 43.102	2.33 15.63	12 253	3.14[a]
A. 8	4 regressions by technological groups of RP on TP	Surplus over A.5 Residual	1.703 60.702	0.62 22.01	-16 293	0.52
A. 9	4 regressions by technological groups of RP on TP and $(TP)^2$	Surplus over A.6 Residual	3.012 52.546	1.09 19.05	-24 289	0.69
A.10	4 regressions by technological groups on TP, $(TP)^2$ and $(TP)^3$	Surplus over A.7 Residual	4.411 47.513	1.60 17.23	-32 285	0.83

[a] Significant at the 1% point.

Table 5.4
Regressions on TP and $(TP)^2$

	U.N.	Industries	Con-stant	TP	$(TP)^2$	N	$\bar{R}^2$	F-ratio
B. 1	20, 21, 22	Food, beverages, tobacco	2.43 (0.84)	−2.55 (2.66)	2.86 (1.25)	32	0.45	13.74
B. 2	23, 24, 29	Textiles, shoes, apparel, leather	1.20 (0.28)	0.98 (0.57)	−0.04 (0.14)	33	0.27	7.21
B. 3	25, 27, 28	Paper, wood, cork	2.30 (0.50)	−5.04 (1.77)	3.21 (0.61)	18	0.89	67.12
B. 4	30	Rubber	1.47 (0.45)	−0.81 (2.07)	2.89 (0.98)	7	0.97	122.74
B. 5	31	Chemical	−4.13 (3.87)	31.83 (5.78)	−0.98 (0.58)	56	0.80	106.43
B. 6	33	Cement, glass, ceramics	0.71 (0.57)	3.10 (0.79)	0.20 (0.06)	26	0.98	481.26
B. 7	34	Basic metals	1.43 (5.99)	6.84 (2.59)	−0.24 (0.11)	22	0.21	3.79
B. 8	35	Metallic construction	2.34 (0.48)	−1.59 (1.11)	0.30 (0.08)	21	0.95	211.58
B. 9	36	Machinery	2.05 (1.04)	5.42 (2.97)	−1.67 (1.28)	41	0.05	2.09
B.10	37	Electrical equipment	5.49 (5.37)	1.79 (4.60)	1.01 (0.33)	29	0.86	90.31
B.11	38	Transportation equipment	−15.63 (16.11)	69.27 (37.65)	−23.97 (14.40)	10	0.16	1.91
B.12	32, 39	Petroleum and miscellaneous	3.94 (2.44)	0.62 (7.52)	−0.02 (4.04)	6	0.00	0.05
		All industries	−3.17 (1.52)	16.01 (1.25)	−0.51 (0.07)	301	0.47	135.37

Table 5.5
Regression on TP, $(TP)^2$ and $(TP)^3$

U.N.	Industries	Con-stant	TP	$(TP)^2$	$(TP)^3$	N	$\bar{R}^2$	F-ratio
20, 21, 22	Food, bever-ages, tobacco	3.07 (1.20)	−7.31 (6.92)	9.10 (8.46)	−1.98 (2.66)	32	0.44	9.21
23, 24, 29	textiles, shoes, apparel, leather	0.92 (0.37)	2.85 (1.70)	−0.56 (1.31)	0.25 (0.22)	33	0.28	5.32
25, 27, 28	Paper, wood, cork	0.69 (0.39)	5.54 (2.02)	−7.14 (1.76)	2.34 (0.40)	18	0.96	160.58
30	Rubber	1.72 (1.09)	−3.49 (10.29)	8.38 (20.51)	−2.14 (57.97)	7	0.96	62.86
31	Chemical	−1.90 (4.40)	23.40 (9.78)	2.27 (3.10)	−0.24 (0.22)	56	0.79	71.52
33	Cement, glass, ceramics	2.21 (0.56)	−3.08 (1.59)	3.31 (0.74)	−0.22 (0.05)	26	0.99	560.07
34	Basic metals	−1.63 (7.34)	11.99 (7.44)	−1.33 (1.47)	0.04 (0.05)	22	0.19	2.65
35	Metallic construction	2.18 (0.91)	−0.61 (4.70)	−0.50 (3.71)	0.05 (0.26)	21	0.95	133.57
36	Machinery	2.23 (1.68)	4.21 (9.50)	−0.10 (11.70)	−0.44 (3.24)	41	0.03	1.36
37	Electrical equipment	−5.61 (5.55)	29.38 (8.92)	−4.07 (1.50)	0.22 (0.06)	29	0.90	89.13
38	Transportation equipment	10.69 (19.48)	−92.60 (90.82)	164.89 (99.88)	−53.49 (28.08)	10	0.40	2.96
32, 39	Petroleum and miscella-neous	3.33 (5.36)	5.37 (35.53)	−7.52 (54.46)	2.91 (21.06)	6	0.00	0.03
	All industries	1.89 (1.62)	3.93 (52.18)	1.47 (0.31)	−0.07 (0.01)	301	0.54	117.33

PART II

INTERNATIONAL COMPARISONS
OF INDUSTRIAL STRUCTURE

This second part is devoted to a certain number of international comparisons of the industrial structure of the Common Market countries. The calculations are based on the data reproduced in the statistical appendix.

Given the absence of official and comparable concentration ratios by industry [1], we thought we might do a good job by computing approximate concentration ratios for the three-digit manufacturing industries as defined by the N.I.C.E., i.e. the industrial classification accepted by the members of the European Communities. To do this, we simply had to use the frequency distributions [2] established by the statistical office of the Communities for each three-digit industry and to run a rather simple program, as explained in the statistical appendix.

It is an easy step to derive, from the same material, average sizes of companies and establishments and also approximate average sizes of the largest companies and establishments. The latter are particularly useful for international comparisons, as will be made clear below.

We hope that the statistical appendix will prove useful for the profession, facilitating more refined quantitative research in this much neglected area. The usefulness of this type of data being established, we also dare hope that the authorities will soon decide to provide more precise and more homogeneous statistical information on industrial structures. For this is a prerequisite for better advice in the field of anti-trust policy.

---

[1] Official and comparable concentration ratios exist only for a selected number of products. See *Hearings before the Subcommittee on Antitrust and Monopoly of the Committee on the Judiciary,* U.S. Senate, 19th Congress, 2nd Session, Part 7A, Appendix to Part 7 (Washington, 1969), pp. 3971–77.

[2] Most unfortunately, frequency distributions are not available for Germany. See the introduction to the statistical appendix.

CHAPTER 6

INTERNATIONAL COMPARISONS

6.1. Introduction

This chapter reports on what seems to be a first attempt to compare industrial organization among European countries. To our knowledge systematic international comparisons of concentration ratios for the entire manufacturing industry are available only for the United States and Great Britain, on the one hand, and for the United States and Canada, on the other hand. [1] These analyses have claimed that industrial organization is very similar. A comparison industry by industry shows that an industry with high concentration in one country will have high concentration in the other country. An over-all comparison leads to the conclusion that monopolistic structure is the same on the average.

We want to find out whether these similarities also exist among the E.E.C. members. On a first trial, we made a few direct comparisons, along lines suggested by J.S.Bain in *International Differences in Industrial Structure*. It soon turned out, however, that these rather naïve comparisons of concentration ratios are not very meaningful – and probably meaningless when the countries involved are of different size. The smaller a country, the smaller

[1] See P.S.Florence, *The Logic of British and American Industry* (London, 1953), pp. 130–35; G.Rosenbluth, Measures of concentration, *Business Concentration and Price Policy* (1955), p. 57; W.Shepherd, A comparison of industrial concentration in the United States and Britain, *Rev. of Economics and Statistics* (1961); B.P.Pashigian, Market concentration in the United States and Great Britain, *J. of Law and Economics* (October 1968). In his well-known book, *International Differences in Industrial Structure* (New Haven, 1966), J.S.Bain made an heroic attempt to compare several countries using a variety of statistical sources.

the number of companies in a given industry and the higher its
concentration ratio. A priori, one might therefore expect Luxemburg to display the greatest concentration on the average and
Italy the smallest.

We had, therefore, to refine the analysis in order to verify
(a) the existence of a relationship between concentration ratios
and market size and (b) whether this relationship explains the
observed differences in concentration.

6.2. Direct comparisons [2]

Comparing company concentration ratios industry by industry,
for a pair of countries, it is immediately apparent from fig. 6.1
that an industry with high concentration in one country will have
high concentration in the other country. [3] The scatter is indeed
oriented to the Northeast.

For countries of comparable size (Netherlands/Belgium and
France/Italy), the points are grouped around the 45° line. But
when we compare Belgium and Luxemburg, we see that Luxemburg generally has much higher concentration ratios: the points
are clearly shifted to the right. For Italy and France, compared
with Belgium, the scatter is also, although less clearly, located
mainly below the diagonal. Furthermore, Italian and French concentration ratios have a smaller range: they hardly get above the
limit value of 80%.

We thus arrive at the rather trivial conclusion that manufacturing industry has the highest concentration in Luxemburg. Let us
take a closer look at the other countries and compute the ratios
(times 100) with respect to Belgium of paired concentration ratios.

---

[2] All computations in this chapter are based on data for three-digit industries.

[3] Each point in fig. 6.1 represents a pair of company concentration ratios, for a
given three-digit industry. The data are taken from table A.1 of the statistical appendix,
and measure the (approximate) percent of persons employed by the four largest companies.

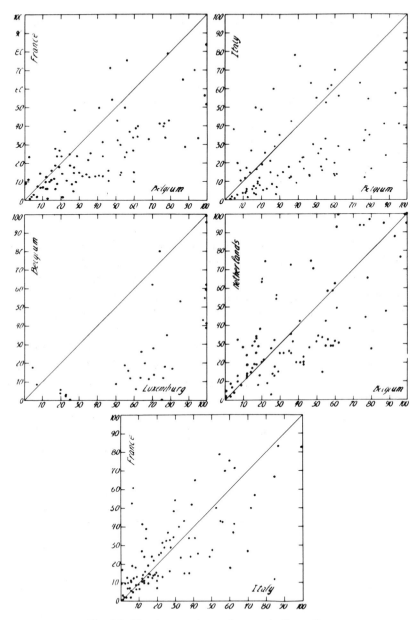

Fig. 6.1. Direct comparisons of concentration ratios.

The main features of the resulting frequency distributions are described in table 6.1.

Table 6.1

Distributions of ratios (X 100) of the concentration ratio (four largest companies) of one country to the Belgian concentration ratio, by industry

	Number of industries	Median	Quartiles
Netherlands	93	100	58–146
France	93	64	43– 94
Italy	93	50	33–106

The central tendency is towards a comparable concentration level in the Netherlands, and towards a lower level in France and Italy. An analysis of the empirical frequency distributions shows that the probability of having a lower concentration ratio (than the Belgian) is 45% for the Netherlands, 75% for France and 72% for Italy.

Italy and France display comparable median values, but France is somewhat higher. This is confirmed by the fact that when we compare France to Italy, the median of the ratios France-Italy is 100 with quartiles of 70.5 and 141.5.

A comparison of *establishment* concentration ratios leads to similar conclusions, as shown in table 6.2.

As for the ratios France-Italy, however, we obtain a median of

Table 6.2

Distributions of ratios (X 100) of the concentration ratio (four largest establishments) of one country to the Belgian concentration ratio, by industry

	Number of industries	Median	Quartiles
Netherlands	89	97	60–150
France	92	41	28– 61
Italy	91	44	28– 85

85, with quartiles of 60 and 120: French establishments appear to be somewhat less concentrated than Italian establishments. For companies we had the opposite result.

For short, these direct comparisons suggest the following ordering. Luxemburg would come first, followed by Belgium and the Netherlands. France and Italy would have a less monopolistic structure, France having somewhat more concentrated firms and Italy somewhat more concentrated establishments.

These conclusions are to be considered as very provisional. Indeed, for international comparisons of monopolistic structure to be meaningful, one has to eliminate the influence of market size, i.e. to put the data on a comparable basis. To this normalization problem we now turn.

6.3. Concentration ratios and market size

Direct comparisons suggest that countries of comparable size have comparable market organizations. It is tempting to deduce from this that the observed differences between countries like France and Belgium or Italy and Belgium are simply due to differences in market size. This is an important question which cannot be left unanswered and forces one to investigate the possible relationship between concentration and market size.

As a first check, we represented concentration ratios as a function of the total number of companies on semi-logarithmic paper. In most cases, Luxemburg is located to the utmost left and at the highest level. The opposite is true for Italy. In other words, concentration seems to be a decreasing function of the number of firms, i.e. of market size.

Before proceeding to more rigourous tests, it might be appropriate to make clear in what sense the number of companies n is a measure of market size. First, it should be emphasized that we are thinking of *relative* market size, not absolute market size, as concentration is defined in terms of market shares. Relative market size is defined as the ratio of quantity demanded to the size of the smallest efficient producer.

This is a theoretical concept. If all firms in an industry were efficient and of the same size, relative market size would be measured, as Pashigian points out [4], by n and the four-firm concentration ratio would be equal to $4/n$. If firms are of different (possibly non-efficient) sizes, n is only a proxy. But it is a good proxy.

If, for example, one is ready to accept that the average size of firms $\overline{F}$ (in an industry) is a good estimate of minimum efficient scale, then n is again a good measure, since $n = M/\overline{F}$, where M is the absolute market size. If one does not want to make this (admittedly crude) assumption, it might be sufficient to notice that n is highly correlated with other estimates of market size based on empirical measures of minimum efficient scale, such as those derived from the survivor technique. [5] In what follows, we proceed therefore on the assumption that n or $M/\overline{F}$ are acceptable proxies.

One possible line of attack is then to try to specify a functional relationship between the four-firm concentration ratio (C) and n, after imposing the restriction that C be smaller than 1 and greater than 0. [6]

Following Pashigian's suggestion, we admit that C is related to relative market size (x) according to

$$C = \frac{1}{1 + e^{-[f(x) + u]}} \qquad (6.1)$$

where u is an error term not correlated with x and such that $E(u) = 0$. The exponent of e goes from minus infinity to plus infinity and C varies between 0 and 1. A transformation of (6.1) leads to

$$\log\left[\frac{C}{1-C}\right] = f(x) + u . \qquad (6.2)$$

---

[4] *Op. cit.*, pp. 299–300.
[5] See Pashigian, *op. cit.*, pp. 300–01.
[6] In the equations that follow, C is the four-firm concentration divided by 100.

With x measured by n, Pashigian specifies f as

$$\log \left[\frac{C}{1-C} \right] = a_0 + a_1 \ (n-4)^{-a_2} + u \ . \tag{6.3}$$

As fig. 6.2 suggests a similar non-linear relationship, we have tested specification (6.2), but without success, for each of our five countries. For certain countries, the iterative procedure used did not converge. For the other countries, the coefficients were not statistically significant.

An alternative approach is then to specify (6.2) in another way, using absolute market size and minimum size of firms. As C is measured in terms of persons employed, we decided to measure absolute market size by total employment (E) and minimum size of firms by employment per company ($\bar{F}$) [7]. As an approximation to the true relationship, we assume the concentration ratio to be negatively related to E and positively to $\bar{F}$, i.e.

$$\log \left[\frac{C}{1-C} \right] = a_0 + a_1 \ \log E + a_2 \ \log \bar{F} + u \ . \tag{6.4}$$

This specification is preferred to a simple regression on $\log n$, to correct for possible intercountry differences in average firm size not related to differences in minimum efficient scale. The presence of a large number of inefficient firms in large countries may indeed bias $\bar{F}$ downwards and therefore affect the intercept (through the upward bias in n). It is hoped that the introduction of average firm size and total market size separately will take account of this, as it is equivalent (given that $n = E/\bar{F}$) to

$$\log \left[\frac{C}{1-C} \right] = (a_0' + a_2' \ \log \bar{F}) + a_1' \log n \ . \tag{6.4a}$$

Table 6.3 presents the regression results by country. All slope coefficients ($\hat{a}_1$ and $\hat{a}_2$) are significantly different from zero. They indicate a positive influence of minimum size ($\bar{F}$) and a negative influence of absolute market size (E). Our two independent

---

[7] See statistical appendix, table A.3.

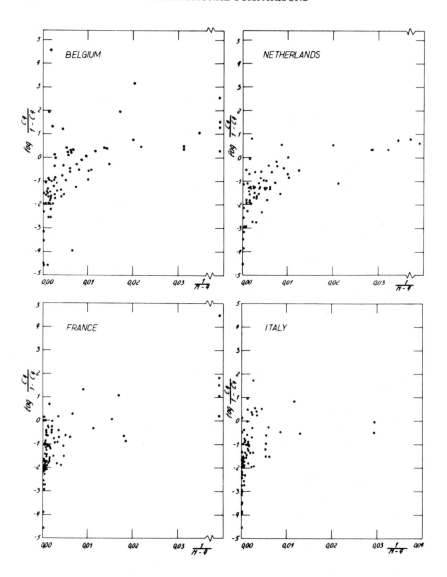

Fig. 6.2. Relation between log $[C/(1-C)]$ and $1/(n-4)$.

Table 6.3

Concentration ratios and (relative) market size. Equation (6.4).

	France	Italy	Netherlands	Belgium
a_0	1.628	1.315	1.374	0.729
	(0.785)	(0.906)	(0.657)	(0.821)
a_1	−0.517	−0.499	−0.639	−0.499
	(0.076)	(0.083)	(0.074)	(0.098)
a_2	0.699	0.748	1.018	0.914
	(0.054)	(0.063)	(0.050)	(0.073)
F	96.08[b]	98.89[b]	219.91[b]	79.33[b]
D.F.	2,88	2,90	2,88	2,86
$\bar{R}^2$	0.679	0.680	0.829	0.640
χ^2	1.947[c]	1.543[c]	4.227[a]	9.972[b]
D.F.	1	1	1	1

[a] Significant at the 5% point.
[b] Significant at the 1% point.
[c] Non-significant at the 5% point, i.e. absence of multicollinearity.

variables account for 65% or more of the variance of the dependent variable.

The existence of a very clear and important influence of market size on concentration is thus established. What would be the degree of concentration in these countries if market sizes were equal? This is the question to be answered in the next section.

6.4. Comparisons with equal market size

Given a negative linear relationship between $\log[C/(1-C)]$ and relative market size ($\log x$), what are the possible cases we could run into, as far as the results of an estimation by regression methods are concerned, for two countries A and B? How are these results to be interpreted in each case?

Case 1. Equality of slopes and of intercepts (fig. 6.3). If countries A and B turn out to have the same slopes and intercepts, the

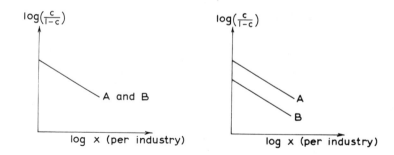

Figs. 6.3 and 6.4. Concentration and relative market size: possible cases.

level of concentration is the same in both countries whenever an industry has the same relative market size. Observed differences in concentration ratios between these countries (for the same industries) could be explained entirely by differences in relative market sizes.

Case 2. Equality of slopes and inequality of intercepts (fig. 6.4). Country A has a higher intercept. If market sizes were equal, country A industries would have higher concentration ratios than country B industries: concentration is systematically higher in A than in B. After correction for the influence of market size, country A stays above country B: "true" (whatever this may mean) concentration ratios are higher in A than in B, and this difference has to be explained by other arguments. Observed differences in concentration ratios cannot be explained entirely by differences in market sizes.

Notice that the *observed* concentration ratios may, in the case just described, nevertheless be systematically lower in A than in B, if the A industries have systematically larger market sizes. These observed concentration ratios would have been even lower if market size had been the only force at work, i.e. if A had had the same intercept as B.

When country A industries have in general a smaller market size than country B industries, then a direct comparison of observed concentration ratios must reveal a higher degree of concentration

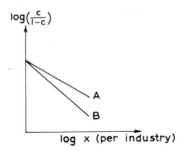

Fig. 6.5. Concentration and relative market size: possible cases.

in *A* for our argument to be consistent (starting from the hypothesis that *A* has the higher intercept).

Case 3. Inequality of slopes and equality of intercepts (fig. 6.5). At a given market size, country *A* industries are more concentrated than country *B* industries. The difference increases with market size. If this situation were to be encountered, we would have to find an explanation for the fact that market size decrease concentration less in *A* than in *B*. (This explanation might be very hard to find.)

Case 4. Inequality of slopes and of intercepts (figs. 6.6 and 6.7). This is really a combination of cases 2 and 3, with the resulting difficulty of finding plausible explanations for differences in inter-

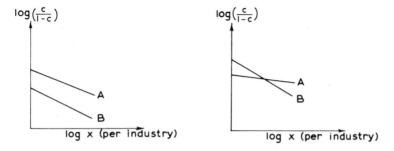

Figs. 6.6 and 6.7. Concentration and relative market size: possible cases.

Table 6.4
Covariance analysis (test of equality of slopes)

	a_1 combined	a_2 combined	F-ratio (for homogeneity)
France-Italy-Belgium-Netherlands	−0.517 (0.041)	0.853 (0.030)	3.209[a] (D.F. = 6,352)
France-Italy	−0.512 (0.056)	0.723 (0.041)	0.193 (D.F. = 2,178)
Belgium-Netherlands	−0.566 (0.062)	0.968 (0.044)	1.042 (D.F. = 2,174)
Belgium-Italy	−0.473 (0.063)	0.839 (0.047)	1.480 (D.F. = 2,176)
France-Netherlands	−0.572 (0.053)	0.871 (0.037)	9.570[b] (D.F. = 2,176)
Belgium-France	−0.492 (0.062)	0.817 (0.046)	3.017 (D.F. = 2,174)
Italy-Netherlands	−0.533 (0.055)	0.886 (0.039)	6.328[b] (D.F. = 2,178)
France-Italy-Belgium	−0.487 (0.049)	0.796 (0.036)	1.757 (D.F. = 4,264)

[a] Significant at the 5% point.
[b] Significant at the 1% point.

cepts and differences in slopes (which implies one country is more concentrated in one subset of industries and the other country in another subset).

It would be nice if our regression results stayed within cases 1 and 2. Case 2 is particularly attractive, because it remains relatively simple while allowing for breathtaking conclusions.

Let us return to table 6.3. Instead of one independent variable, we have two independent variables to measure the influence of market size. For the rest, the reasoning above applies without difficulty.

We will first test the equality of slopes (a_1 and a_2) with the help of the now familiar covariance analysis. Running a combined regression for all countries, we find clear indication (see the first F-test in table 6.4) that the slopes are not homogeneous.

Are there any homogeneous subgroups? We consider first pairs of countries, and find a non-transitive ordering. Table 6.4 indicates that:

Italy = France = Belgium = Netherlands $\neq$ Italy

and also

France = Italy = Belgium = Netherlands $\neq$ France.

The Netherlands are the heterogeneous element while the three other countries seem to have the same slope coefficient. To see this more clearly, the latter countries are taken together in the last row of table 6.4 and get indeed a very low F-ratio.

The next thing to do is to test the equality of intercepts. Slopes being different, standard covariance analysis cannot be used. We will therefore set up a test that applies both in the case of homogeneous and in the case of non-homogeneous slopes.

To test the null hypothesis that the intercepts of countries A and B are equal ($a_0^A - a_0^B = 0$), we are going to use the variables

$$\sqrt{T_A}\,(\hat{a}_0^A - a_0^A) \quad \text{and} \quad \sqrt{T_B}(\hat{a}_0^B - a_0^B)$$

whose distribution tends towards a normal distribution with zero mean when the number of observations T increases indefinitely. [8] Their difference

$$\sqrt{T_A}\,(\hat{a}_0^A - a_0^A) - \sqrt{T_B}(\hat{a}_0^B - a_0^B)$$

has the same property. The variances of $\hat{a}_0^A$ and $\hat{a}_0^B$ are σ_A^2 and σ_B^2 and a_0^A and a_0^B are fixed. Therefore, the variances of our variables are $T_A \sigma_A^2$ and $T_B \sigma_B^2$ and — under the hypothesis of independence — the variance of their difference is $(T_A \sigma_A^2 + T_B \sigma_B^2)$. The variable

[8] See E.Malinvaud, *Méthodes statistiques de l'économetrie* (Dunod, Paris, 1964), pp. 205–207.

$$\frac{\sqrt{T_A}\,(\hat{a}_0^A - a_0^A) - \sqrt{T_B}\,(\hat{a}_0^B - a_0^B)}{\sqrt{T_A\,\sigma_A^2 + T_B\,\sigma_B^2}} \tag{6.5}$$

has thus an asymptotically standard normal distribution. For $T_A = T_B$, expression (6.5) becomes

$$\frac{(\hat{a}_0^A - a_0^A) - (\hat{a}_0^B - a_0^B)}{\sqrt{\sigma_A^2 + \sigma_B^2}} = \frac{(\hat{a}_0^A - \hat{a}_0^B) - (a_0^A - a_0^B)}{\sqrt{\sigma_A^2 + \sigma_B^2}} \tag{6.6}$$

and we can test the null hypothesis

$$H_0: \qquad a_0^A - a_0^B = 0 \tag{6.7}$$

replacing σ_A^2 and σ_B^2 by their estimates.

In our regressions (table 6.3) the number of observations is not equal from country to country ($T_A \neq T_B$). We can nevertheless test an approximation of H_0, since we have from (6.5)

$$\frac{(\sqrt{T_A}\,\hat{a}_0^A - \sqrt{T_B}\,\hat{a}_0^B) - (\sqrt{T_A}\,a_0^A - \sqrt{T_B}\,a_0^B)}{\sqrt{T_A\,\sigma_A^2 + T_B\,\sigma_B^2}} \tag{6.8}$$

which allows testing $\sqrt{T_A}\,a_0^A - \sqrt{T_B}\,a_0^B = 0$. Indeed

$$\sqrt{T_B} = \sqrt{T_A} + m, \qquad \text{where} \qquad m \gtrless 0$$

and

$$\sqrt{T_A}\,a_0^A - (\sqrt{T_A} + m)\,a_0^B = 0$$

$$\sqrt{T_A}\,(a_0^A - a_0^B) = m a_0^B\ .$$

The null hypothesis becomes

$$H_0: \qquad a_0^A - a_0^B = \frac{m}{\sqrt{T_A}}\, a_0^B \qquad\qquad (6.9)$$

which tends towards (6.7) as T_A increases with m constant. When a_0^B is zero, H_0 reduces to a simple test of significance of a_0^A.

Consider the subgroup Belgium-France-Italy. Within this group, France is the only country, according to table 6.3, to have an intercept that is significantly different from zero. If one is ready to accept the strong hypothesis that the Belgian and Italian intercepts are in fact zero, there results the classification

  — case 1 (equality of slopes and intercepts) = Belgium-Italy

  — case 2 (equality of slopes and different intercepts) =
       France-Belgium and France-Italy

On the other hand, the Netherlands also have a significant intercept. Comparing it with the French intercept, we obtain according to (6.6)

$$\frac{1.628 - 1.374}{0.616225 + 0.431649} = \frac{0.254}{1.024} = 0.248 .$$

We conclude that there is equality, with the result that two more cases show up:

  — case 3 (inequality of slopes and equality of intercepts) =
       France-Netherlands

  — case 4 (inequality of slopes and intercepts) =
       Netherlands-Belgium and Netherlands-Italy.

In one word, French industry appears as systematically more concentrated than its partners when market sizes are equalized. An increase in market size leads to a faster decrease in concentration in the Netherlands. Belgium and Italy have a comparable (low) concentration level. Fig. 6.8 illustrates this.

Notice that these findings are compatible with our direct comparisons in terms of observed concentration ratios, because French

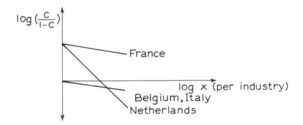

Fig. 6.8. Concentration and relative market size: results.

and Italian industries have systematically larger market sizes. To take the case of France: France appeared, in the direct comparisons, as less concentrated than, say, Belgium. This is not in contradiction with the idea that, with equal market sizes, France is more concentrated than Belgium. If France had had the same intercept as Belgium (and the same slope), i.e. if market size had been the only force at work, the observed French concentration ratios would have been even lower than they are (probably in the neighbourhood of the Italian ratios).

6.5. A possible explanation

Let it be clear that we have no rigorous explanation to offer for the faster decrease in concentration in the Netherlands. The phenomenon is due to the presence of a group of extremely concentrated industries (such as sugar, artificial fibres, petroleum, cement, steel, steel tubes, forgings, electric wires, electronic material). One would have to study the history of these industries to explain this particular situation. In the case of the cement industry, the facts are clear and well known: the Dutch production is under the control of an international Belgo-German agreement, which regulates the expansion of the Dutch firms and organizes the Dutch market (fixing import quotas, sales conditions, etc. [9]).

Similar circumstances might have arisen in the other cases, but a verification of this feeling would lead us to case studies, which are beyond the scope of this book.

We prefer to concentrate our efforts on the question why France is systematically more concentrated than its neighbours (remembering that Germany is not included in our analysis). Again, we do not want to undertake a detailed historical analysis. All we can do here is to try to formulate an hypothesis and to collect as much evidence as we can from the available material.

Our efforts will tend towards making the point that the closed and traditionally cartelized nature of French industry is an important factor (possibly among others) in the explanation. The argument is based on the idea that concentration is complementary to cartelization rather than substitutable.

We developed this idea elsewhere. [10] The argument runs as follows. In the literature, cartels and corporate mergers are generally considered as two easily substitutable ways of restricting competition. Mergers would simply be more "durable" agreements: if one type of agreement is illegal, firms will tend to resort to the other type, given their propensity to monopolize. The literature of course recognizes the legal and sociological difficulties inherent to merger activities: if cartels are legal, entrepreneurs would therefore be less interested in embarking in merger activities. Roughly speaking, substitutability seems nevertheless to be the dominant characterization. [11]

[9] See L.Phlips, La concurrence dans le Marché commun du ciment, *Bull. de l'Institut de Recherches Économiques et Sociales* (1960, No. 6), or *De l'intégration des marchés*, chap. 9 (Louvain, 1962).

[10] L.Phlips, Le problème de la concentration des sociétés européennes, in: *Les ententes à l'échelle européenne*, Collection de l'Institut d'Administration des Entreprises de l'Université de Paris (Dunod, 1967) pp. 121–41.

[11] The following list of references is intended to give a representative sample (in chronological order): E.Fridrichowicz, Kartelle, *Z. für die gesamte Staatswissenschaft* LI (1895) 648; *Report of the Committee on Trusts* of the British Ministry of Reconstruction, 1919, cited by E.Eggmann, *Der Staat und die Kartelle* (Zürich, 1945), pp. 123–24; A.R.Burns, *The Decline of Competition* (New York, 1936), pp. 18–19; F.Machlup, *The Political Economy of Monopoly* (Baltimore, 1952), p. 232; J.Houssiaux, *Le Pouvoir de Monopole* (Paris, 1958), pp. 315–16 and 389–90; J.Heinz Müller, Zu Salins These von

On economic grounds, complementarity seems to be a better description of the relationship between collusion and merger, at least *if we restrict the argument to "monopolistic" mergers.* By this we mean mergers for monopoly, i.e. mergers intended to increase the control of the market, or, empirically speaking, mergers intended to increase the concentration ratio of the industry. These mergers are the more profitable, the more the market concerned is closed, organized and regulated. In a cartelized market, the agreements on prices, sales conditions, entry restrictions, etc. are the best guarantees for the profitability of a monopolistic take-over. (On the contrary, *non*-monopolistic mergers might be more profitable and more feasible in a competitive environment.)

Before returning to France, it might be interesting to give a rapid survey of the available empirical evidence (however small).

A first implication of our hypothesis is that no significant correlation should be expected between the degree of price competition and the *total* number of (monopolistic and non-monopolistic) corporate mergers. This is exactly what J.W.Markham found in his survey of the evidence on mergers. He concludes, "The relationship between merger activity and wholesale price movements lends no support to the hypothesis that mergers are motivated by generally declining prices brought on by outbreaks of competition." [12]

Monopolistic mergers, on the contrary should flourish in non-competitive industries or environments, and particularly during periods where collusion is authorized or encouraged. This implication is largely confirmed by the history of the merger movement

---

Footnote 11 continued
der Unentrinnbarkeit der Konzentration, *Z. für die gesamte Staatswissenschaft* 118 (1962) 283–84; A.Nicols, The monopoly basis of success, *Revue suisse d'économie politique et de statistique* (1962, No. 4), 514; E.Salin, Kartellverbot und Konzentration, *Kyklos* 16 (1963) 193; C.D.Edwards, Control of the single firm: its place in anti-trust policy, *Law and Contemporary Problems* 30 (1965) 466.

The only reference (we could find) that insists on the fact that cartelization facilitates concentration is A.Wolfer, Das Kartellproblem im Lichte der deutschen Kartellliteratur, *Schriften des Vereins für Sozialpolitik*, ed. E.Lederer, Bd. 180, 2. Teil (Munich and Leipzig, 1931), pp. 9–13.

[12] J.W.Markham, Survey of the evidence and findings on mergers, in: *Business Concentration and Price Policy* (Princeton, 1955) p. 154.

in Europe. On the continent, the cement industry offers a good example of the creation of dominant positions inside cartels through monopolistic acquisitions. These acquisitions initiated exactly from the moment the stability of the cartels had been guaranteed by governmental intervention (forbidding any creation of new capacity). In Germany, the movement started in 1916; in the other Common Market countries, in 1932–35. [13]

Truly enough, several industries were monopolized through spectacular mergers at the end of the 19th and the beginning of the 20th century as a result of heavy price competition. But the conditions were such that cartelization was impossible. [14]

A similar objection could be made about the great mergers in the United States between 1887 and 1919, which were clearly monopolistic, whereas the Sherman Act is dated 1890. Isn't there a clear link? The answer is no. Our suggestion is that these mergers were realized under conditions very similar to those underlying the contemporaneous wave in England. Some support can be derived from the following observation by Stigler, "Why was merger preferred to collusion? Part of the answer lies in the prima facie illegality of collusion after 1890. This point should not be pressed, however. The effectiveness of the Sherman law in dealing with conspiracies was not clear until 1899, when the Addyston Pipe case was decided; and there was a contemporaneous wave of amalgamations in England, where conspiracies were unenforcible but not actionable." [15]

As for *non-monopolistic* mergers, these should dominate in economies enforcing a broad anti-cartel legislation, i.e. a legislation according which cartels, agreements and restrictive and predatory practices are illegal, but without antimerger stipulations.

This implication is consistent with Stigler's [16] and Markham's [17]

---

[13] See L.Phlips, *De l'integration des marchés* (Louvain, 1962), pp. 226–29, and H.O. Lenel, Vom Stand der Konzentrationsdebatte . . ., *Ordo* 13 (1962) 302.

[14] See P.L.Cook, *Effects of Mergers* (London, 1958), pp. 425–32.

[15] Monopoly and oligopoly by merger, *Readings in Industrial Organization and Public Policy* (Homewood, 1958), pp. 75–76.

[16] *Op. cit.,* p. 78.

[17] *Op. cit.,* pp. 169–78 and pp. 180–82.

findings that the merger movement in the U.S. has lost its monopolistic character between 1919 and 1947: the great majority of
mergers were not for monopoly or oligopoly but for other reasons.
We should also mention a recent study by M.Didier and E.Malin-
vaud [18] which reaches the (very tentative) conclusion that concentration did not increase in France since 1955, i.e. during a period
of increased competition, although merger activity was rather
spectacular.

Finally, we want to quote a passage from J.S.Bain's study on
International Differences in Industrial Structure [19], which compares eight nations in the 1950's. Bain writes, "A further tentative
generalization is to the effect that in these countries of distinctly
higher seller concentration (i.e. France, Italy, Canada, India and
Sweden in ascending order), with the exception of Canada and
possibly of India, as well as in Japan, the stronger monopolistic
tendencies inherent in the higher degree of seller concentration
observed appear to be reinforced by government policies con-
doning cartelization and by the widespread operation of cartels —
a circumstance which distinguishes these countries from the
United States and from Canada and in large part from the
United Kingdom. The restriction of competition would appear
further to be reinforced by the existence in several of these countries of super-control entities of the sort that brings a group of
vertically related companies in different industries under a single
control or influence, and that reduces "horizontal" competition
at several industry levels by confining supplier-buyer transactions
within a vertically related complex of entreprises." The general
argument of this passage is in line with our own hypothesis. It
should be remembered, however, as to the ranking of the countries, that Bain did not eliminate the influence of market size.

We now have to provide evidence to the point that the higher
concentration level in France (for equal market sizes) has a monopolistic character.

[18] La concentration de l'industrie s'est-elle accentuée depuis le début du siècle?,
Economie et statistique (June 1969) 3–10.
[19] (Yale University Press, New Haven, 1966), pp. 120–21.

To begin with, we might point out that by equalizing market sizes, we in fact (see equation (6.4)) equalized total employment (M) and average size of firms ($\bar{F}$). If this average size really measures minimum efficient scale (which is of course questionable), this means that with equal minimal efficient dimensions, French industries are more concentrated. This might indicate that the supplement of concentration was not obtained for efficiency reasons. But we do not want to press this point.

More direct evidence is obtained by comparing the size of companies and of establishments among countries. If the previous analysis is correct, one would expect France to have the largest companies.

To make meaningful international comparisons, one should avoid using national averages taken over the whole industry, for these averages are affected by market size. As was the case for concentration ratios, these averages are biased downwards in the larger countries: the more firms, the smaller average. Meaningful direct comparisons are possible, however, if limited to the largest firms, e.g. the four largest companies.

Choosing Belgium as the point of reference, dividing the average size of the four largest companies of each industry in a country by the corresponding number in Belgium, and taking the median, we find that the largest firms are indeed bigger in France than in the other countries (see table 6.5).

If now we turn to the size of the four largest establishments, and go through the same computations, we obtain table 6.6. France

Table 6.5

Distributions of ratios ($\times$ 100) of the average size of the four largest companies in one country to the average size of the four largest companies in Belgium, per industry.

Country	Number of industries	Median	Quartiles
France	88	274	178–559
Italy	89	236	131–467
Netherlands	87	119	61–231

Table 6.6

Distributions of ratios (X 100) of the average size of the four largest establishments in one country to the average size of the four largest establishments in Belgium, per industry

Country	Number of industries	Median	Quartiles
France	84	213	117–344
Italy	86	201	109–307
Netherlands	85	111	63–175

comes out, once more, with the largest median, but this is markedly lower than for companies (table 6.6).

Table 6.7 gives the averages, per country, of the average size of the four largest companies and establishments. The rankings are the same as in the two preceding tables and lead to the interesting conclusion that, while the largest firms are three times as large in France than in Belgium. on the average, the largest establishments are only twice as large. In Italy, firms are 2.4 times bigger than in Belgium, while establishments are 1.4 times as large.

It is interesting, then, to compare company and establishment concentration within each country. Let us divide the company concentration ratio by the establishment ratio, for each industry. (If total employment per industry were the same for company and establishment data, these computations would also give the ratio

Table 6.7

Number and average size of firms and establishments

	France	Italy	Netherlands	Belgium
Total number of firms	371,052	577,089	76,957	81,735
Total number of establishments	385,762	597,190	82,555	82,005
Average of average size of four largest companies	3,105	2,332	1,005	988
Average of average size of four largest establishments	1,730	1,373	862	821

Table 6.8
Average company-plant concentration

	France	Italy	Nether-lands	Bel-gium	Luxem-burg
$\dfrac{C_4 \text{ companies}}{C_4 \text{ establishments}}$	1.80	1.46	1.17	1.11	1.00
$\dfrac{C_8 \text{ companies}}{C_8 \text{ establishments}}$	1.56	1.34	1.13	1.06	1.00
$\dfrac{C_{20} \text{ companies}}{C_{20} \text{ establishments}}$	1.35	1.20	1.09	1.02	1.00
$\dfrac{C_{50} \text{ companies}}{C_{50} \text{ establishments}}$	1.20	1.12	1.04	1.01	1.00

of the size of firms over the size of establishments. In fact, total employment is often very different, as a comparison of tables A.3 and A.4 immediately reveals.) Table 6.8 gives the national averages. Being ratios of percentages, these are directly comparable among countries. France comes out first again.

The divergence between company and establishment concentration has been proposed, in the antitrust literature, as an indicator of the monopolistic nature of the level of concentration. Stated as bluntly, this suggestion cannot be accepted without qualifications.

First of all, it should be clear that some divergence is to be expected and to be considered as normal. Multiplant economies, i.e. economies resulting from the operation of several establishments under common ownership and control, are a very real possibility. They may be due to the possibility of reducing selling and distribution costs, greater efficiency in supervision and control, reductions in the costs of factors of production and what not. As these economies are probably larger, the larger the country, one should expect the largest countries to have the largest divergence, as is indeed roughly the case in table 6.8.

On the other hand, it would be wrong to think that, inside a

Table 6.9

Contingency table for France, company concentration and divergence between company and plant concentration.

C_4 comp. \ C_4 estab. \ C_4 comp.	<1.5		1.5–2		>2		N_i
<25	31	25.11	15	14.95	9	14.95	55
25–50	8	11.87	7	7.07	11	7.07	26
>50	3	5.02	3	2.99	5	2.99	11
N_j	42		25		25		$N = 92$

Contingency = 0.300; $\chi^2 (4) = 9.35$.

country, divergence is largest in industries with high concentration. Simple correlations between the four-firm concentration ratio (C_4 companies) and the ratio company C_4/establishment C_4 turn out to be equal to

0.303 in France (92 observations),
0.317 in Italy (93 observations),
0.095 in the Netherlands (91 observations),
0.112 in Belgium (89 observations).

A concentration-divergence relationship seems to exist in France and Italy but even there it is certainly not very strong, as is confirmed by the contingency tables given in tables 6.9 and 6.10, which lead to non-significant contingency coefficients.

If we talk about divergence here, it is rather because we consider it to be related to cartelization. We cannot avoid being impressed by the detailed French figures, in particular the values

Table 6.10

Contingency table for Italy, company concentration and divergence between company and plant concentration

C_4 comp. \\ C_4 comp. / C_4 estab.	<1.5		$1.5-2$		>2		N_i
<25	42	36.77	9	10.42	6	9.81	57
$25-50$	12	12.90	3	3.66	5	3.44	20
>50	6	10.32	5	2.92	5	2.75	16
N_j	60		17		16		$N = 93$

Contingency = 0.280; $\chi^2(4) = (8.37)$.

taken in industries where divergence is higher than two. These industries are put together in table 6.11: those with the highest divergence are known to be heavily cartelized and/or protected.

To sum up, we did provide some evidence to the point that France is the most concentrated of the countries analysed and that it is so because it is the most protected and the most cartelized. The evidence is perhaps not too impressive: it simply does not contradict the hypothesis, which is after all the only way we have to "verify" hypotheses.

Table 6.11
Divergence between company and plant concentration in particular industries

No. N.I.C.E.	Industry	France	Italy	Netherlands	Belgium
202	Milk	3.63	2.53	1.54	1.00
214	Soft drinks	2.45	1.26	1.12	1.00
233	Cotton	3.83	2.51	1.50	1.60
234	Silk	2.83	1.68	1.14	1.00
236	Other textile fibres	2.32	1.19	1.28	1.00
238	Textile finishing	2.52	2.50	1.17	1.00
252	Semifinished wood products	2.32	1.60	1.11	1.02
271	Pulp, paper and board	2.26	2.27	1.55	1.57
303	Artificial and synthetic fibres	2.15	2.10	1.59	1.10
311	Basic chemicals	3.07	1.85	(1.00)	1.79
312	Industrial and agricultural chemicals	2.23	2.67	1.13	1.36
332	Glass	2.65	1.76	(1.00)	1.88
333	China, pottery	2.11	2.27	(1.00)	1.34
334	Cement, lime, plaster	4.37	3.18	1.02	1.35
341	Steel mills	2.04	2.06	1.00	1.84
344	Primary non-ferrous metals	5.06	1.91	1.01	1.41
345	Foundries	2.57	1.00	1.18	1.09
355	Metal tools	2.63	1.11	1.63	1.07
369	Other machinery	2.12	1.00	1.23	1.01
372	Motors, generators, etc.	2.18	1.51	1.21	1.18
375	Electronic material	3.77	1.12	1.28	1.19
378	Batteries	2.58	1.17	1.08	1.00
379	Repair and fixing of electrical appliances	3.68	1.54	(1.00)	1.00
382	Railroad and street cars	4.21	1.00	–	1.19
386	Aircraft	2.88	1.33	1.12	1.00

CHAPTER 7

CONCLUSIONS

Whereas the central theme of this book focuses on the economic performance of concentrated industries, two related topics are also covered to some extent. One of these refers to the validity of international comparisons in the field, not only as to economic performance but also with regard to industrial structure as such. Another (related) topic takes up the question whether measures of industrial concentration have any meaning in very small export-oriented and "open" economies, i.e. whether they measure market power as they are supposed to do in large and "closed" economies such as the U.S. economy.

It may be convenient to start with the second point. On formal grounds, covariance analysis (and its refinements such as Zellner's approach to "seemingly unrelated" regressions) is a natural and satisfactory approach to a comparative analysis of several countries. It allows to test the homogeneity of the regression results and thus the presence of aggregation bias. Furthermore, this technique allows to compensate to some extent the heterogeneity and the resulting loss in information that characterize industrial statistics in Europe. On economic grounds, however, matters are more complex. International comparisons of effects of concentration, and of concentration itself, have to take account of the fact that concentration ratios are influenced by market size.

Chapter 6 is devoted to this problem. A direct international comparison of concentration ratios, industry by industry, reveals that small countries tend to be more concentrated on the average than large countries. The ordering is as follows:

Luxemburg > Belgium = Netherlands > France > Italy.

This ordering suggests that market size has a strong influence on concentration ratios. It is indeed verified that concentration is a decreasing function of relative market size.

We therefore proceed to international comparisons after eliminating this influence, to discover more meaningful "true" values. With equal market sizes, French industries appear (perhaps surprisingly) as more concentrated on the average than Belgian and Italian industries. The Dutch have an intermediate position, with oligopolistic industries as concentrated as in France, but with a more rapidly decreasing level of concentration as the number of firms increases.

It is then argued that France is more concentrated than its partners (remembering that Germany is not included in the analysis) because it has (or had) a closed and strongly cartelized economy. Complementary evidence gives some support to this view. The largest firms are, on the average, the biggest in France. The difference in size between French companies and, say, Belgian companies is larger than the difference in size between French establishments and, say, Belgian establishments. Finally, the divergence between company and plant concentration is highest in France.

Given the influence of market size on "observed" concentration ratios, some caution is in order in the interpretation of international comparisons of performance-concentration relationships. Bearing this in mind, we now turn to the results of the analysis of four performance indicators: price flexibility (inflation), profits, wages and research efforts.

Concerning the first, a certain literature — which is in contradiction with standard economic theory — suggests that more concentrated industries are responsible for what has been called "*administrative inflation*": during upswings of the business cycle, more concentrated industries would use their monopolistic power to increase selling prices more than would be justified by increases in demand or costs. Our analysis (chapter 2) of Belgian, Dutch and

French wholesale prices over the period 1958–65 shows very clearly that this was not the case. Over this period, more concentrated industries behaved exactly like less concentrated industries. A covariance analysis reveals an impressive homogeneity as to (a) the absence of any relationship between price increases and concentration ratios, (b) an increase in prices with unit wage costs and unit materials costs, and (c) the influence of labor intensity on price changes in response to changes in unit wage costs.

This does not necessarily imply that concentrated industries adopt competitive prices: the level of prices, at any phase of the business cycle, might still be too "high", leading to "excessive" *profits*. Here economic theory predicts a positive relationship between rates of return (on equity) and concentration ratios.

We had a very hard time (in chapter 3) to derive orthodox results. A lot of experimenting was needed to find the right thresholds above which concentration, barriers to entry and profits can be said to be high and also to find the appropriate levels of aggregation over time and over industries.

Thresholds have to be put the lower, the larger the country, as far as concentration is concerned, because of the bias in "observed" concentration ratios due to market size. Barriers to entry can be treated the same way, whatever the size of the country, while the partition of profits into "high" and "low" has to take account of national accounting practices. Suitable thresholds seem to lie around values of 50 and 30, for the concentration ratio, and 7 and 2, for the rates of return, in Belgium and Italy respectively.

Averaging rates of return over a period of several years turns out to be dangerous, in the sense that nothing seems to be gained while losses in information might be important. When averages are used, one should be careful to stay within the same phase of the business cycle. This conclusion is in conflict with our initial intention to use the averaging process in order to eliminate fluctuations over the business cycle, based on the finding that the inter-industry pattern of rates of return is more stable over the business cycle in highly concentrated industries.

Rather than justifying the use of time averages of rates of return, this greater stability may help to explain why, for Italy at least, a positive profit-concentration relationship shows up only, but then very clearly, in recession years. The more as this positive relationship appears to be typical for industries that are highly concentrated and highly protected by technological barriers to entry.

For Belgium, no significant results could be obtained, except for a negative (sic!) linear relationship between profits and concentration in industries where both concentration and barriers are low, and a higher average level of profits in high barrier industries.

The computations for Italy and Belgium are based on rates of return on equity after taxes. For Belgium all joint-stock companies are included, while for Italy the data include only larger companies (with a capital of more than 100 million lire). This may be part of the explanation why orthodox results are obtained for Italy and not for Belgium, as small companies may overstate rates of return relatively more than larger companies.

For France, the only profit data available give rates of return on value of shipments, and these do not seem to be relevant to the problem at hand.

In chapters 4 and 5, we turn to possible relationships on the production side between concentration and wages on the one hand, and concentration and research efforts on the other hand.

Whether they extract higher profits or not, concentrated industries do pay higher *wages* in all countries under study (chapter 4). An increase of the concentration ratio by 10 points leads, *ceteris paribus*, to an increase of the hourly wage rate of 0.70 B.F. ($ 0.014) in Belgium, 1.26 B.F. ($ 0.025) in France and 1.44 B.F. ($ 0.029) in Italy.

This net effect could be explained by the presence of higher profits, which would tend to confirm that something is wrong with the Belgian (and French) data on profits used in chapter 3. As for the differences among countries, we suspect these could have been reduced if we had been able to introduce a variable measuring geographical concentration. The more concentrated industries are probably located in high wage regions, especially in larger countries such as France and Italy.

Chapter 5 reports the results of an analysis of research efforts in a sample of 301 Belgian firms. It was readily confirmed that research increases with the size of firms. However, as in the United States, manufacturing industry can be partitioned into three types of industries: there is a very progressive group, comprising the chemical and the electronics industry, a moderately progressive group (rubber, cement, glass, . . .) and a very large non-progressive group.

On the other hand, research personnel increases at an increasing rate with the size of firms, which is not that surprising, given that the vast majority of the firms in the sample are relatively small, when compared with the U.S.

As for concentration, no significant relationship with research efforts was obtained, as in many other studies of the subject, when no distinction was made between more or less progressive groups. But when the sample was partitioned into a chemical sector, an electronics sector, a moderately progressive sector and the rest, each group being allowed to have its own slope, an interesting result came up: when the environment is dynamic, then concentration is a favorable factor (after elimination of the influence of firm size). This again tends to show that more concentrated industries do realize higher profits, which are used to promote research efforts.

Do concentration ratios measure market power in the Benelux countries? This has been a recurrent question, the answer to which cannot be delayed any longer, this being the final page. (Needless to say it is an embarrassing question.)

Surveying the whole study, we notice first that the homogeneity of the results on (the absence of) administrative inflation in France, Belgium and the Netherlands does not imply that Belgian and Dutch concentration ratios are as good as the French are supposed to be. Homogeneity of regression coefficients does not mean identity of causal relationships, the more as in this case we have an alleged absence of relationship. On the other hand, the completely unorthodox results on profits in Belgium may be thought to result from the fact that Belgian concentration ratios (or Dutch or

Luxemburger, for that matter) measure anything but market power (if any). If so, we would come to the paradox that the highest figures (in the context of the Common Market) have the least economic meaning.

Look however at chapters 4 and 5. There, perfectly clear and plausible results are obtained, precisely for Belgium. Furthermore, to be consistent, these results call for a positive profit-concentration relationship. All in all, the measurement or aggregation errors seem therefore to be on the profit side. And we conclude that the results obtained on the wage and the research front tend to strengthen our initial belief that the Beneluxian concentration ratios are not worse than their French, Italian . . . or American counterparts. That this was indeed our initial belief can be derived from the troubles we supported valiantly in preparing the statistical appendix that follows.

STATISTICAL APPENDIX

The following tables give the results of calculations made on data taken from the 1963 Industrial Census which was organized in all Common Market countries and put at our disposal by the Statistical Office of the Communities. The interested reader will find here some information on the Census, the industrial classification used and on the calculations made (in particular on the estimation of the concentration ratios).

The 1963 Industrial Census [1]

In principle, the census refers to the year 1962. However, as this was the first Common Market census, it had to be based on national censuses which were carried out by the national statistical institutes. As a consequence, the results do not always refer to the same date. The data on the number of companies, establishment and persons employed, which are used here, refer to the following dates:
— Italy = 6 June 1961,
— Netherlands = end of September 1962,
— Belgium = 31 December 1962,
— Luxemburg = 31 December 1962 (for the number of companies and establishments) and 30 September 1962 (for the number of persons employed),
— France = 2 January 1963.
Each country published (or is about to publish) these results in its own industrial classification independently. [2]

---

[1] See *Statistiques Industrielles* (Office Statistique des Communautés Europeennes, Brussels, 1967-J-A) and the recent Résultats définitifs de l'enquête industrielle de 1963, *Etudes et enquêtes statistiques* (1969/2).

A *company* ("entreprise") is defined as the smallest independent unit from a legal point of view. It may comprise one single establishment or several establishments which are not legally autonomous.

An *establishment* ("unité locale") is an isolated plant used for a particular economic activity. As Luxemburg has only one or two companies with more than one establishment, this country did not distinguish between companies and establishments. This is the reason why the Luxemburg data on establishments are identical with those on companies.

The N.I.C.E. industrial classification

The census is based on the Nomenclature des industries établies dans les communautés européennes (N.I.C.E.) which is the classification accepted by all Common Market countries and was published in its final form in 1963. [3] This classification is inspired by the U.N.O. international classification and by the (rather divergent) national classifications.

The N.I.C.E. covers (1) extractive industry, (2–3) manufacturing industry, (4) construction and (5) electricity, gaz and water. We limited ourselves to manufacturing industry.

The comparisons made in chapter 6 are based exclusively on three-digit industries. In the tables, the reader will also find information on a few two-digit industries for which a three-digit subclassification is lacking (industries 20A, 220, 260, 280 and 320).

Tables A.1 and A.2

Tables A.1 and A.2 give estimated concentration ratios for the 4, 8, 20 and 50 largest companies and establishments, by industry, for five E.E.C. countries. Germany had to be excluded, as the system adopted by this country to protect the statistical secret

[2] See references in part I.

[3] See *Statistiques industrielles*, Office Statistique des Communautés Européennes, Brussels, Livraison supplémentaire (June 1963).

led to a relatively large number of blanks in the frequency distributions, which made it impossible to calculate concentration ratios.

All concentration ratios are based on numbers of persons employed. We were fully aware of the fact that shipments would have been a better measure, but the available frequency distributions were too incomplete to provide acceptable estimates.

Frequency distributions provide the number of companies, the number of establishments and the number of persons employed corresponding to each size class. The census distinguishes the following 14 size classes: 1, 2–4, 5–9, 10–19, 20–49, 50–99, 100–199, 200–499, 500–999, 1,000–1,999, 2,000–4,999, 5,000 –9,999, 10,000–19,999, 20,000 and more persons employed.

Concentration ratios are defined as the percent of the total dimension of an industry (here the total number of persons employed) accounted for by the 4 (8, 20 or 50) largest companies or establishments. They are equal to 100 if the number of companies or establishments in an industry is smaller than or equal to 4 (8, 20, or 50). Otherwise, they are smaller than 100. How are these ratios to be computed from frequency distributions? We used a method suggested by J.S.Bain in *International Differences in Industrial Structure.* [4]

Consider the number of companies [5] belonging to the last size class (i.e. the class with the largest companies). There are three possibilities. [6]

(a) This number of companies happens to be equal to four. The concentration ratio is the ratio of the total dimension of these companies to the total dimension of the industry.

(b) The number of companies is smaller than four. Add the number of companies of the previous size class. According as the total is equal, smaller or larger than four, we have cases (a'), (b') or (c') (discussed below).

---

[4] (New Haven, 1966), pp. 27–28.

[5] The reasoning is the same for establishments.

[6] The reasoning is the same for the computation of the concentration ratio of the 8, 20 and 50 largest companies (or establishments) as for the computation of the ratio of the four largest, which is analysed here.

(c) The number of companies is larger than four. One has to compute a maximal and a minimal estimate of the concentration ratio.

Maximal estimate. Assign to all companies (in the class) except four the dimension of the lower limit of the size class. The dimensions of the four largest is obtained by substracting the previous result from the total dimension of the class. The maximal estimate of the concentration ratio is the ratio of the dimension of the four largest companies to the total dimension of the industry.

Minimal estimate. Compute the average dimension of the companies in the class. The minimal estimate of the concentration ratio is the ratio of this average dimension multiplied by four to the total dimension of the sector.

The concentration ratio (for case (c)) is the arithmetic average of the maximal and minimal estimates.

Case (b) refers to cases (a'), (b') and (c') to be detailed now.

(a') The number of companies belonging to the last and the preceding size class is equal to four. No problem.

(b') This number is smaller than four. Add the number of companies of the preceding class. According as the sum is equal, inferior or larger than four, we are back in cases (a'), (b') or (c').

(c') The number of companies belonging to the last and to some preceding classes is greater than four. One has to compute a maximal and a minimal estimate of the concentration ratio.

Maximal estimate. Assign the dimension of the lower limit of the (smallest) size class considered to all companies (in this class) except four minus the number of companies belonging to the larger size classes. Substraction gives the total dimension of the companies of the class that belong to the four largest of the industry. (If this substraction implies an average size larger than the upper limit of the class, assign a dimension equal to this upper limit.) The maximal estimate is the ratio of the dimension of the four largest companies, computed as explained, to the total dimension of the sector.

Minimal estimate. Compute the average size of the companies of the (smallest) size class considered. Multiply this by four minus the number of companies belonging to the larger size classes. Add this product to the dimension of the larger size classes and divide the sum by the total dimension of the sector.

The concentration ratio (for case (c')) is the arithmetic average of the maximal and minimal estimates.

Comparing tables A.1 and A.2, the reader will discover that the concentration ratios for establishments are in several cases larger than the concentration ratios for companies, in the same industry. This is theoretically impossible. Leaving aside errors of estimation, an explanation is to be found in the fact that a company is classified in one industry only, (the one of its "principal" activity), while the establishments depending from this company may be classified in different industries, if they happen to produce goods belonging to different industries.

Tables A.3 and A.4

The average number of persons employed per company (or establishment) was needed to obtain the results given in tables 6.3 and 6.4. An international comparison of the size of firms (or establishments) based on tables A.3 and A.4 would not be very illuminating, though, as these averages are of course influenced by the size of the countries. Direct international comparisons of size of firms (or establishments) should rather be based on the data given in tables A.5 and A.6, where we estimated the average size of the 4, 8, 20 and 50 largest firms and establishments.

Tables A.5 and A.6

These data allow meaningful direct international comparisons. They were obtained by multiplying the total dimension (employment) of each industry by the concentration ratio and dividing by the relevant number of companies or establishments. The resulting estimate is a crude one because of rounding errors (which might have some importance when concentration ratios are very small) and errors in the estimation of the concentration ratios. Nevertheless, these estimates do serve their purpose well.

When an industry has less than 4 (or 8, or 20, or 50) components, no average size is given.

On the state of industrial statistics in the E.E.C.

The statistical office of the E.E.C. provided invaluable help in making the census results available to us and in giving competent advice on the way of handling these. The following brief remarks should be interpreted as constructive proposals to increase the usefulness of the work done and in no way as a criticism of it.

It is our hope, first of all, that it will soon be possible to include Germany in similar analyses. For obvious reasons, this country should have her place in international comparisons of this type.

The reader will also have noticed the absence of regional data. In the study of the wage structure and other problems of production and productivity, this type of data would be of great help and make it possible to disentangle regional and industry effects (see chapter 4).

It was our intention to make an international study of the relationship between concentration and research (expenses for R & D, R & D personnel, etc.). Again, this turned out to be impossible because of a lack of comparable data, in particular of comparable industrial classifications. A questionnaire on R & D should be added in any industrial census to be organized.

This leads to a question of timing. It is somewhat discouraging to work, in 1970, on a 1963 census, in a period where concentration seems to be changing rapidly, or more precisely where merger activity seems to be increasing (whether this is sufficient to markedly change the pattern of concentration is not clear). More recent and homogeneous statistical information is badly needed.

Furthermore, the interested reader will recognize the necessity of following the evolution of concentration over time: time series are indispendable for this purpose. We have the strong impression that time series on the evolution of industrial structure are either inexistent or strictly non-comparable between countries. The impressive amount of available time-series seems, indeed, to be collected for the sole purpose of analyzing the business cycle. As a result, to take one example, wholesale price and production time series are, in general, constructed on the basis of non-structural criteria, such as sensitivity as business cycle indicators. Price or production indexes defined according to the industrial classifications utilized in industrial censuses are most often completely inexistent.

We would therefore conclude to the necessity of:

(1) organizing, in the E.E.C. countries, an annual industrial survey, in the spirit of the American Annual survey of manufactures or the Dutch Produktiestatistieken, on the basis of the N.I.C.E. classification;

(2) organizing a Common Market industrial census at regular intervals; and to include in it regional aspects and R & D problems;

(3) speeding up the unification of industrial statistics on prices, production, productivity, etc. along the lines followed in the field of wage statistics, where valuable results have been obtained.

Table A.1

Company concentration ratios (percent of persons employed by the 4, 8, 20 and 50 largest companies)[1]

No. N.I.C.E.	Industry	France	Italy	Nether-lands	Bel-gium	Luxem-burg
20A	Animal and vegetable fats and oils	61	7	58	75	–
		69	9	82	83	–
		81	12	96	92	–
		90	17	100	98	–
201	Meat slaughtering and processing plants	24	17	28	18	5
		31	22	38	23	7
		40	30	53	32	13
		52	43	68	42	25
202	Milk	16	27	17	15	100
		22	34	25	22	100
		31	42	39	36	100
		43	50	57	56	100
203	Canned fruits and vegetables	15	20	31	60	–a
		23	26	46	75	–
		41	38	67	90	–
		60	55	83	99	–
204	Canned and cured seafoods	13	23	19	43	–
		23	39	32	60	–
		41	67	53	83	–
		68	88	81	96	–
205	Corn milling	10	3	57	28a	71
		14	4	79	42	92
		19	7	92	62	100
		26	12	97	77	100
206	Bread and related products	15	16	8	9	7b
		24	20	11	10	10
		38	25	15	13	17
		58	30	21	17	28
207	Sugar	42	63	94	74	–
		54	80	100	83	–
		73	95	100	96	–
		91	100	100	100	–

[1] The four numbers corresponding to each industry and country measure the percent of total employment accounted for by the 4, 8, 20 and 50 largest companies respectively. See notes at end of tables.

Table A.1 (cont.)

No. N.I.C.E.	Industry	France	Italy	Nether-lands	Bel-gium	Luxem-burg
208	Cocoa, chocolate,	15	35	25	30	$-^c$
	confectionery products	24	44	38	39	–
		40	59	60	57	–
		61	75	82	80	–
209	Other food preparations	12	8	19	16	57^d
		19	11	27	25	80
		30	20	37	43	100
		43	31	49	60	100
211	Fermentation alcohol,	13	15	25	32	$-^e$
	yeast, liquors	22	23	35	52	–
		36	34	53	74	–
		51	48	76	87	–
212	Wines	11	13	–	$-^f$	46^f
		17	18	–	–	77
		30	27	–	–	100
		47	37	–	–	100
213	Beer and malt	24	49	64	20	66
		35	71	84	32	93
		56	94	98	51	100
		80	100	100	71	100
214	Soft drinks	22	18	26	35	78
		31	25	37	47	100
		42	34	57	68	100
		53	43	76	87	100
220	Tobacco	100	78	31	37	$-^g$
		100	80	50	59	–
		100	84	84	84	–
		100	89	98	95	–
232	Wool	14	19	20	20	$-^g$
		22	24	33	31	–
		35	33	56	51	–
		51	44	86	76	–
233	Cotton	19	15	27	25	–
		24	23	42	36	–
		34	39	70	54	–
		50	57	94	77	–

See notes at end of tables

Table A.1 (cont.)

No. N.I.C.E.	Industry	France	Italy	Nether-lands	Bel-gium	Luxem-burg
234	Silk	14	12	73	36	–
		19	18	91	48	–
		29	28	100	70	–
		42	46	100	93	–
235	Linen and hemp	28	50	34	17	–
		38	59	48	28	–
		56	72	61	43	–
		79	85	77	55	–
236	Other textile fibres, (jute, etc.), cordage	49	29	55	28	–
		65	45	71	48	–
		78	66	87	80	–
		90	79	97	97	–
237	Hosiery	7	4	28	10	–
		12	7	40	15	–
		23	12	60	27	–
		39	19	86	45	–
238	Textile finishing	37	26	75	22	–
		43	36	88	36	–
		53	48	97	60	–
		68	62	100	87	–
239	Other textile industries	10	12	24	12	–
		14	16	35	18	–
		21	21	53	32	–
		33	30	72	52	–
241	Foot-wear	13	4	31	16	–[g]
		17	6	36	24	–
		26	11	47	39	–
		38	18	69	57	–
242	Shoe repair	17	0	1	0	9
		26	0	1	1	14
		40	1	3	2	26
		58	1	5	4	49
243	Wearing apparel	2	2	7	4	20[h]
		4	3	11	6	28
		7	5	19	10	40
		13	9	29	18	52

See notes at end of tables

Table A.1 (cont.)

No. N.I.C.E.	Industry	France	Italy	Nether- lands	Bel- gium	Luxem- burg
244	Mattresses and bedding	25	21	3	25	_i
		32	27	6	38	−
		47	38	11	57	−
		64	49	18	71	−
245	Fur goods	10	15	15	14	71
		15	21	24	23	92
		22	32	39	41	100
		31	44	58	54	100
251	Sawmills and planing mills	2	3	10	7	61
		4	6	16	10	80
		7	11	35	18	96
		12	19	63	31	100
252	Semifinished wood products	10a	13	63	60	−
		14	19	74	69	−
		21	32	89	84	−
		30	52	100	98	−
253	Frames, carpentry, floors	1	2	19	12	−
		2	2	25	19	−
		3	4	37	31	−
		5	6	50	46	−
254	Wood packing	_b	3	25	17	_j
		−	5	35	25	−
		−	10	56	45	−
		−	16	78	74	−
255	Other wood products	9	10	8	18	77k
		15	15	14	25	92
		27	24	28	38	100
		39	37	44	53	100
259	Cork products, cane chairs, brushes	11	6	29	15	_j
		15	10	38	22	−
		21	19	53	35	−
		31	28	71	52	−
260	Wood furniture	3	1	4	5	20
		5	2	7	9	30
		9	4	13	16	52
		14	7	23	28	79

See notes at end of tables

Table A.1 (cont.)

No. N.I.C.E.	Industry	France	Italy	Netherlands	Belgium	Luxemburg
271	Pulp, paper and board	26	22	59	56	_g
		38	32	71	79	–
		56	51	89	99	–
		80	70	100	100	–
272	Paper and board	5	7	13	27	–
	products	8	11	23	34	–
		15	19	41	49	–
		29	33	64	68	–
280	Printing and	7	10	8	9	50
	publishing	10	13	12	16	64
		18	18	20	27	82
		28	26	33	41	97
291	Tannery, tawery	16	13	28	46	_g
		25	20	38	70	–
		41	32	61	87	–
		59	45	86	94	–
292	Leather products	6	6	12	12	58
		10	9	19	19	92
		17	14	31	30	100
		27	23	51	44	100
301	Synthetic rubber and	50	53	42	55	99[l]
	asbestos	57	59	62	71	100
		68	67	80	86	100
		79	75	93	95	100
302	Plastic materials	6	9	19	17	_m
		10	12	29	26	–
		19	21	46	45	–
		32	31	66	71	–
303	Artificial and synthetic	83	87	100	100	–
	fibres	95	99	100	100	–
		100	100	100	100	–
		100	100	100	100	–
304	Starch, glue and	83	100	55	_b	–
	gelatin	91	100	72	–	–
		99	100	96	–	–
		100	100	100	–	–

See notes at end of tables

Table A.1 (cont.)

No. N.I.C.E.	Industry	France	Italy	Netherlands	Belgium	Luxemburg
311	Production and trans-	35	29	30	62	70[n]
	formation of basic	47	44	47	82	91
	chemicals	59	64	71	98	100
		74	77	92	100	100
312	Industrial and agricultu-	18	60	18	27	−[o]
	ral chemicals	27	64	30	37	−
		41	69	47	56	−
		57	77	69	79	−
313	Chemicals for domestic	15	16	33	53	86
	consumption	22	24	48	61	98
		32	35	64	73	100
		46	51	81	85	100
320	Petroleum	66	41	95	87[c]	−
		88	60	99	100	−
		93	83	100	100	−
		97	95	100	100	−
331	Baked clay products	11	6	9	23	−[p]
		17	9	15	32	−
		28	15	28	49	−
		44	25	50	68	−
332	Glass	39	14	49	61	−[q]
		47	19	70	73	−
		64	28	83	90	−
		78	40	90	97	−
333	China, pottery, fire-	24	17	20	43	98[r]
	proof products	35	24	27	57	100
		53	36	39	76	100
		71	51	51	93	100
334	Cement, lime, plaster	40	32	94	76	−[h]
		51	42	97	94	−
		70	52	100	100	−
		87	64	100	100	−
335	Concrete products	24	13	15	29	100
		29	16	21	33	100
		35	21	32	44	100
		44	28	50	59	100

See notes at end of tables

Table A.1 (cont.)

No. N.I.C.E.	Industry	France	Italy	Netherlands	Belgium	Luxemburg
339	Stone and non-metallic mineral products	10	4	14	12	68[s]
		16	7	22	17	78
		22	12	39	25	93
		30	18	58	33	100
341	Steel mills (according to E.C.C.S. treaty)	40	56	100	62	100
		64	66	100	78	100
		91	78	100	97	100
		100	88	100	100	100
342	Steel tubes	70	58	88	93	—
		84	63	100	100	—
		96	71	100	100	—
		100	80	100	100	—
343	Wire-drawing, rolling, cold finishing, etc.	33	27	38	68	—
		48	40	57	76	—
		69	62	81	91	—
		85	82	94	100	—
344	Primary non-ferrous metals	54	30	71	48	—[t]
		65	42	87	75	—
		78	55	97	97	—
		91	66	100	100	—
345	Foundries (ferrous and non-ferrous)	19	7	33	17	81[u]
		25	10	54	27	97
		37	20	74	48	100
		51	33	90	70	100
351	Forgings, punching, stamping, etc.	14	18	93	61	—
		24	31	100	84	—
		45	59	100	100	—
		71	81	100	100	—
352	Second transformation of metals	2	5	21	21	—[v]
		4	9	31	28	—
		8	15	45	40	—
		15	24	60	54	—
353	Metallic construction	18	8	13	19	55[w]
		25	12	19	31	67
		41	19	30	45	83
		60	29	43	58	94

See notes at end of tables

Table A.1 (cont.)

No. N.I.C.E.	Industry	France	Italy	Nether-lands	Bel-gium	Luxem-burg
354	Boiler-works	15	37	32	27	–[v]
		20	52	40	40	–
		31	74	57	60	–
		42	93	69	83	–
355	Metal tools	7	5	13	12	63
		10	8	20	21	92
		15	12	35	33	100
		24	20	52	50	100
359	Auxiliary activities	10	1	2	0	25
	of metallic industries	13	1	3	1	35
		23	2	5	2	47
		42	3	9	5	68
361	Farm machinery and	34	14	29	59	100
	equipment	42	21	41	69	100
		52	34	60	83	100
		66	52	84	91	100
362	Office machines	67	85	67	–[d]	100
		84	94	81	–	100
		92	96	89	–	100
		96	98	94	–	100
363	Metal-cutting machine	13	9	20	39[e]	100
	tools	19	14	32	67	100
		30	24	51	84	100
		45	38	74	94	100
364	Textile machinery,	23	33	29	55	–
	sewing machines	35	44	43	70	–
		51	60	63	85	–
		69	75	79	96	–
365	Food products machinery	13	12	25	36	–
		19	20	34	46	–
		32	37	49	68	–
		48	58	72	87	–
366	Mining, steel-work	14	20	20	41	100
	machinery, cranes, etc.	21	30	33	59	100
		35	45	53	75	100
		54	62	76	87	100

See notes at end of tables

Table A.1 (cont.)

No. N.I.C.E.	Industry	France	Italy	Nether- lands	Bel- gium	Luxem- burg
367	Transmission equipment	72	63	75	47	–
		87	68	87	72	–
		99	78	99	95	–
		100	89	100	100	–
368	Other specific	33	25	34	51	–
	machinery	46	33	45	65	–
		67	44	70	83	–
		89	59	90	94	–
369	Other non-electric	27	12	38	19	100
	machinery	38	17	48	33	100
		51	28	59	55	100
		65	43	70	73	100
371	Electric wires	52	39	95	100	100
		67	53	100	100	100
		88	72	100	100	100
		99	91	100	100	100
372	Motors, generators,	42	12	46	77	–
	transformers, switchgear,	57	18	61	83	–
	etc.	69	30	81	91	–
		81	45	95	97	–
373	Electric accessories,	27	70	59	59	100
	tools, welding	36	87	72	67	100
	apparatus, etc.	49	94	91	78	100
		60	99	100	88	100
374	Electrical measuring	34	41	77	96	100
	instruments	50	55	83	99	100
		72	71	96	100	100
		88	83	100	100	100
375	Electronic material,	43	35	97	79	–
	radio and television	51	47	98	85	–
		65	66	99	91	–
		79	90	100	96	–
376	Domestic electric	25	43	35	36	–
	appliances	39	55	57	50	–
		56	78	86	82	–
		74	91	99	98	–

See notes at end of tables.

Table A.1 (cont.)

No. N.I.C.E.	Industry	France	Italy	Netherlands	Belgium	Luxemburg
377	Lamps and lighting fixtures	75	60	32	56	–
		83	71	49	67	–
		93	83	69	85	–
		95	91	87	98	–
378	Batteries	79	55	66	78	–
		90	78	85	91	–
		97	98	97	100	–
		99	100	100	100	–
379	Repair and fixing of electrical appliances	53	6	5	1	75
		58	10	7	3	87
		64	15	14	7	98
		70	21	20	16	100
381	Shipbuilding and repairing	37	62	29	58	–
		50	72	42	66	–
		67	82	59	80	–
		78	89	73	93	–
382	Railroad and street cars	34	38	–[a]	77	–
		63	61	–	88	–
		93	97	–	99	–
		100	100	–	100	–
383	Automobiles and parts	50	72	42	41	–[x]
		62	76	56	54	–
		77	80	62	69	–
		85	86	74	83	–
384	Independent repair of automobiles, motorcycles and cycles	1	1	2	3	23
		1	1	4	5	32
		2	2	8	8	53
		4	3	12	13	75
385	Motorcycles, cycles and parts	43	55	31	50	–
		52	65	46	60	–
		64	79	74	73	–
		77	90	95	85	–
386	Aircraft construction and repair	57	74	100[b]	99	–[x]
		70	92	100	100	–
		87	100	100	100	–
		98	100	100	100	–

See notes at end of tables.

Table A.1 (cont.)

No. N.I.C.E.	Industry	France	Italy	Nether- lands	Bel- gium	Luxem- burg
389	Transportation equip- ment, n.e.c.	0	17	27	80	74[y]
		1	20	43	91	86
		1	27	66	100	94
		2	33	82	100	100
391	Measuring devices, con- trols	29	24	47	88	–
		36	38	63	93	–
		48	58	83	97	–
		62	82	95	99	–
392	Surgical and medical instruments	7	20	13	7	–[g]
		12	29	22	12	–
		20	39	39	20	–
		29	52	57	32	–
393	Ophtalmic goods and photographic equipment	29	27	15	53	–[g]
		44	37	23	66	–
		67	51	33	79	–
		85	67	44	87	–
394	Watches and clocks	24	38	9	3	23
		33	42	11	5	41
		46	47	14	11	74
		65	51	20	15	100
395	Jewelry, silverware and lapidary work	9	8	14	26	64
		13	11	21	34	93
		22	17	35	47	100
		36	26	52	61	100
396	Musical instruments	32	23	23	43	–[g]
		45	32	35	59	–
		61	46	52	77	–
		79	65	68	91	–
397	Games, toys and sporting goods	11	20	32	7	–
		18	30	48	14	–
		31	47	71	34	–
		47	69	92	51	–
399	Miscellaneous products, n.e.c.	12	17	14	12	76[z]
		19	23	26	19	89
		27	32	48	35	97
		37	46	66	55	100

See notes at end of tables.

Table A.2
Establishment concentration ratios (percent of persons employed by the 4, 8, 20 and 50 largest establishments)[1]

No. N.I.C.E.	Industry	France	Italy	Netherlands	Belgium	Luxemburg
20A	Animal and vegetable fats and oils	29	4	58	70	–
		42	6	73	81	–
		64	10	91	92	–
		81	15	100	96	–
201	Meat slaughtering and processing plants	14	15	24	18	5
		24	20	31	23	7
		36	27	47	31	13
		49	40	64	42	25
202	Milk	5	11	11	15	100
		7	16	16	22	100
		13	26	26	36	100
		22	35	43	55	100
203	Canned fruits and vegetables	9	12	30	44	–[a]
		16	17	44	68	–
		30	27	63	86	–
		48	44	83	98	–
204	Canned and cured seafoods	8	21	16	43	–
		14	34	28	60	–
		29	58	46	83	–
		55	82	69	97	–
205	Corn milling	7	2	42	28[a]	71
		11	3	63	41	92
		15	5	85	61	100
		22	9	95	77	100
206	Bread and related products	10	12	5	9	7[b]
		18	15	7	10	10
		31	21	11	13	17
		50	25	17	17	28
207	Sugar	22	18	45	61	–
		32	31	72	72	–
		50	58	100	89	–
		74	85	100	100	–

[1] The four numbers corresponding to each industry and country measure the percent of total employment accounted for by the 4, 8, 20 and 50 largest establishments respectively.

See notes at end of tables.

Table A.2 (cont.)

No. N.I.C.E.	Industry	France	Italy	Nether-lands	Bel-gium	Luxem-burg
208	Cocoa, chocolate,	12	28	24	30	_c
	confectionery products	19	37	38	39	–
		34	51	58	57	–
		56	68	78	80	–
209	Other food	7	6	12	16	57d
	preparations	12	9	18	25	80
		23	17	29	43	100
		36	27	42	60	100
211	Fermentation alcohol,	9	8	20	31	_e
	yeast, liquors	16	13	29	50	–
		27	22	48	74	–
		40	36	72	87	–
212	Wines	10	9	–	_f	46f
		15	13	–	–	77
		25	22	–	–	100
		41	31	–	–	100
213	Beer and malt	15	32	51	20	66
		24	49	71	32	93
		41	81	94	51	100
		65	100	100	71	100
214	Soft drinks	9	14	23	35	78
		15	19	34	47	100
		25	27	53	68	100
		37	37	72	87	100
220	Tobacco	18	17	23	27	_g
		34	31	39	48	–
		75	56	67	76	–
		100	76	92	94	–
232	Wool	13	9	18	16	_g
		19	14	26	25	–
		29	24	48	44	–
		43	37	81	72	–
233	Cotton	5	6	18	16	–
		8	10	32	26	–
		15	19	55	44	–
		27	34	85	69	–

See notes at end of tables.

Table A.2 (cont.)

No. N.I.C.E.	Industry	France	Italy	Nether-lands	Bel-gium	Luxem-burg
234	Silk	5	7	64	36	–
		8	12	81	47	–
		15	21	100	70	–
		25	35	100	93	–
235	Linen and hemp	18	24	35	16	–
		25	37	49	28	–
		43	58	62	43	–
		69	77	92	55	–
236	Other textile fibres, (jute, etc.), cordage	21	25	43	28	–
		36	42	61	48	–
		59	66	82	80	–
		79	80	96	97	–
237	Hosiery	5	3	21	10	–
		9	5	30	15	–
		17	10	49	27	–
		31	16	68	45	–
238	Textile finishing	15	10	64	22	–
		21	17	84	36	–
		34	31	95	60	–
		53	49	100	87	–
239	Other textile industries	9	13	19	12	–
		12	17	27	18	–
		19	22	46	32	–
		29	31	66	52	–
241	Foot-wear	7	3	18	16	–[g]
		12	5	24	23	–
		20	9	36	38	–
		32	16	54	56	–
242	Shoe repair	15	0	1	0	9
		23	0	1	1	14
		34	1	2	2	26
		49	1	4	4	49
243	Wearing apparel	1	2	3	3	20[h]
		2	3	5	5	28
		5	6	10	10	40
		9	9	18	17	52

See notes at end of tables.

Table A.2 (cont.)

No. N.I.C.E.	Industry	France	Italy	Netherlands	Belgium	Luxemburg
244	Mattresses and bedding	14	19	3	25	$-^i$
		21	24	6	38	–
		38	34	11	57	–
		57	46	18	71	–
245	Fur goods	8	15	14	14	71
		13	21	22	23	92
		20	32	37	41	100
		29	46	55	54	100
251	Sawmills and planing mills	2	3	8	6	61
		3	5	15	9	80
		6	9	31	17	96
		11	15	50	29	100
252	Semifinished wood products	4^a	8	57	59	–
		7	14	71	68	–
		14	27	8?	83	–
		23	48	99	98	–
253	Frames, carpentry, floors	1	1	18	12	–
		2	2	22	19	–
		3	4	33	31	–
		5	6	47	46	–
254	Wood packing	$-^b$	4	21	17	$-^j$
		–	6	30	25	–
		–	10	50	45	–
		–	16	73	74	–
255	Other wood products	9	9	8	18	77^k
		15	13	13	25	92
		28	22	26	38	100
		40	35	42	53	100
259	Cork products, cane chairs, brushes	9	6	22	15	$-^j$
		11	9	32	22	–
		17	17	47	35	–
		25	27	66	52	–
260	Wood furniture	2	1	4	5	20
		4	2	7	9	30
		8	4	12	16	52
		13	7	20	27	79

See notes at end of tables.

Table A.2 (cont.)

No. N.I.C.E.	Industry	France	Italy	Nether-lands	Bel-gium	Luxem-burg
271	Pulp, paper and board	12	10	38	36	_g
		19	17	57	57	–
		35	33	79	94	–
		59	56	100	100	–
272	Paper and board products	4	6	11	20	–
		6	10	19	29	–
		12	17	36	45	–
		22	30	59	67	–
280	Printing and publishing	5	7	6	8	50
		8	11	10	15	64
		14	15	17	27	82
		23	23	29	40	97
291	Tannery, tawery	11	13	28	46	_g
		20	19	40	69	–
		36	31	60	87	–
		54	44	85	94	–
292	Leather products	5	6	11	12	58
		8	8	17	19	92
		15	14	29	30	100
		25	22	48	44	100
301	Synthetic rubber and asbestos	32	35	34	55	99l
		41	44	55	71	100
		55	57	74	86	100
		70	68	89	95	100
302	Plastic materials	7	6	14	16	_m
		11	10	24	25	–
		19	18	40	44	–
		32	28	61	70	–
303	Artificial and synthetic fibres	39	41	63	91	–
		56	64	94	100	–
		84	95	100	100	–
		99	100	100	100	–
304	Starch, glue and gelatin	62	97	48	_b	–
		77	100	67	–	–
		92	100	92	–	–
		100	100	100	–	–

See notes at end of tables.

Table A.2 (cont.)

No. N.I.C.E.	Industry	France	Italy	Netherlands	Belgium	Luxemburg
311	Production and transformation of basic chemicals	11	15	38	35	70[n]
		18	27	53	58	91
		29	43	70	90	100
		46	63	89	100	100
312	Industrial and agricultural chemicals	8	22	16	20	—[o]
		14	29	24	30	—
		25	38	41	48	—
		42	50	61	73	—
313	Chemicals for domestic consumption	8	10	28	50	86
		12	14	38	58	98
		19	26	55	70	100
		31	41	74	83	100
320	Petroleum	21	26	86	87[c]	—
		37	44	94	100	—
		72	68	99	100	—
		91	88	100	100	—
331	Baked clay products	6	2	9	15	—[p]
		9	4	14	24	—
		17	8	25	42	—
		32	14	44	63	—
332	Glass	15	8	50	32	—[q]
		23	13	69	49	—
		40	24	81	78	—
		65	37	89	95	—
333	China, pottery, fireproof products	11	8	39	32	98[r]
		20	13	57	47	100
		35	23	72	70	100
		58	41	86	90	100
334	Cement, lime, plaster	9	10	92	56	—[p]
		18	15	95	81	—
		35	26	99	99	—
		62	45	100	100	—
335	Concrete products	14	6	11	28	100
		19	9	18	33	100
		24	13	29	43	100
		34	21	43	59	100

See notes at end of tables.

Table A.2 (cont.)

No. N.I.C.E.	Industry	France	Italy	Netherlands	Belgium	Luxemburg
339	Stone and non-metallic mineral products	5	4	13	6	68[s]
		8	6	21	11	78
		13	10	37	19	93
		21	15	55	28	100
341	Steel mills (according to E.C.C.S. treaty)	20	25	100	34	100
		33	38	100	53	100
		60	55	100	87	100
		89	76	100	100	100
342	Steel tubes	51	35	83	93	–
		66	50	100	100	–
		87	69	100	100	–
		98	80	100	100	–
343	Wire-drawing, rolling, cold finishing, etc.	20	27	28	59	–
		31	38	47	72	–
		51	58	77	88	–
		73	80	92	99	–
344	Primary non-ferrous metals	11	16	70	34	–[t]
		19	25	85	59	–
		39	43	96	92	–
		65	62	100	100	–
345	Foundries (ferrous and non-ferrous)	7	14	28	16	81[u]
		13	18	43	25	97
		23	27	66	46	100
		39	40	86	70	100
351	Forgings, punching, stamping, etc.	14	17	91	61	–
		23	29	100	84	–
		43	56	100	100	–
		67	80	100	100	–
352	Second transformation of metals	2	5	19	18	–[v]
		3	8	28	26	–
		7	14	42	39	–
		13	22	57	54	–
353	Metallic construction	14	5	11	18	55[w]
		21	8	16	29	67
		35	15	27	45	83
		55	25	40	58	94

See notes at end of tables.

Table A.2 (cont.)

No. N.I.C.E.	Industry	France	Italy	Netherlands	Belgium	Luxemburg
354	Boiler-works	8	42	27	27	_v
		13	54	36	40	–
		21	72	54	60	–
		33	92	76	83	–
355	Metal tools	3	5	8	11	63
		5	7	14	19	92
		10	11	26	32	100
		18	18	42	49	100
359	Auxiliary activities of metallic industries	10	1	2	0	25
		13	1	3	1	35
		23	2	5	2	47
		33	3	9	5	68
361	Farm machinery and equipment	22	16	27	59	100
		32	23	38	69	100
		45	36	57	83	100
		60	52	81	91	100
362	Office machines	43	29	46	_d	100
		57	56	65	–	100
		75	78	78	–	100
		90	88	89	–	100
363	Metal-cutting machine tools	7	12	19	39e	100
		12	17	29	67	100
		21	26	47	84	100
		36	40	71	94	100
364	Textile machinery, sewing machines	23	13	38	52	–
		34	25	51	67	–
		48	43	67	84	–
		67	63	80	95	–
365	Food products machinery	9	12	20	35	–
		14	20	30	45	–
		26	35	46	68	–
		43	56	68	87	–
366	Mining, steel-work machinery, cranes, etc.	8	14	20	37	100
		14	22	34	57	100
		25	34	53	74	100
		43	53	75	87	100

See notes at end of tables.

Table A.2 (cont.)

No. N.I.C.E.	Industry	France	Italy	Netherlands	Belgium	Luxemburg
367	Transmission equipment	54	51	72	47	–
		72	59	85	72	–
		94	72	98	95	–
		100	85	100	100	–
368	Other specific machinery	23	19	34	51	–
		36	29	45	65	–
		61	40	68	83	–
		85	56	89	94	–
369	Other non-electric machinery	13	16	31	18	100
		20	22	38	32	100
		35	31	50	55	100
		51	44	63	73	100
371	Electric wires	32	33	75	100	100
		50	49	89	100	100
		75	72	100	100	100
		93	90	100	100	100
372	Motors, generators, transformers, switchgear, etc.	19	8	38	65	–
		28	13	50	78	–
		42	24	69	88	–
		62	39	89	96	–
373	Electric accessories, tools, welding apparatus, etc.	20	54	60	59	100
		28	69	72	67	100
		40	83	90	78	100
		54	96	100	88	100
374	Electrical measuring instruments	30	28	64	81	100
		47	38	73	93	100
		66	54	88	100	100
		84	67	99	100	100
375	Electronic material, radio and television	11	32	76	66	–
		20	46	88	81	–
		35	69	97	89	–
		56	88	100	95	–
376	Domestic electric appliances	16	44	43	36	–
		27	61	55	50	–
		45	77	78	82	–
		66	91	96	98	–

See notes at end of tables.

Table A.2 (cont.)

No. N.I.C.E.	Industry	France	Italy	Netherlands	Belgium	Luxemburg
377	Lamps and lighting fixtures	44	33	51	_f	–
		61	52	66	–	–
		82	71	80	–	–
		95	86	92	–	–
378	Batteries	31	46	61	78	–
		50	73	83	91	–
		84	96	96	100	–
		98	100	100	100	–
379	Repair and fixing of electrical appliances	14	4	19	1	75
		20	6	24	3	87
		30	11	30	7	98
		42	17	38	16	100
381	Ship building and repairing	32	32	27	58	–
		46	49	39	67	–
		66	72	54	81	–
		78	85	68	94	–
382	Railroad and street cars	8	39	100	65	–
		16	57	100	82	–
		32	87	100	98	–
		55	100	100	100	–
383	Automobiles and parts	38	41	41	41	_x
		50	55	47	53	–
		61	68	56	69	–
		72	78	67	83	–
384	Independent repair of automobiles, motorcycles and cycles	2	1	1	3	23
		4	1	2	5	32
		5	2	5	8	53
		7	3	9	13	75
385	Motorcycles, cycles and parts	27	48	29	50	–
		39	58	44	60	–
		56	74	69	73	–
		73	87	91	85	–
386	Aircraft construction and repair	20	57	89	99	_x
		33	80	100	100	–
		55	98	100	100	–
		81	100	100	100	–

See notes at end of tables.

Table A.2 (cont.)

No. N.I.C.E.	Industry	France	Italy	Nether- lands	Bel- gium	Luxem- burg
389	Transportation equip- ment, n.e.c.	0 1 1 2	15 19 27 33	25 41 64 81	80 91 100 100	74[y] 86 94 100
391	Measuring devices, controls	23 28 38 52	23 36 55 79	41 59 80 93	85 92 96 99	– – – –
392	Surgical and medical instruments	6 10 17 26	20 28 39 52	14 23 36 54	7 12 20 32	–[g] – – –
393	Ophtalmic goods and photographic equipment	27 41 60 82	22 31 46 62	13 20 29 41	53 66 79 87	–[g] – – –
394	Watches and clocks	20 29 41 61	33 37 43 48	8 10 13 19	3 5 11 15	23 41 74 100
395	Jewelry, silverware and lapidary work	8 12 20 32	7 10 16 24	15 21 35 52	26 34 47 61	64 93 100 100
396	Musical instruments	24 35 51 74	20 29 44 64	23 33 47 63	43 59 77 91	–[g] – – –
397	Games, toys and sporting goods	9 16 28 42	18 28 45 67	24 43 66 90	7 14 34 51	– – – –
399	Miscellaneous products, n.e.c.	12 16 24 34	16 21 30 44	14 24 44 63	12 19 35 55	76[z] 89 97 100

See notes at end of tables.

Table A.3

Total employment (E), total number of companies (n) and average size of companies ($\bar{F} = E/n$)

No. N.I.C.E.	Industry		France	Italy	Netherlands	Belgium	Luxemburg
20A	Animal and vegetable fats and oils	E	15,563	36,851	6,361	4,497	—
		n	465	9,012	38	65	—
		$\bar{F}$	33	4	167	69	—
201	Meat slaughtering and processing plants	E	31,471	24,129	22,778	8,018	1,366
		n	1,205	1,588	584	936	401
		$\bar{F}$	26	15	39	9	3
202	Milk	E	77,075	33,562	30,067	7,979	507
		n	3,474	3,234	372	368	4
		$\bar{F}$	22	10	81	22	127
203	Canned fruits and vegetables	E	23,580	45,306	11,511	5,371	—[a]
		n	598	902	189	74	—
		$\bar{F}$	39	50	61	73	—
204	Canned and cured seafoods	E	9,779	5,434	3,128	1,638	—
		n	245	187	229	72	—
		$\bar{F}$	40	29	14	23	—
205	Corn milling	E	29,212	46,498	3,554	5,630[a]	162
		n	5,978	13,606	116	698	14
		$\bar{F}$	5	3	31	8	12
206	Bread and related products	E	29,292	63,079	70,968	49,007	1,781[b]
		n	1,052	13,822	10,691	13,658	463
		$\bar{F}$	28	5	7	4	4

See notes at end of tables.

Table A.3 (cont.)

No. N.I.C.E.	Industry		France	Italy	Nether-lands	Belgium	Luxem-burg
207	Sugar	E	25,125	18,402	9,272	5,719	—
		n	92	36	6	33	—
		$\bar{F}$	273	511	1,545	173	—
208	Cocoa, chocolate, confectionery products	E	25,933	24,896	13,875	8,916	—[c]
		n	1,089	721	266	370	—
		$\bar{F}$	24	35	52	24	—
209	Other food preparations	E	31,605	46,732	22,176	11,766	247[d]
		n	1,858	3,461	1,818	820	19
		$\bar{F}$	17	14	12	14	13
211	Fermentation alcohol, yeast, liquors	E	27,006	18,118	4,378	1,962	—[e]
		n	4,515	1,245	177	189	—
		$\bar{F}$	6	15	25	10	—
212	Wines	E	13,185	21,578	—	685	245[f]
		n	1,605	2,104	—	50	16
		$\bar{F}$	8	10	—	14	15
213	Beer and malt	E	21,209	7,444	6,781	19,680	673
		n	211	38	41	328	11
		$\bar{F}$	101	196	164	60	61
214	Soft drinks	E	10,879	16,328	3,306	3,229	212
		n	1,014	1,954	215	170	9
		$\bar{F}$	11	8	15	19	24

See notes at end of tables.

Table A.3 (cont.)

No. N.I.C.E.	Industry		France	Italy	Netherlands	Belgium	Luxemburg
220	Tobacco	E	14,870	30,778	15,811	9,339	-g
		n	1	564	134	282	-
		F	14,870	55	118	33	-
232	Wool	E	106,823	146,401	18,875	30,847	-g
		n	2,009	9,567	123	254	-
		F	53	15	153	121	-
233	Cotton	E	133,347	155,312	36,309	35,458	-
		n	1,031	2,525	138	530	-
		F	129	62	263	67	-
234	Silk	E	46,039	57,752	5,512	5,838	-
		n	2,956	1,691	17	88	-
		F	16	34	324	66	-
235	Linen and hemp	E	23,404	15,461	2,749	10,540	-
		n	339	687	254	1,574	-
		F	69	22	11	7	-
236	Other textile fibres (jute, etc.), cordage	E	19,812	7,862	5,534	7,979	-
		n	473	588	100	101	-
		F	41	13	55	79	-
237	Hosiery	E	93,379	122,451	19,425	20,721	-
		n	3,932	21,849	278	571	-
		F	24	6	70	36	-

See notes at end of tables.

Table A.3 (cont.)

No. N.I.C.E.	Industry		France	Italy	Netherlands	Belgium	Luxemburg
238	Textile finishing	E	38,254	44,101	5,966	9,758	—
		n	505	802	53	140	—
		$\bar{F}$	76	54	113	70	—
239	Other textile industries	E	46,690	56,866	14,134	15,104	—
		n	3,682	11,681	530	827	—
		$\bar{F}$	13	5	27	18	—
241	Foot-wear	E	90,512	105,029	20,469	16,127	—[g]
		n	2,618	5,673	389	526	—
		$\bar{F}$	34	19	53	31	—
242	Shoe repair	E	2,606	69,996	11,755	6,586	237
		n	581	56,286	6,030	5,048	172
		$\bar{F}$	4	1	2	1	1
243	Wearing apparel	E	289,780	302,747	93,229	70,535	1,400[h]
		n	54,069	107,254	6,233	13,757	455
		$\bar{F}$	5	3	15	5	3
244	Mattresses and bedding	E	9,201	6,450	16,141	1,631	—[i]
		n	695	1,772	3,381	305	—
		$\bar{F}$	13	4	5	5	—
245	Fur goods	E	9,400	7,278	1,874	3,820	97
		n	2,654	1,253	343	661	11
		$\bar{F}$	4	6	5	6	9

See notes at end of tables.

Table A.3 (cont.)

No. N.I.C.E.	Industry		France	Italy	Netherlands	Belgium	Luxemburg
251	Sawmills and planing mills	E	46,581	23,409	4,747	6,448	405
		n	8,879	4,251	217	770	30
		$\bar{F}$	5	6	22	8	14
252	Semifinished wood products	E	76,265[a]	18,102	2,814	6,055	—
		n	5,943	357	52	77	—
		$\bar{F}$	13	51	54	79	—
253	Frames, carpentry, floors	E	144,305	138,149	13,645	4,852	—
		n	49,181	57,634	758	1,124	—
		$\bar{F}$	3	2	18	4	—
254	Wood packing	E	—[b]	23,791	5,618	2,041	⌐[j]
		n	—	4,734	261	213	—
		$\bar{F}$	—	5	22	96	—
255	Other wood products	E	4,293	18,812	5,970	4,940	71[k]
		n	2,125	2,576	1,022	1,029	14
		$\bar{F}$	2	7	6	4	5
259	Cork products, cane chairs, brushes	E	22,877	14,562	3,949	2,625	⌐[j]
		n	5,405	2,840	424	631	—
		$\bar{F}$	4	5	9	4	—
260	Wood furniture	E	87,743	135,558	28,548	23,378	516
		n	16,225	28,396	3,176	3,478	119
		$\bar{F}$	5	5	9	7	4

See notes at end of pages.

Table A.3 (cont.)

No. N.I.C.E.	Industry		France	Italy	Netherlands	Belgium	Luxemburg
271	Pulp, paper and board	E	53,680	44,710	14,648	8,578	—g
		n	210	598	37	28	—
		F	256	75	396	306	—
272	Paper and board products	E	70,339	39,148	19,158	16,863	—
		n	2,095	1,989	357	454	—
		F	34	20	54	37	—
280	Printing and publishing	E	180,098	112,578	72,893	35,633	806
		n	11,181	9,028	2,917	3,687	62
		F	16	12	25	10	13
291	Tannery, tawery	E	20,401	20,363	3,996	3,693	—g
		n	615	1,207	124	119	—
		F	33	17	32	31	—
292	Leather products	E	36,324	29,087	7,415	4,368	12
		n	9,179	4,702	664	801	9
		F	4	6	11	5	1
301	Synthetic rubber and asbestos	E	90,164	60,199	12,660	8,280	1,282
		n	1,347	2,872	183	186	6
		F	67	21	69	45	214
302	Plastic materials	E	46,026	43,872	8,951	6,430	—m
		n	2,321	2,703	362	220	—
		F	20	16	25	29	—

See notes at end of pages.

Table A.3 (cont.)

No. N.I.C.E.	Industry		France	Italy	Netherlands	Belgium	Luxemburg
303	Artificial and synthetic fibres	E	33,923	35,565	17,898	4,528	—
		n	28	14	4	1	—
		F	1,212	2,540	4,475	4,528	—
304	Starch, glue and gelatin	E	3,870	689	4,297	—[b]	—
		n	30	5	28	—	—
		F	129	138	153	—	—
311	Production and transformation of basic chemicals	E	125,155	77,303	19,413	17,448	321[n]
		n	1,035	1,030	133	50	13
		F	121	75	146	349	25
312	Industrial and agricultural chemicals	E	45,076	82,001	17,709	14,072	—[o]
		n	1,246	1,736	421	427	—
		F	36	47	42	33	—
313	Chemicals for domestic consumption	E	108,622	79,495	19,858	20,768	63
		n	2,490	2,325	371	374	9
		F	44	34	54	56	7
320	Petroleum	E	32,718	13,712	9,552	2,204[c]	—
		n	157	134	21	6	—
		F	208	102	455	367	—
331	Baked clay products	E	27,587	78,705	13,374	10,653	—[p]
		n	1,143	1,754	236	420	—
		F	24	45	57	25	—

See notes at end of tables.

Table A.3 (cont.)

No. N.I.C.E.	Industry		France	Italy	Netherlands	Belgium	Luxemburg
332	Glass	E	60,257	49,813	6,236	27,856	$-q$
		n	1,212	2,405	255	195	—
		F	50	21	24	143	—
333	China, pottery, fireproof products	E	36,191	50,538	9,336	7,722	1,185[r]
		n	1,141	2,157	274	135	6
		F	32	24	34	57	198
334	Cement, lime, plaster	E	18,709	30,836	1,284	4,928	$-p$
		n	277	1,111	19	23	—
		F	68	28	68	214	—
335	Concrete products	E	36,386	56,727	22,066	16,906	412
		n	2,240	4,226	678	829	5
		F	16	13	33	20	82
339	Stone and non-metallic mineral products	E	20,610	49,215	3,811	7,307	304[s]
		n	3,934	6,371	474	1,570	32
		F	5	8	8	5	10
341	Steel mills (according to E.C.C.S. treaty)	E	233,813	112,344	16,850	89,240	26,921
		n	54	398	3	36	3
		F	4,330	282	5,617	2,479	8,974
342	Steel tubes	E	13,757	31,653	2,052	1,045	—
		n	58	442	6	6	—
		F	237	72	342	174	—

See notes at end of tables.

Table A.3 (cont.)

No. N.I.C.E.	Industry		France	Italy	Netherlands	Belgium	Luxemburg
343	Wire-drawing, rolling cold finishing, etc.	E	28,397	7,342	5,248	11,482	—
		n	273	183	147	54	—
		$\bar{F}$	104	40	36	213	—
344	Primary nonferrous metals	E	55,989	38,942	4,066	22,103	–t
		n	279	1,125	33	36	—
		$\bar{F}$	201	35	123	614	—
345	Foundries (ferrous and non-ferrous)	E	100,608	51,893	10,140	16,583	200u
		n	1,932	2,131	178	388	9
		$\bar{F}$	52	24	57	43	22
351	Forgings, punching, stamping, etc.	E	24,185	5,432	870	96	—
		n	304	185	7	17	—
		$\bar{F}$	80	29	124	6	—
352	Second transformation of metals	E	123,111	41,749	8,786	11,375	–v
		n	11,610	5,392	774	969	—
		$\bar{F}$	11	8	11	12	—
353	Metallic construction	E	33,595	62,995	31,220	19,222	1,848w
		n	407	3,295	1,252	1,051	103
		$\bar{F}$	83	19	25	18	18
354	Boiler-works	E	76,589	3,569	8,618	5,030	–v
		n	3,183	80	172	198	—
		$\bar{F}$	24	45	50	25	—

See notes at end of tables.

Table A.3 (cont.)

No. N.I.C.E.	Industry		France	Italy	Netherlands	Belgium	Luxemburg
355	Metal tools	E	186,566	113,172	53,946	33,858	205
		n	14,458	5,353	1,217	1,748	14
		$\bar{F}$	13	21	44	19	15
359	Auxiliary activities of metallic industries	E	634	145,519	15,602	5,261	382
		n	389	52,778	4,902	3,380	157
		$\bar{F}$	2	3	3	2	2
361	Farm machinery and equipment	E	37,873	19,857	3,043	4,320	27
		n	794	624	110	154	1
		$\bar{F}$	48	32	28	28	27
362	Office machines	E	31,215	32,534	6,604	—d	7
		n	667	349	212	—	4
		$\bar{F}$	47	93	31	—	2
363	Metal-cutting machine tools	E	64,455	44,139	5,399	6,758e	75
		n	1,649	1,400	208	169	2
		$\bar{F}$	39	32	26	40	38
364	Textile machinery, sewing machines	E	18,841	37,033	1,864	6,148	—
		n	539	419	246	163	—
		$\bar{F}$	35	88	8	38	—
365	Food products machinery	E	23,946	20,491	10,544	4,483	—
		n	976	430	212	128	—
		$\bar{F}$	25	48	50	35	—

See notes at end of tables.

Table A.3 (cont.)

No. N.I.C.E.	Industry		France	Italy	Netherlands	Belgium	Luxemburg
366	Mining, steel-work machinery, cranes, etc.	E	53,896	31,183	11,060	15,947	368
		n	745	504	201	201	3
		F	72	62	55	79	123
367	Transmission equipment	E	3,266	23,246	2,195	1,449	—
		n	28	225	26	27	—
		F	117	103	84	54	—
368	Other specific machinery	E	6,940	15,830	3,388	2,832	—
		n	168	511	111	107	—
		F	41	31	31	26	—
369	Other non-electric machinery	E	130,891	63,380	47,023	13,569	218
		n	2,203	3,711	1,098	652	4
		F	59	17	43	21	55
371	Electric wires	E	13,780	6,953	7,911	2,989	23
		n	68	118	11	5	1
		F	204	59	719	598	23
372	Motors, generators, transformers, switchgear, etc.	E	92,543	74,496	15,371	24,642	—
		n	679	1,549	107	228	—
		F	136	48	144	11	—
373	Electric accessories tools, welding apparatus, etc.	E	63,020	30,811	2,010	627	4
		n	2,108	88	42	92	1
		F	30	350	48	7	4

See notes at end of tables.

Table A.3 (cont.)

No. N.I.C.E.	Industry		France	Italy	Nether-lands	Belgium	Luxem-burg
374	Electrical measuring instruments	E	12,546	34,564	13,603	18,643	1
		n	201	400	66	53	1
		F	62	86	206	352	1
375	Electronic material, radio and television	E	97,762	22,273	67,513	14,820	—
		n	880	179	58	482	—
		F	111	124	1,164	31	—
376	Domestic electric appliances	E	29,311	19,074	6,227	3,061	—
		n	823	169	75	95	—
		F	36	113	83	32	—
377	Lamps and lighting fixtures	E	6,419	17,119	3,224	1,761	—
		n	60	285	154	68	—
		F	107	60	21	26	—
378	Batteries	E	10,812	2,892	1,120	1,260	—
		n	115	27	35	15	—
		F	87	107	32	84	—
379	Repair and fixing of electrical appliances	E	37,345	46,287	5,150	1,613	266
		n	4,038	9,171	1,286	986	25
		F	9	5	4	2	11
381	Shipbuilding and repairing	E	64,018	57,752	58,666	11,465	—
		n	1,202	692	1,028	166	—
		F	53	83	57	69	—

See notes at end of tables.

Table A.3 (cont.)

No. N.I.C.E.	Industry		France	Italy	Netherlands	Belgium	Luxemburg
382	Railroad and street cars	E	21,859	13,445	—ᵃ	6,766	—
		n	59	38	—	31	—
		$\bar{F}$	370	354	—	22	—
383	Automobiles and parts	E	323,065	172,595	18,257	22,560	—ˣ
		n	3,307	715	617	377	—
		$\bar{F}$	98	241	30	60	—
384	Independent repair of automobiles, motorcycles and cycles	E	93,363	125,461	66,180	19,018	1,654
		n	32,822	47,413	11,648	6,830	190
		$\bar{F}$	3	3	6	3	9
385	Motorcycles, cycles and parts	E	20,669	29,217	6,296	3,735	—
		n	494	271	95	361	—
		$\bar{F}$	42	108	66	10	—
386	Aircraft construction and repair	E	89,575	6,970	6,122ᵇ	16,836	—ˣ
		n	152	21	5	6	—
		$\bar{F}$	589	332	1,224	281	—
389	Transportation equipment, n.e.c.	E	61,095	6,936	2,477	482	206ʸ
		n	39,362	2,981	316	18	32
		$\bar{F}$	2	2	8	27	6
391	Measuring devices, controls	E	66,993	2,778	4,223	2,274	—
		n	2,295	168	123	62	—
		$\bar{F}$	29	17	34	37	—

See notes at end of tables.

Table A.3 (cont.)

No. N.I.C.E.	Industry		France	Italy	Netherlands	Belgium	Luxemburg
392	Surgical and medical instruments	E	14,484	6,021	2,914	1,398	−g
		n	3,480	1,013	530	583	−
		F	4	6	5	2	−
393	Ophtalmic goods and photographic equipment	E	5,132	15,450	2,259	1,346	−g
		n	295	598	531	176	−
		F	17	26	4	8	−
394	Watches and clocks	E	19,804	10,651	3,939	1,068	47
		n	587	4,038	1,476	875	32
		F	34	3	3	1	1
395	Jewelry, silverware and lapidary work	E	22,173	29,816	3,699	2,206	14
		n	3,823	4,418	644	533	9
		F	6	7	6	4	1
396	Musical instruments	E	3,322	7,174	2,322	345	−g
		n	384	646	408	68	−
		F	9	11	6	5	−
397	Games, toys and sporting goods	E	24,988	7,454	1,038	308	−
		n	1,820	361	97	155	−
		F	14	21	11	2	−
399	Miscellaneous products, n.e.c.	E	19,856	10,052	1,631	2,646	807[z]
		n	2,697	938	277	644	39
		F	7	11	6	4	21

See notes at end of tables.

Table A.4

Total employment (E), total number of establishments (n) and average size of establishments ($\bar{S} = E/n$)

No. N.I.C.E.	Industry		France	Italy	Netherlands	Belgium	Luxemburg
20A	Animal and vegetable fats and oils	E	13,667	39,153	5,986	4,497	—
		n	527	9,839	45	67	—
		S	26	4	133	67	—
201	Meat slaughtering and processing plants	E	35,476	25,582	22,576	8,018	1,366
		n	1,483	2,311	658	936	401
		S	24	11	34	9	3
202	Milk	E	73,774	30,457	29,582	7,979	507
		n	3,974	3,634	487	370	4
		S	19	8	61	22	127
203	Canned fruits and vegetables	E	23,203	45,927	11,483	5,354	—[a]
		n	674	1,115	218	83	—
		S	34	41	53	65	—
204	Canned and cured seafoods	E	11,198	5,416	3,037	1,638	—
		n	306	229	254	72	—
		S	37	24	12	23	—
205	Corn milling	E	28,944	45,621	3,396	5,702[a]	162
		n	6,054	14,149	130	699	14
		S	5	3	26	8	12
206	Bread and related products	E	31,057	60,288	71,954	49,032	1,781[b]
		n	1,177	14,705	10,956	13,659	463
		S	26	4	7	4	4

See notes at end of tables.

Table A.4 (cont.)

No. N.I.C.E.	Industry		France	Italy	Netherlands	Belgium	Luxemburg
207	Sugar	E	22,854	17,572	9,084	5,536	—
		n	181	132	24	40	—
		S	126	132	379	139	—
208	Cocoa, chocolate, confectionery products	E	27,101	21,885	16,588	8,916	—[c]
		n	1,144	772	305	370	—
		S	24	28	54	24	—
209	Other food preparations	E	33,650	47,246	21,795	11,663	247[d]
		n	2,029	3,833	1,935	820	19
		S	17	12	18	14	13
211	Fermentation alcohol, yeast, liquors	E	25,810	18,441	4,202	2,099	—[e]
		n	4,628	1,423	204	191	—
		S	6	13	11	11	—
212	Wines	E	13,486	21,523	—	685	245[f]
		n	1,660	2,483	—	50	16
		S	8	9	—	14	15
213	Beer and malt	E	20,318	6,228	5,872	19,666	673
		n	268	57	51	328	11
		S	76	109	115	9	61
214	Soft drinks	E	7,609	16,013	3,013	3,197	212
		n	1,067	2,105	224	170	9
		S	7	8	13	22	24

See notes at end of tables.

Table A.4 (cont.)

No. N.I.C.E.	Industry		France	Italy	Netherlands	Belgium	Luxemburg
220	Tobacco	E	13,478	26,561	16,822	9,322	−g
		n	36	771	171	291	−
		S	396	34	98	65	−
232	Wool	E	105,489	143,100	18,687	30,406	−g
		n	2,217	9,787	145	260	−
		S	48	15	129	117	−
233	Cotton	E	123,205	164,333	35,552	35,217	−
		n	1,408	2,861	179	548	−
		S	88	57	199	64	−
234	Silk	E	45,427	59,514	5,756	5,854	−
		n	3,281	1,931	20	89	−
		S	14	31	288	66	−
235	Linen and hemp	E	22,298	14,230	3,019	10,540	−
		n	401	739	261	1,574	−
		S	56	19	12	7	−
236	Other textile fibres (jute, etc.), cordage	E	17,512	9,855	5,737	7,979	−
		n	535	638	110	101	−
		S	33	15	52	79	−
237	Hosiery	E	92,715	123,731	18,699	20,721	−
		n	4,113	22,364	339	572	−
		S	23	6	55	36	−

See notes at end of tables.

Table A.4 (cont.)

No. N.I.C.E.	Industry		France	Italy	Nether-lands	Belgium	Luxem-burg
238	Textile finishing	E	40,687	39,174	7,260	9,758	—
		n	610	904	67	140	—
		S	67	43	108	70	—
239	Other textile industries	E	48,144	61,611	13,938	15,137	—
		n	3,900	12,033	587	828	—
		S	12	5	24	18	—
241	Foot-wear	E	86,338	104,401	19,039	16,049	—[g]
		n	2,700	5,784	435	527	—
		S	32	18	44	30	—
242	Shoe repair	E	2,609	69,905	12,006	6,586	237
		n	657	56,703	6,223	5,048	172
		S	4	1	2	1	1
243	Wearing apparel	E	300,185	309,094	93,640	70,640	1,400[h]
		n	54,782	108,494	6,702	13,766	455
		S	5	3	14	5	3
244	Mattresses and bedding	E	9,177	6,274	17,623	1,631	—[i]
		n	728	1,841	3,620	305	—
		S	13	3	5	5	—
245	Fur goods	E	9,202	7,368	1,900	3,820	97
		n	2,666	1,308	356	661	11
		S	3	6	5	6	9

See notes at end of tables.

Table A.4 (cont.)

No. N.I.C.E.	Industry		France	Italy	Netherlands	Belgium	Luxemburg
251	Sawmills and planing mills	E	47,447	23,611	4,887	6,439	405
		n	9,045	4,540	252	774	30
		S	5	5	19	8	14
252	Semifinished wood products	E	76,453[a]	19,262	3,033	5,868	—
		n	6,225	398	60	77	—
		S	12	48	51	76	—
253	Frames, carpentry, floors	E	144,150	138,220	14,034	4,852	—
		n	49,204	58,269	808	1,124	—
		S	3	2	17	4	—
254	Wood packing	E	—[b]	24,299	5,756	2,041	—[j]
		n	—	4,804	283	213	—
		S	—	5	20	10	—
255	Other wood products	E	4,374	17,916	5,930	4,940	71[k]
		n	2,129	2,627	1,059	1,029	14
		S	2	7	6	4	5
259	Cork products, cane chairs, brushes	E	22,318	15,059	4,001	2,625	—[j]
		n	5,487	2,914	446	631	—
		S	4	5	9	4	—
260	Wood furniture	E	89,055	135,886	28,908	23,418	516
		n	16,486	29,102	3,359	3,480	119
		S	5	5	9	7	4

See notes at end of tables.

Table A.4 (cont.)

No. N.I.C.E.	Industry		France	Italy	Nether-lands	Belgium	Luxem-burg
271	Pulp, paper and board	E	51,730	46,106	14,023	8,209	—g
		n	350	739	48	36	—
		S	148	62	292	228	—
272	Paper and board products	E	73,438	39,635	19,926	17,382	—
		n	2,362	2,141	414	462	—
		S	31	19	48	38	—
280	Printing and publishing	E	175,937	110,212	72,620	35,287	806
		n	11,770	9,447	3,349	3,689	62
		S	15	12	22	10	13
291	Tannery, tawery	E	20,224	21,258	3,968	3,709	—g
		n	663	1,270	131	120	—
		S	31	17	30	31	—
292	Leather products	E	36,769	29,197	7,484	4,352	12
		n	9,261	4,809	697	801	9
		S	4	6	11	5	1
301	Synthetic rubber and asbestos	E	90,747	53,191	12,969	8,264	1,282l
		n	1,556	3,057	212	187	6
		S	58	17	61	44	214
302	Plastic materials	E	52,060	44,214	9,522	6,771	—m
		n	2,520	2,863	411	224	—
		S	21	15	23	30	—

See notes at end of tables.

Table A.4 (cont.)

No.; N.I.C.E.	Industry		France	Italy	Netherlands	Belgium	Luxemburg
303	Artificial and synthetic fibres	E	31,875	32,718	17,045	4,528	—
		n	86	42	13	5	—
		S	371	779	1,311	906	
304	Starch, glue and gelatin	E	3,628	175	4,492	—b	—
		n	52	6	31	—	—
		S	70	29	145	—	—
311	Production and transformation of basic chemicals	E	126,395	89,470	27,267	15,545	321n
		n	1,789	1,396	170	59	13
		S	71	64	160	263	25
312	Industrial and agricultural chemicals	E	49,340	51,389	18,289	14,307	—o
		n	1,574	2,084	519	447	—
		S	31	25	35	32	—
313	Chemicals for domestic consumption	E	103,958	76,229	19,222	21,635	63
		n	2,988	2,602	437	386	9
		S	35	29	44	56	7
320	Petroleum	E	31,661	14,329	8,712	2,204c	—
		n	238	219	30	6	—
		S	133	65	290	367	—
331	Baked clay products	E	27,682	79,548	13,377	10,612	—p
		n	1,293	2,170	300	431	—
		S	21	37	45	25	—

See notes at end of tables.

Table A.4 (cont.)

No. N.I.C.E.	Industry		France	Italy	Netherlands	Belgium	Luxemburg
332	Glass	E	59,353	50,454	6,246	27,006	—q
		n	1,352	2,547	267	206	—
		$\bar{S}$	44	20	23	131	—
333	China, pottery, fire-proof products	E	38,537	49,806	10,456	7,914	1,185[r]
		n	1,233	2,284	295	145	6
		$\bar{S}$	31	22	35	55	198
334	Cement, lime, plaster	E	18,988	29,919	1,302	4,684	—p
		n	403	1,381	24	28	—
		$\bar{S}$	47	22	54	167	—
335	Concrete products	E	38,914	57,202	23,034	17,124	412
		n	2,527	4,712	827	835	5
		$\bar{S}$	15	12	28	21	82
339	Stone and non-metallic mineral products	E	20,993	49,401	3,879	6,913	304[s]
		n	4,088	6,799	518	1,579	32
		$\bar{S}$	5	7	7	4	10
341	Steel mills (according to E.C.C.S. treaty)	E	196,706	107,288	18,595	73,247	26,921
		n	179	524	4	48	3
		$\bar{S}$	1,099	205	4,649	1,526	8,974
342	Steel tubes	E	21,258	40,932	1,943	1,603	—
		n	92	509	7	7	—
		$\bar{S}$	231	80	278	229	—

See notes at end of tables.

Table A.4 (cont.)

No. N.I.C.E.	Industry		France	Italy	Nether-lands	Belgium	Luxem-burg
343	Wire-drawing, rolling, cold finishing, etc.	E	29,918	8,549	5,441	14,297	—
		n	364	214	158	63	—
		S	82	40	34	227	—
344	Primary non-ferrous metals	E	52,382	40,241	4,025	22,074	—[t]
		n	442	1,218	38	44	—
		S	119	33	106	502	—
345	Foundries (ferrous and non-ferrous)	E	109,565	61,556	10,730	16,850	200[u]
		n	2,153	2,239	194	390	9
		S	51	27	55	43	22
351	Forgings, punching, stamping, etc.	E	27,004	5,593	856	96	—
		n	355	194	8	17	—
		S	76	29	107	6	—
352	Second transformation of metals	E	131,802	41,962	8,884	11,444	—[v]
		n	11,880	5,500	809	972	—
		S	11	8	11	12	—
353	Metallic construction	E	32,490	62,647	33,095	19,584	1,848[w]
		n	433	3,503	1,355	1,054	103
		S	75	18	24	19	18
354	Boiler works	E	76,216	4,325	8,768	5,030	—[v]
		n	3,341	90	188	198	—
		S	22	48	47	25	—

See notes at end of tables.

Table A.4 (cont.)

No. N.I.C.E.	Industry		France	Italy	Netherlands	Belgium	Luxemburg
355	Metal tools	E	193,928	114,630	53,352	33,929	205
		n	14,955	5,648	1,345	1,753	14
		S	13	20	40	19	15
359	Auxiliary activities of metallic industries	E	635	147,049	15,966	5,261	382
		n	390	53,397	5,028	3,380	157
		S	2	3	3	2	2
361	Farm machinery and equipment	E	39,845	21,334	3,094	4,320	27
		n	868	664	119	154	1
		S	46	32	26	28	27
362	Office machines	E	28,748	25,003	6,768	—d	7
		n	747	456	259	—	4
		S	38	55	26	—	2
363	Metal cutting machine tools	E	64,871	47,635	5,413	6,698e	75
		n	1,844	1,486	219	169	2
		S	35	32	25	40	38
364	Textile machinery, sewing machines	E	17,983	36,369	2,236	6,327	—
		n	573	479	264	166	—
		S	31	76	8	38	—
365	Food products machinery	E	24,230	20,298	10,068	4,603	—
		n	1,047	484	233	129	—
		S	23	42	43	36	—

See notes at end of tables.

Table A.4 (cont.)

No. N.I.C.E.	Industry		France	Italy	Netherlands	Belgium	Luxemburg
366	Mining, steel-work, machinery, cranes, etc.	E	54,763	29,191	11,458	16,526	368
		n	949	610	218	204	3
		S	58	48	53	81	123
367	Transmission equipment	E	3,146	23,398	1,907	1,449	—
		n	37	261	27	27	—
		S	85	90	71	54	—
368	Other specific machinery	E	6,969	15,096	3,373	2,832	—
		n	188	537	116	107	—
		S	37	28	29	26	—
369	Other non-electric machinery	E	131,699	71,509	46,770	13,737	218
		n	2,582	3,962	1,237	653	4
		S	51	18	38	21	55
371	Electric wires	E	24,561	8,578	5,979	2,989	23
		n	123	136	18	6	1
		S	200	63	332	498	23
372	Motors, generators, transformers, switch-gear, etc.	E	90,702	76,844	16,375	24,394	—
		n	913	1,740	144	233	—
		S	99	44	114	195	—
373	Electric accessories, tools, welding apparatus, etc.	E	65,403	7,880	2,417	627	4
		n	2,277	96	46	92	1
		S	29	82	53	7	4

See notes at end of tables

Table A.4 (cont.)

No. N.I.C.E.	Industry		France	Italy	Netherlands	Belgium	Luxemburg
374	Electrical measuring instruments	E	16,742	38,148	13,798	19,311	1
		n	257	491	86	61	1
		S	65	78	160	317	1
375	Electronic material, radio and television	E	88,150	23,060	55,455	12,534	—
		n	1,072	219	91	483	—
		S	82	105	609	26	—
376	Domestic electric appliances	E	32,260	34,284	8,891	3,061	—
		n	917	230	102	95	—
		S	35	149	87	32	—
377	Lamps and lighting fixtures	E	5,683	14,400	8,019	3,638	—
		n	80	317	173	69	—
		S	71	45	46	53	—
378	Batteries	E	12,018	2,495	960	1,260	—
		n	149	31	37	15	—
		S	81	80	26	84	—
379	Repair and fixing of electrical appliances	E	23,839	49,390	8,270	1,613	266
		n	4,163	9,835	1,468	986	25
		S	6	5	6	2	11
381	Ship building and repairing	E	99,337	51,308	53,772	14,005	—
		n	1,375	779	1,091	170	—
		S	72	66	49	82	—

See notes at end of tables.

Table A.4 (cont.)

No. N.I.C.E.	Industry		France	Italy	Nether-lands	Belgium	Luxem-burg
382	Railroad and street cars	E	86,498	21,726	3,232	4,934	—
		n	367	63	1	32	—
		S	236	345	3,232	154	—
383	Automobiles and parts	E	298,758	129,570	17,842	22,622	—x
		n	3,576	815	665	382	—
		S	83	159	27	59	—
384	Independent repair of automobiles, motor-cycles and cycles	E	100,396	130,205	66,843	19,018	1,654
		n	33,069	48,311	12,391	6,830	190
		S	3	3	5	3	9
385	Motorcycles, cycles and parts	E	22,247	26,511	6,200	3,735	—
		n	543	302	111	361	—
		S	41	88	56	10	—
386	Aircraft construction and repair	E	96,221	12,047	6,169	16,427	—x
		n	267	43	9	7	—
		S	360	280	685	2,347	—
389	Transportation equip-ment, n.e.c.	E	61,404	6,971	2,350	482	206y
		n	39,399	3,018	317	18	32
		S	2	2	7	27	6
391	Measuring devices, controls	E	67,002	2,704	4,096	2,274	—
		n	2,496	177	131	63	—
		S	27	15	31	36	—

See notes at end of tables.

Table A.4 (cont.)

No. N.I.C.E.	Industry		France	Italy	Netherlands	Belgium	Luxemburg
392	Surgical and medical instruments	E	14,497	6,497	3,065	1,398	$-g$
		n	3,530	1,056	562	583	–
		S	4	6	5	2	–
393	Ophtalmic goods and photographic equipment	E	5,230	15,644	2,418	1,346	$-g$
		n	309	667	610	176	–
		S	17	23	4	8	–
394	Watches and clocks	E	20,031	10,433	3,993	1,068	47
		n	635	4,133	1,522	875	32
		S	32	3	3	1	1
395	Jewelry, silverware and lapidary work	E	21,938	30,016	3,970	2,206	14
		n	3,886	4,542	668	533	9
		S	6	7	6	4	1
396	Musical instruments	E	3,324	7,232	2,277	345	$-g$
		n	406	675	428	68	–
		S	8	11	5	5	–
397	Games, toys and sporting goods	E	24,706	7,309	984	308	–
		n	1,891	369	107	155	–
		S	13	20	9	2	–
399	Miscellaneous products, n.e.c.	E	19,942	10,322	1,626	2,646	807^z
		n	2,756	998	285	644	39
		S	8	10	6	4	21

See notes at end of tables.

Table A.5

Estimated average number of persons employed by the 4, 8, 20 and 50 largest companies[1]

No. N.I.C.E.	Industry	France	Italy	Netherlands	Belgium	Luxemburg
20A	Animal and vegetable fats and oils	2,360	645	922	843	–
		1,342	415	652	467	–
		630	240	305	207	–
		280	125	–	88	–
201	Meat slaughtering and processing plants	1,888	1,025	1,594	361	17
		1,220	664	1,082	231	12
		629	362	604	128	9
		327	208	310	67	7
202	Milk	3,083	2,265	1,278	299	127
		2,120	1,426	940	219	–
		1,195	705	586	144	–
		663	336	343	89	–
203	Canned fruits and vegetables	884	2,265	892	806	–[a]
		678	1,472	662	504	–
		483	861	386	242	–
		283	498	191	106	–
204	Canned and cured seafoods	318	312	149	176	–
		281	265	125	123	–
		200	182	83	68	–
		133	96	51	32	–
205	Corn milling	730	349	506	394[a]	29
		511	232	351	296	19
		278	163	163	175	–
		152	112	69	87	–
206	Bread and related products	1,098	2,523	1,419	1,103	31[b]
		879	1,577	976	613	22
		557	788	532	319	15
		340	378	298	167	10
207	Sugar	2,638	2,898	2,179	1,058	–
		1,696	1,840	–	593	–
		917	874	–	275	–
		457	–	–	–	–

[1] The four numbers corresponding to each industry and country measure the average number of persons employed by the 4, 8, 20 and 50 largest companies respectively. See notes at end of tables.

Table A.5 (cont.)

No. N.I.C.E.	Industry	France	Italy	Nether-lands	Bel-gium	Luxem-burg
208	Cocoa, chocolate,	972	2,178	867	669	$-^c$
	confectionery products	778	1,369	659	435	–
		519	734	416	254	–
		316	373	228	143	–
209	Other food preparations	948	935	1,053	471	35^d
		751	643	748	368	25
		474	467	410	253	–
		272	290	217	141	–
211	Fermentation alcohol	878	679	274	157	$-^e$
	yeast, liquors	743	521	192	125	–
		486	308	116	73	–
		275	174	67	34	–
212	Wines	363	701	–	$-^f$	28^f
		280	486	–	–	24
		198	291	–	–	–
		124	160	–	–	–
213	Beer and malt	1,273	912	1,085	984	111
		928	661	712	787	78
		594	350	332	502	–
		339	–	–	279	–
214	Soft drinks	598	735	215	283	41
		422	510	153	190	27
		228	278	94	110	–
		115	140	50	56	–
220	Tobacco	–	6,002	1,225	864	$-^g$
		–	3,078	988	689	–
		–	1,293	664	392	–
		–	548	310	177	–
232	Wool	3,739	6,954	944	1,542	$-^g$
		2,938	4,392	779	1,195	–
		1,869	2,416	529	787	–
		1,090	1,288	325	469	–
233	Cotton	6,334	5,824	2,451	2,216	–
		4,000	4,465	1,906	1,596	–
		2,267	3,029	1,271	957	–
		1,333	1,771	683	546	–

See notes at end of tables.

Table A.5 (cont.)

No. N.I.C.E.	Industry	France	Italy	Netherlands	Belgium	Luxemburg
234	Silk	1,611	1,733	1,006	525	–
		1,093	1,299	627	350	–
		668	809	–	204	–
		387	531	–	109	–
235	Linen and hemp	1,638	1,933	234	445	–
		1,112	1,140	165	369	–
		655	557	84	227	–
		370	263	42	116	–
236	Other textile fibres, (jute, etc.), cordage	2,427	570	770	559	–
		1,610	442	491	479	–
		773	259	241	319	–
		357	124	107	155	–
237	Hosiery	1,634	1,225	1,360	518	–
		1,401	1,071	971	389	–
		1,074	735	583	280	–
		728	465	334	186	–
238	Textile finishing	3,538	2,867	1,119	537	–
		2,056	1,985	656	439	–
		1,014	1,058	289	293	–
		520	547	119	170	–
239	Other textile industries	1,167	1,706	848	453	–
		817	1,137	618	340	–
		490	597	375	242	–
		308	341	204	157	–
241	Foot-wear	2,942	1,050	1,586	645	–[g]
		1,923	788	921	484	–
		1,177	578	481	314	–
		688	378	282	184	–
242	Shoe repair	111	40	29	5	5
		85	32	18	5	4
		52	25	17	5	3
		30	15	12	5	2
243	Wearing apparel	1,449	1,514	1,632	705	70[f]
		1,449	1,135	1,282	529	49
		1,014	757	886	353	28
		753	545	541	254	15

See notes at end of tables.

Table A.5 (cont.)

No. N.I.C.E.	Industry	France	Italy	Nether-lands	Bel-gium	Luxem-burg
244	Mattresses and bedding	575	339	121	102	_[i]
		368	218	121	77	–
		216	123	89	46	–
		118	63	58	23	–
245	Fur goods	235	273	70	134	17
		176	191	56	95	11
		103	116	37	78	–
		58	64	22	41	–
251	Sawmills and planing	233	176	119	128	62
	mills	233	176	95	81	41
		163	129	83	58	19
		112	90	60	40	–
252	Semifinished wood	1,907[a]	588	433	908	–
	products	1,335	430	260	522	–
		801	290	125	254	–
		458	188	56	119	–
253	Frames, carpentry,	361	691	648	146	–
	floors	351	345	426	115	–
		216	276	252	75	–
		144	166	136	45	–
254	Wood packing	_[b]	178	351	87	_[j]
		–	149	246	64	–
		–	119	157	46	–
		–	76	88	30	–
255	Other wood products	97	470	119	222	14[k]
		80	353	104	154	8
		58	226	84	94	–
		33	139	53	52	–
259	Cork products, cane	629	218	286	98	_[j]
	chairs, brushes	429	182	188	72	–
		240	138	105	46	–
		142	82	56	27	–
260	Wood furniture	658	339	285	292	26
		548	339	250	263	19
		395	271	186	187	13
		246	190	131	140	8

See notes at end of tables.

Table A.5 (cont.)

No. N.I.C.E.	Industry	France	Italy	Nether-lands	Bel-gium	Luxem-burg
271	Pulp, paper and board	3,489	2,459	2,161	1,200	_g
		2,550	1,788	1,300	847	–
		1,503	1,140	652	425	–
		859	626	–	–	–
272	Paper and board products	879	685	623	1,138	–
		703	538	551	717	–
		528	372	393	413	–
		408	258	245	229	–
280	Printing and publishing	3,152	2,814	1,458	802	101
		2,251	1,829	1,093	713	64
		1,621	1,013	729	481	33
		1,009	585	481	292	16
291	Tannery, tawery	816	662	280	425	_g
		638	509	190	323	–
		418	326	122	161	–
		241	183	69	69	–
292	Leather products	545	436	222	131	2
		454	327	176	104	1
		309	234	115	66	–
		196	134	76	38	–
301	Synthetic rubber and asbestos	11,271	7,976	1,329	1,139	317[l]
		6,424	4,440	981	735	–
		3,066	2,017	506	356	–
		1,425	903	235	157	–
302	Plastic materials	690	987	425	273	_m
		575	658	324	209	–
		437	461	206	145	–
		295	272	118	91	–
303	Artificial and synthetic fibres	7,039	7,735	4,475	–	–
		4,028	4,401	–	–	–
		1,696	–	–	–	–
		–	–	–	–	–
304	Starch, glue and gelatin	803	172	591	_b	–
		440	–	387	–	–
		192	–	206	–	–
		–	–	–	–	–

See notes at end of tables.

Table A.5 (cont.)

No. N.I.C.E.	Industry	France	Italy	Netherlands	Belgium	Luxemburg
311	Production and transformation of basic chemicals	10,951	5,604	1,456	2,704	56[n]
		7,353	4,252	1,141	1,788	37
		3,692	2,474	689	855	–
		1,852	1,190	357	349	–
312	Industrial and agricultural chemicals	2,028	12,300	797	950	–o
		1,521	6,560	664	651	–
		924	2,829	416	394	–
		514	1,263	244	222	–
313	Chemicals for domestic consumption	4,073	3,180	1,638	2,752	14
		2,987	2,385	1,191	1,584	8
		1,738	1,391	635	758	–
		999	811	322	353	–
320	Petroleum	5,398	1,405	2,269	479[c]	–
		3,599	1,028	1,182	–	–
		1,521	569	478	–	–
		–	261	–	–	–
331	Baked clay products	759	1,181	301	613	–p
		586	885	251	426	–
		386	590	187	261	–
		243	394	134	145	–
332	Glass	5,875	1,743	764	4,248	–q
		3,540	1,183	546	2,542	–
		1,928	697	259	1,254	–
		940	399	112	540	–
333	China, pottery, fire-proof products	2,171	2,148	467	830	290[r]
		1,583	1,516	315	550	–
		959	910	182	293	–
		514	515	95	144	–
334	Cement, lime, plaster	1,871	2,467	302	936	–p
		1,193	1,619	156	579	–
		655	802	–	246	–
		326	395	–	–	–
335	Concrete products	2,183	1,844	827	1,226	103
		1,319	1,135	579	697	–
		637	596	353	372	–
		320	318	221	199	–

See notes at end of tables.

Table A.5 (cont.)

No. N.I.C.E.	Industry	France	Italy	Netherlands	Belgium	Luxemburg
339	Stone and non-metallic	515	493	133	219	52[s]
	mineral products	412	432	105	155	30
		227	296	74	91	14
		124	178	44	48	–
341	Steel mills (according	23,381	15,728	–	13,832	–
	to E.C.C.S. treaty)	18,705	9,268	–	8,701	–
		10,638	4,381	–	4,328	–
		4,676	1,977	–	–	–
342	Steel tubes	2,407	4,590	451	243	–
		1,444	2,493	–	–	–
		660	1,124	–	–	–
		275	506	–	–	–
343	Wire-drawing, rolling	2,343	496	499	1,952	–
	cold finishing, etc.	1,704	367	374	1,091	–
		980	228	213	522	–
		483	120	99	230	–
344	Primary nonferrous	7,559	2,921	722	2,652	–[t]
	metals	4,549	2,044	442	2,072	–
		2,184	1,071	197	1,072	–
		1,019	514	–	–	–
345	Foundries (ferrous and	4,779	908	837	705	41[u]
	nonferrous)	3,144	649	684	560	24
		1,861	519	375	398	–
		1,026	342	183	232	–
351	Forgings, punching,	846	244	202	15	–
	stamping, etc.	726	210	–	10	–
		544	160	–	–	–
		343	88	–	–	–
352	Second transformation of	616	522	461	597	–[v]
	metals	616	470	340	398	–
		492	313	198	228	–
		369	200	105	123	–
353	Metallic construction	1,512	1,260	1,015	913	254[w]
		1,050	945	741	745	155
		689	598	468	432	77
		403	365	268	230	35

See notes at end of tables.

Table A.5 (cont.)

No. N.I.C.E.	Industry	France	Italy	Nether- lands	Bel- gium	Luxem- burg
354	Boiler-works	2,872	330	689	340	$-^v$
		1,915	232	468	252	–
		1,187	132	246	151	–
		643	66	119	83	–
355	Metal tools	3,265	1,415	1,753	1,016	32
		2,332	1,132	1,350	889	24
		1,399	679	944	559	–
		896	453	561	339	–
359	Auxiliary activities of metallic industries	16	364	78	5	24
		10	182	59	5	17
		7	146	39	5	9
		6	87	28	5	5
361	Farm machinery and equipment	3,219	695	221	637	–
		1,988	521	156	373	–
		985	338	91	179	–
		500	207	51	79	–
362	Office machines	5,229	6,913	479	$-^d$	2
		3,278	3,823	669	–	–
		1,436	1,562	294	–	–
		599	638	124	–	–
363	Metal-cutting machine tools	2,095	993	270	659^e	–
		1,531	772	216	566	–
		967	530	138	284	–
		580	335	80	127	–
364	Textile machinery, sewing machines	1,083	3,055	135	845	–
		824	2,037	100	538	–
		480	1,111	59	261	–
		260	555	29	118	–
365	Food products ma- chinery	778	615	659	403	–
		569	512	448	258	–
		383	379	258	152	–
		230	238	152	78	–
366	Mining, steel-work ma- chinery, cranes, etc.	1,886	1,559	553	1,635	–
		1,415	1,169	456	1,176	–
		943	702	293	598	–
		582	387	168	277	–

See notes at end of tables.

Table A.5 (cont.)

No. N.I.C.E.	Industry	France	Italy	Netherlands	Belgium	Luxemburg
367	Transmission equipment	588	3,661	412	170	–
		355	1,976	239	130	–
		162	907	109	69	–
		–	414	–	–	–
368	Other specific machinery	573	989	288	361	–
		399	653	191	230	–
		232	348	119	118	–
		124	187	61	53	–
369	Other non-electric machinery	8,835	1,901	4,467	645	55
		6,217	1,347	2,821	560	–
		3,338	887	1,387	373	–
		1,702	545	658	198	–
371	Electric wires	1,791	678	1,879	747	–
		1,154	461	989	–	–
		606	250	–	–	–
		273	127	–	–	–
372	Motors, generators, transformers, switchgear, etc.	9,717	2,235	1,768	4,744	–
		6,594	1,676	1,172	2,557	–
		3,193	1,117	623	1,121	–
		1,499	670	292	478	–
373	Electric accessories, tools, welding apparatus, etc.	4,254	5,392	296	92	–
		2,836	3,351	181	53	–
		1,544	1,448	91	24	–
		756	610	–	12	–
374	Electrical measuring instruments	1,066	3,543	2,619	4,474	–
		784	2,376	1,411	2,307	–
		452	1,227	653	932	–
		221	574	272	–	–
375	Electronic material, radio and television	10,509	1,949	16,372	2,927	–
		6,232	1,309	8,270	1,575	–
		3,177	735	3,342	674	–
		1,545	401	1,350	285	–
376	Domestic electric appliances	1,832	2,050	545	275	–
		1,429	1,311	444	191	–
		821	744	268	126	–
		434	347	123	60	–

See notes at end of tables.

Table A.5 (cont.)

No. N.I.C.E.	Industry	France	Italy	Netherlands	Belgium	Luxemburg
377	Lamps and lighting	1,204	2,568	258	247	–
	fixtures	666	1,519	197	147	–
		298	710	111	75	–
		128	312	56	35	–
378	Batteries	2,135	398	185	246	–
		1,216	282	119	143	–
		524	142	54	–	–
		214	–	–	–	–
379	Repair and fixing of	4,948	694	64	5	50
	electrical appliances	2,708	579	52	5	29
		1,195	347	36	5	13
		523	194	21	5	–
381	Ship building and	5,922	8,952	4,253	1,662	–
	repairing	4,001	5,198	3,080	946	–
		2,145	2,368	1,731	457	–
		999	1,028	857	213	–
382	Railroad and street	1,858	1,277	–[a]	1,303	–
	cars	1,721	1,025	–	744	–
		1,016	652	–	335	–
		437	–	–	–	–
383	Automobiles and parts	40,383	31,067	1,917	2,313	–[x]
		25,038	16,397	1,278	1,523	–
		12,438	6,904	566	778	–
		5,492	2,969	270	374	–
384	Independent repair of	233	314	331	143	95
	automobiles, motor-	117	157	331	119	66
	cycles and cycles	93	125	265	76	38
		75	75	159	49	25
385	Motorcycles, cycles	2,222	4,017	488	467	–
	and parts	1,343	2,374	362	280	–
		661	1,154	233	136	–
		318	526	120	63	–
386	Aircraft construction	12,764	1,289	1,531[b]	4,167	–[x]
	and repair	7,838	802	–	–	–
		3,897	349	–	–	–
		1,756	–	–	–	–

See notes at end of tables.

Table A.5 (cont.)

No. N.I.C.E.	Industry	France	Italy	Netherlands	Belgium	Luxemburg
389	Transportation equipment, n.e.c.	55	295	167	96	38[y]
		42	173	133	55	22
		31	94	82	–	10
		24	46	41	–	–
391	Measuring devices, controls	4,857	167	496	500	–
		3,015	132	333	264	–
		1,608	81	175	110	–
		831	46	80	45	–
392	Surgical and medical instruments	253	301	95	24	–[g]
		217	218	80	21	–
		145	117	57	14	–
		84	63	33	9	–
393	Ophtalmic goods and photographic equipment	372	1,043	85	178	–[g]
		282	715	65	111	–
		172	394	37	53	–
		87	207	20	24	–
394	Watches and clocks	1,188	1,012	89	8	3
		817	559	54	7	2
		455	250	28	6	2
		257	109	16	5	–
395	Jewelry, silverware and lapidary work	499	596	129	143	2
		360	410	97	94	2
		244	253	65	52	–
		160	155	38	27	–
396	Musical instruments	266	413	136	37	–[g]
		187	287	102	25	–
		101	165	60	14	–
		52	93	32	6	–
397	Games, toys and sporting goods	687	373	83	5	–
		562	280	62	5	–
		387	175	37	5	–
		235	103	19	3	–
399	Miscellaneous products, n.e.c.	596	427	57	79	153[z]
		472	289	53	63	90
		268	161	39	46	39
		147	92	22	29	–

See notes at end of tables.

Table A.6

Estimated average number of persons employed by the 4, 8, 20 and 50 largest establishments. [1]

No. N.I.C.E.	Industry	France	Italy	Netherlands	Belgium	Luxemburg
20A	Animal and vegetable	991	392	868	787	–
	fats and oils	718	294	546	455	–
		437	196	272	207	–
		221	117	–	86	–
201	Meat slaughtering and	1,242	959	1,355	361	17
	processing plants	1,064	640	875	231	12
		639	345	531	124	9
		348	205	289	67	7
202	Milk	922	838	814	299	127
		646	609	592	219	–
		480	396	385	144	–
		325	213	254	88	–
203	Canned fruit and	522	1,378	861	589	–[a]
	vegetables	464	976	632	455	–
		348	620	362	230	–
		223	404	191	105	–
204	Canned and cured	224	284	121	112	–
	seafoods	196	230	106	78	–
		162	157	70	43	–
		123	89	42	20	–
205	Corn milling	507	228	357	399[a]	29
		398	171	267	292	19
		172	114	144	174	–
		127	82	65	88	–
206	Bread and related	776	1,809	899	1,103	31[b]
	products	699	1,130	630	613	22
		463	633	396	319	15
		311	301	245	167	10
207	Sugar	1,257	791	1,022	844	–
		914	681	818	498	–
		571	510	454	246	–
		338	299	–	–	–

[1] The four numbers corresponding to each industry and country measure the average number of persons employed by the 4, 8, 20 and 50 largest establishments respectively. See notes at end of tables.

Table A.6 (cont.)

No. N.I.C.E.	Industry	France	Italy	Nether-lands	Bel-gium	Luxem-burg
208	Cocoa, chocolate,	813	1,532	995	669	_c
	confectionery products	644	1,012	788	435	–
		461	558	481	254	–
		304	298	259	143	–
209	Other food preparations	589	708	654	467	35d
		505	531	490	364	25
		387	401	316	251	–
		242	255	183	140	–
211	Fermentation alcohol,	581	369	210	163	_e
	yeast, liquors	516	300	152	131	–
		348	203	101	78	–
		206	133	61	37	–
212	Wines	337	1,159	–	_f	28f
		253	837	–	–	24
		169	567	–	–	–
		111	319	–	–	–
213	Beer and malt	762	498	749	983	111
		610	381	521	787	78
		417	252	276	501	–
		264	125	117	279	–
214	Soft drinks	171	560	173	280	41
		143	380	128	188	27
		95	216	80	109	–
		56	118	43	56	–
220	Tobacco	607	1,129	967	629	_g
		573	1,029	820	559	–
		505	744	564	354	–
		–	404	310	175	–
232	Wool	3,428	3,220	841	1,216	_g
		2,505	2,504	607	950	–
		1,530	1,717	448	669	–
		871	1,059	303	438	–
233	Cotton	1,540	2,465	1,600	1,409	–
		1,232	2,054	1,422	1,145	–
		924	1,561	978	775	–
		665	1,117	604	486	–

See notes at end of tables.

Table A.6 (cont.)

No. N.I.C.E.	Industry	France	Italy	Nether-lands	Bel-gium	Luxem-burg
234	Silk	570	1,041	921	527	–
		454	893	583	344	–
		341	625	288	205	–
		227	417	–	109	–
235	Linen and hemp	1,003	854	264	422	–
		697	658	185	369	–
		479	413	94	227	–
		308	220	56	116	–
236	Other textile fibres, (jute, etc.), cordage	919	616	617	559	–
		788	517	437	479	–
		517	325	235	319	–
		277	158	110	155	–
237	Hosiery	1,159	928	982	518	–
		836	773	701	389	–
		788	619	458	280	–
		575	396	254	186	–
238	Textile finishing	1,526	979	1,162	537	–
		1,068	832	762	439	–
		691	607	345	293	–
		431	384	145	170	–
239	Other textile industries	1,083	2,002	662	454	–
		722	1,309	470	341	–
		457	678	321	242	–
		279	382	184	157	–
241	Foot-wear	1,511	783	857	642	–[g]
		1,295	653	571	461	–
		863	470	343	305	–
		553	334	206	180	–
242	Shoe repair	98	34	30	5	5
		75	26	15	5	4
		44	24	12	5	3
		26	16	10	5	2
243	Wearing apparel	751	1,545	702	530	70[h]
		750	1,159	585	442	49
		750	927	468	353	28
		540	556	337	240	15

See notes at end of tables.

Table A.6 (cont.)

No. N.I.C.E.	Industry	France	Italy	Nether- lands	Bel- gium	Luxem- burg
244	Mattresses and bedding	321	298	132	102	_[i]
		241	188	132	77	–
		174	107	97	46	–
		105	58	63	23	–
245	Fur goods	184	276	67	134	17
		150	193	52	110	11
		92	118	35	78	–
		53	68	21	41	–
251	Sawmills and planing mills	237	177	98	97	62
		178	148	92	72	41
		142	106	76	55	19
		104	71	49	37	–
252	Semifinished wood pro- ducts	765[a]	385	432	853	–
		669	337	269	499	–
		535	260	130	244	–
		352	185	60	115	–
253	Frames, carpentry, floors	360	346	632	146	–
		360	346	386	115	–
		216	276	232	75	–
		144	166	132	45	–
254	Wood packing	_[b]	243	302	87	_[j]
		–	182	216	64	–
		–	121	144	46	–
		–	78	84	30	–
255	Other wood products	98	403	119	222	14[k]
		82	291	96	154	8
		61	197	77	94	–
		30	125	50	52	–
259	Cork products, cane chairs, brushes	502	226	220	98	_[j]
		307	169	160	72	–
		190	128	94	46	–
		112	81	53	27	–
260	Wood furniture	490	340	289	293	26
		445	340	253	263	19
		356	272	173	187	13
		232	190	116	126	8

See notes at end of tables.

Table A.6 (cont.)

No. N.I.C.E.	Industry	France	Italy	Netherlands	Belgium	Luxemburg
271	Pulp, paper and board	1,552	1,153	1,332	739	_g
		1,228	980	999	585	–
		905	761	554	386	–
		610	516	–	–	–
272	Paper and board products	734	595	548	869	–
		551	495	473	630	–
		441	337	359	391	–
		323	238	235	233	–
280	Printing and publishing	2,199	1,929	1,089	706	101
		1,759	1,515	908	662	64
		1,232	827	617	476	33
		809	507	421	282	16
291	Tannery, tawery	556	691	278	427	_g
		506	505	198	320	–
		364	329	119	161	–
		218	187	67	70	–
292	Leather products	462	438	206	131	2
		370	292	159	103	1
		277	204	109	65	–
		185	128	72	38	–
301	Synthetic rubber and asbestos	7,260	4,654	1,102	1,136	317[l]
		4,651	2,926	892	733	–
		2,496	1,516	480	355	–
		1,270	723	231	137	–
302	Plastic materials	911	663	333	271	_m
		716	553	286	212	–
		440	398	190	149	–
		333	248	116	95	–
303	Artificial and synthetic fibres	3,108	3,354	2,685	1,030	–
		2,231	2,617	2,003	–	–
		1,339	1,554	852	–	–
		631	–	–	–	–
304	Starch, glue and gelatin	562	42	539	_b	–
		349	–	376	–	–
		167	–	207	–	–
		73	–	90	–	–

See notes at end of tables.

Table A.6 (cont.)

No. N.I.C.E.	Industry	France	Italy	Netherlands	Belgium	Luxemburg
311	Production and transformation of basic chemicals	3,476	3,355	2,590	1,360	56[n]
		2,844	3,020	1,806	1,127	37
		1,833	1,924	954	700	–
		1,163	1,127	485	311	–
312	Industrial and agricultural chemicals	987	2,826	732	715	–[o]
		863	1,863	548	537	–
		617	976	375	343	–
		414	514	223	209	–
313	Chemicals for domestic consumption	2,079	1,906	1,346	2,704	14
		1,559	1,334	913	1,569	8
		988	991	529	757	–
		645	625	284	359	–
320	Petroleum	1,662	931	1,873	479[c]	–
		1,464	788	1,024	–	–
		1,140	487	431	–	–
		576	252	174	–	–
331	Baked clay products	415	398	301	398	–[p]
		311	398	234	318	–
		235	318	167	223	–
		177	223	118	134	–
332	Glass	2,226	1,009	781	2,160	–[q]
		1,706	820	539	1,654	–
		1,187	605	253	1,053	–
		772	373	111	533	–
333	China, pottery, fire-proof products	1,060	996	1,019	633	290[r]
		963	809	745	465	–
		674	573	376	277	–
		447	408	180	142	–
334	Cement, lime, plaster	427	748	299	656	–[p]
		427	561	155	474	–
		332	389	64	232	–
		235	269	26	–	–
335	Concrete products	1,362	858	633	1,199	103
		924	644	518	706	–
		467	372	334	368	–
		265	240	198	202	–

See notes at end of tables.

Table A.6 (cont.)

No. N.I.C.E.	Industry	France	Italy	Netherlands	Belgium	Luxemburg
339	Stone and non-metallic	262	494	126	104	52[s]
	mineral products	210	371	102	95	30
		136	247	72	66	14
		88	148	43	39	–
341	Steel (according to	9,835	6,706	4,649	6,226	–
	E.C.C.S. treaty	8,114	5,096	–	4,853	–
		5,901	2,950	–	3,186	–
		3,501	1,631	–	–	–
342	Steel tubes	2,710	3,582	403	373	–
		1,754	2,558	243	–	–
		925	1,412	–	–	–
		417	655	–	–	–
343	Wire-drawing, rolling,	1,496	577	381	2,109	–
	cold finishing, etc.	1,159	406	320	1,287	–
		763	248	209	629	–
		437	137	100	283	–
344	Primary nonferrous	1,441	1,610	704	1,876	–[t]
	metals	1,244	1,258	387	1,628	–
		1,021	865	193	1,015	–
		681	499	–	–	–
345	Foundries (ferrous and	1,917	2,154	751	674	41[u]
	nonferrous)	1,780	1,385	577	527	24
		1,260	831	354	388	–
		855	492	185	236	–
351	Forgings, punching,	945	238	195	15	–
	stamping, etc.	776	203	107	10	–
		581	157	–	–	–
		362	89	–	–	–
352	Second transformation	659	525	422	517	–[v]
	of metals	494	420	311	372	–
		461	294	187	223	–
		343	185	101	124	–
353	Metallic construction	1,137	783	910	881	254[w]
		853	626	662	710	155
		569	470	447	441	77
		357	313	265	227	35

See notes at end of tables.

Table A.6 (cont.)

No. N.I.C.E.	Industry	France	Italy	Nether-lands	Bel-gium	Luxem-burg
354	Boiler-works	1,524	454	592	340	–[v]
		1,239	292	395	252	–
		800	156	237	151	–
		503	80	133	83	–
355	Metal tools	1,454	1,432	1,067	933	32
		1,212	1,002	934	806	24
		970	630	694	543	–
		698	412	448	333	–
359	Auxiliary activities	16	368	80	5	24
	of metallic industries	10	184	60	5	17
		7	147	40	5	9
		4	88	29	5	5
361	Farm machinery and	2,192	853	209	637	–
	equipment	1,594	613	147	373	–
		897	384	88	179	–
		478	222	50	79	–
362	Office machines	3,090	1,813	778	–[d]	2
		2,048	1,750	550	–	–
		1,078	975	264	–	–
		517	440	120	–	–
363	Metal-cutting machine	1,135	1,429	257	653[e]	–
	tools	973	1,012	196	561	–
		681	619	127	281	–
		467	381	77	126	–
364	Textile machinery,	1,034	1,182	212	823	–
	sewing machines	764	1,137	143	530	–
		432	782	75	266	–
		241	458	36	120	–
365	Food products machinery	545	609	503	403	–
		424	507	378	259	–
		315	355	232	157	–
		208	227	137	80	–
366	Mining, steel-work ma-	1,095	1,022	573	1,529	–
	chinery, cranes, etc.	958	803	487	1,177	–
		685	496	304	611	–
		471	309	172	288	–

See notes at end of tables.

Table A.6 (cont.)

No. N.I.C.E.	Industry	France	Italy	Nether-lands	Bel-gium	Luxem-burg
367	Transmission equip-ment	425	2,983	343	170	–
		283	1,726	203	130	–
		148	842	93	69	–
		–	398	–	-	–
368	Other specific ma-chinery	401	717	287	361	–
		314	547	190	230	–
		213	302	115	118	–
		118	169	60	53	–
369	Other non-electric machinery	4,280	2,860	3,625	618	55
		3,292	1,966	2,222	549	–
		2,305	1,108	1,169	378	–
		1,343	629	589	201	–
371	Electric wires	1,965	708	1,121	747	–
		1,535	525	665	–	–
		921	309	299	–	–
		457	154	–	–	–
372	Motors, generators, transformers, switch-gear, etc.	3,183	1,537	1,556	3,964	–
		3,175	1,249	1,023	2,378	–
		1,905	922	565	1,073	–
		1,125	599	291	468	–
373	Electric accessories, tools, welding apparatus, etc.	3,270	1,064	363	92	–
		1,727	680	218	53	–
		1,308	327	109	24	–
		706	151	48	11	–
374	Electrical measuring instruments	1,256	2,670	2,208	3,910	–
		984	1,812	1,259	2,245	–
		552	1,030	607	966	–
		281	512	273	–	–
375	Electronic material, radio and television	2,424	1,844	10,536	2,068	–
		2,204	1,326	6,100	1,269	–
		1,543	796	2,690	558	–
		987	406	1,109	238	–
376	Domestic electric appliances	1,290	3,771	956	275	–
		1,089	2,614	611	191	–
		726	1,320	347	126	–
		426	624	171	60	–

See notes at end of tables.

Table A.6 (cont.)

No. N.I.C.E.	Industry	France	Italy	Netherlands	Belgium	Luxemburg
377	Lamps and lighting fixtures	625	1,188	1,022	_f	–
		433	936	622	–	–
		233	511	321	–	–
		108	248	148	–	–
378	Batteries	931	287	147	246	–
		751	228	100	143	–
		515	120	46	–	–
		236	–	–	–	–
379	Repair and fixing of electrical appliances	834	494	393	–	50
		596	370	248	–	29
		356	272	124	–	13
		200	168	63	–	–
381	Ship building and repairing	7,947	4,105	3,630	2,031	–
		5,712	3,143	2,621	1,173	–
		3,278	1,847	1,452	567	–
		1,550	872	731	263	–
382	Railroad and street cars	1,730	2,118	–	802	–
		1,730	1,548	–	506	–
		995	945	–	242	–
		952	435	–	–	–
383	Automobiles and parts	28,382	13,281	1,829	2,319	_x
		18,672	8,908	1,048	1,499	–
		9,112	4,405	500	780	–
		4,302	2,021	239	376	–
384	Independent repair of automobiles, motor-cycles and cycles	502	326	167	143	95
		502	163	167	119	66
		351	130	167	76	38
		141	78	120	49	25
385	Motorcycles, cycles and parts	1,502	3,181	450	467	–
		1,085	1,922	341	280	–
		325	981	214	136	–
		324	461	113	63	–
386	Aircraft construction and repair	4,811	1,717	1,373	4,066	_x
		3,969	1,205	771	–	–
		2,646	590	–	–	–
		1,559	–	–	–	–

See notes at end of tables.

Table A.6 (cont.)

No. N.I.C.E.	Industry	France	Italy	Nether- lands	Bel- gium	Luxem- burg
389	Transportation equip-	50	261	147	96	38[y]
	ment, n.e.c.	42	166	120	55	22
		31	94	75	–	10
		25	46	38	–	–
391	Measuring devices,	3,853	155	420	455	–
	controls	2,345	122	302	262	–
		1,273	74	164	109	–
		697	43	76	45	–
392	Surgical and medical	217	325	107	24	–[g]
	instruments	181	227	88	21	–
		123	127	55	14	–
		75	68	33	9	–
393	Ophtalmic goods and	353	860	79	178	–[g]
	photographic equipment	268	606	60	111	–
		157	360	35	53	–
		86	194	20	23	–
394	Watches and clocks	1,002	861	80	8	3
		726	483	50	7	2
		411	224	26	6	2
		244	100	15	3	–
395	Jewelry, silverware and	439	525	149	143	2
	lapidary work	329	375	104	94	2
		219	240	69	52	–
		140	144	41	27	–
396	Musical instruments	199	362	131	37	–[g]
		145	262	94	25	–
		85	159	54	13	–
		49	93	29	6	–
397	Games, toys and sporting	556	329	59	5	–
	goods	494	256	53	5	–
		346	164	32	5	–
		208	98	18	3	–
399	Miscellaneous products,	598	413	57	79	153[z]
	n.e.c.	399	271	49	63	90
		239	155	36	46	39
		136	91	20	29	–

See notes at end of tables.

Notes for tables A.1 to A.6

France

a   Including industry 254.
b   Included in industry 252.

Netherlands

a   Included in industry 386.
b   Including industry 382.

Belgium

a   Including industry 304.
b   Included in industry 205.
c   Refining only, without distribution.
d   Included in industry 363.
e   Including industry 362.
f   An error in the listing made the computation of the concentration ratios impossible.

Luxemburg

a   Included in industry 209.
b   Including industry 208.
c   Included in industry 206.
d   Including industry 203.
e   Included in industry 212.
f   Including industry 211.
g   Included in industry 399.
h   Including industry 244.
i   Included in industry 243.
j   Included in industry 255.
k   Including industries 254 and 259.
l   Including industry 302.
m   Included in industry 301.
n   Including industry 312.
o   Included in industry 311.
p   Included in industry 333.
q   Included in industry 339.
r   Including industries 331 and 334.
s   Including industry 332.
t   Included in industry 345.
u   Including industry 344.
v   Included in industry 353.
w   Including industries 352 and 354.

[x] Included in industry 389.
[y] Including industries 383 and 386.
[z] Including industries 220, 232, 241, 271, 291, 392, 393 and 396.

INDEX